Religion, Identity and Politics in Northern Ireland

It is good to see the complexities of the Northern Irish situation presented with such clarity. All those interested in, and at times bewildered by, the place of religion in Northern Ireland should not only read this book but bring it swiftly to the attention of their students. It will become an excellent teaching tool.
    Grace Davie, Professor of the Sociology of Religion, University of Exeter, UK

This will be a controversial book, for it considers an emotive topic and takes on some well-established arguments, but is likely to establish itself quickly as the definitive study of religion and politics in Northern Ireland. It is clear, lucid and extremely well written and has a refreshing blend of survey data and qualitative interviews. Mitchell establishes once and for all the role religion plays in Northern Ireland's conflict and it is not as simplistic or derivative as most people think.
    John David Brewer, Professor of Sociology, University of Aberdeen, UK

This is a topic which is – in my view – going to become increasingly important both because of the importance of fundamentalist religion globally, and because of the continuation of conflict and crisis in Northern Ireland. This book should find a readership both in courses on the sociology (or politics) of religion in the contemporary world and in courses on Northern Ireland. I strongly recommend it.
    Dr Jennifer Todd, University College Dublin, Republic of Ireland

Has conflict in Northern Ireland kept political dimensions of religion alive, and has religion played a role in fuelling conflict?

Conflict in Northern Ireland is not and never will be a holy war. Yet religion is more socially and politically significant than many commentators presume. In fact, religion has remained a central feature of social identity and politics throughout conflict as well as recent change.

There has been an acceleration of interest in the relationship between religion, identity and politics in modern societies. Building on this debate, Claire Mitchell presents a challenging analysis of religion in contemporary Northern Ireland, arguing that religion is not merely a marker of ethnicity and that it continues to provide many of the meanings of identity, community and politics. In light of the multifaceted nature of the conflict in Northern Ireland, Mitchell explains that, for Catholics, religion is primarily important in its social and institutional forms, whereas for many Protestants its theological and ideological dimensions are more pressing. Even those who no longer go to church tend to reproduce religious stereotypes of 'them and us'. Drawing on a range of unique interview material, this book traces how individuals and groups in Northern Ireland have absorbed religious types of cultural knowledge, belonging and morality, and how they reproduce these as they go about their daily lives. Despite recent religious and political changes, the author concludes that perceptions of religious difference help keep communities in Northern Ireland socially separate and often in conflict with one another.

Religion, Identity and Politics in Northern Ireland

Boundaries of Belonging and Belief

Claire Mitchell

Queen's University Belfast, UK

ASHGATE

Published by
Ashgate Publishing Limited
Gower House
Croft Road
Aldershot
Hants GU11 3HR
England

Ashgate Publishing Company
Suite 420
101 Cherry Street
Burlington, VT 05401-4405
USA

Ashgate website: http://www.ashgate.com

British Library Cataloguing in Publication Data
Mitchell, Claire
    Religion, identity and politics in Northern Ireland :
    boundaries of belonging and belief
    1. Religion and politics - Northern Ireland 2. Religion and
    sociology - Northern Ireland 3. Identity (Psychology) -
    Northern Ireland - Religious aspects 4. Group identity -
    Northern Ireland 5. Northern Ireland - Religion 6. Northern
    Ireland - Politics and government 7. Northern Ireland -
    Social conditions - 1969-
    I. Title
    261.7'09416

Library of Congress Cataloging-in-Publication Data
Mitchell, Claire.
Religion, identity and politics in Northern Ireland : boundaries of
belonging and belief / Claire Mitchell.
        p. cm.
    Includes bibliographical references and index.
    ISBN 0-7546-4154-6 (hardcover : alk. paper)—ISBN 0-7546-4155-4
(pbk. : alk. paper) 1. Christianity—Northern Ireland. 2. Northern
Ireland—Religion. 3. Christianity and politics—Northern Ireland. 4.
Identification (Religion) 5. Group identity—Northern Ireland. I.
Title.

BR796.3.M58 2005
305.6'7416—dc22
                                                                                                    2005007949

ISBN 0 7546 4154 6 (Hbk); 0 7546 4155 4 (Pbk)

Typeset by IML Typographers, Birkenhead, Merseyside
Printed and bound in Great Britain by TJ International Ltd, Padstow, Cornwall.

Contents

List of figures and tables

Figure

Tables

Preface

Researching religion and politics in Northern Ireland is an odd experience. It is at once the least appropriate topic of discussion at any social gathering and one of the most deeply rooted social issues. I try to always keep the topic of my research quiet at parties and in taxis. However, after the surface is scratched, most people in Northern Ireland have a lot of things to say about the relationship between religion and politics. Even where feelings about religion are hostile, the vast majority of people in Northern Ireland have a lot of internalized knowledge about it. Whilst the relationship between religion and politics is complicated, controversial and many find it unsettling, it is difficult to grow up and live in Northern Ireland without absorbing some of its religious reference points and behaviours. This book stems from the desire to explore this notion theoretically and empirically.

It has persistently struck me how religion continues to influence the ideas of many people I know in Northern Ireland who no longer attend church and who do not consider themselves to be particularly religious. Whilst as a convinced social constructionist I believe that individuals can transform their identities, I am confronted with the feeling that these changes are often minimal and reversible. The limitations that pre-existing structures, relationships, patterns of behaviour and expectations place on us are very powerful. They can leave familiar tracks that are easier to walk around in than step out from. In this sense, the book is interested in how individuals and groups in Northern Ireland have absorbed religious types of cultural knowledge, belonging and morality, and how they in turn might reproduce these as they go about their daily lives. It asks how religion itself might help construct social identities and differences rather than simply mask other social phenomena. Of course, over generations religious ideas and functions shift and are redefined. However, the continuities are striking.

One of the things that stimulated this research is the frequent assumption that religion is a backward force and that Northern Ireland is firmly stuck in the past, rehashing Reformation debates. However, religion is far from dying out in the modern world, and it continues to help individuals and groups make sense of their place in many different social contexts. At the heart of this research is the question of what religion might mean to people's social identities and political attitudes in a Northern Ireland where individuals are thoroughly engaged with the realities of life in the twenty-first century. It questions how people can be both religious and modern. Being religious and modern used to be seen as a contradiction in terms by secularization theorists who believed that modernity would cause people to be so rational that they would no longer need religion to explain their experiences. However, there has since been a turn in the sociology of religion which argues that modernity creates such tensions of its own that individuals still draw on religion to help them understand their lives, albeit in different ways than in the past. This book adds to the debate by mapping out in a specific context both well-established and some under-theorized ways in which religion continues to provide meaning to modern social life. Arguing that religion creates a cultural reservoir, from which identities and actions are partially constructed, does not mean that it is a reactionary or irrational force. Rather, religion is called upon by active, reasoning individuals to give meaning to life, social relationships and often to political developments.

Finally, this book is concerned with religious change. Religion is not just a static force that *causes* certain attitudes in a linear fashion. Rather, the religious elements of identification are highly responsive to social and political effects. My thinking on religious meaning and significance has been informed by my own experience of an evangelical socialization in Northern Ireland followed by ten agnostic years in secular Dublin. No study on religion and conflict in Northern Ireland, not least by someone who has grown up there, can claim to be value free. However, thinking analytically about my own religious and political journey, and how it has responded to changes in my social context, has been invaluable in attempting to understand the dynamics of the relationships between religion, identity and social relationships.

I am hugely indebted to many people for their encouragement throughout the process of researching and writing this book. I am particularly grateful to Dr Jennifer Todd, my doctoral supervisor, for teaching me how to think theoretically and practically at the same time, which has changed the way I see the world. Many people in the Department of Politics at University College Dublin: Jean Brennan, Gladys Ganiel, Katy Hayward, Kevin Howard, Finbarr Lane, Tobias Theiler and others, are due thanks for their encouragement and humour as well as substantive contributions to my thinking on religion, conflict and identity. Many people have read parts of the book in various incarnations and I would like to express gratitude to John Brewer, John Coakley, Grace Davie, Tom Garvin, Niamh Hardiman, Bernie Hayes, Iseult Honohan, Tom Inglis, Veronique Mottier and James Tilley for their suggestions and advice, and also to my colleagues in the School of Sociology and Social Policy at Queen's University Belfast. Many thanks to all at ARK and the Northern Ireland Life and Times Survey, and in particular to Paula Devine for her assistance.

I also have a great many personal debts to those close to me who supported me throughout the process. My parents, who made me go to church as a child, and my grandparents, who brought them before me, have no doubt provided the cornerstone of my fascination with religion and society. I am also grateful to Kerry Anthony, Joe Doyle, Wes Forsythe, David Gallagher, Dave O'Leary and Niamh Puirséil for endless pub debates over the issues. Thanks in particular to Tim Millen for the photo on the cover of the book in addition to his reflections on religion and identity.

The fieldwork was conducted as part of my doctoral research which was funded under the Irish Research Council for the Social Sciences and Humanities Government of Ireland Scholarship scheme and I would like to acknowledge their support. Later research was undertaken as Newman Fellow in the Institute for British-Irish Studies at University College Dublin, which was funded by Diageo Ireland.

Above all I would like to thank all of those individuals who gave so freely of their hospitality, time, stories and ideas in interviews and without whose generosity this book would not have been possible. It is not easy to disclose one's feelings about religion and politics in Northern Ireland and I very much appreciate their willingness to participate. I have tried to get inside their shoes, but of course any misrepresentations and mistakes are my own.

I

Introduction

Key points

- *Religion is a marker of social difference.*

- *Religious ideas and symbols help constitute group identities.*

- *Religious practices help construct community.*

- *Religious beliefs can be politically salient.*

- *Religious institutions are politically influential and provide structure to the boundary.*

Conflict in Northern Ireland has not been, is not and will never be a holy war. However, religion is much more socially and politically significant than many commentators have presumed. In a conflict constituted by multiple factors, such as ethnicity and inequality, religion remains one of the central dimensions of social difference. Its political significance derives from five overlapping sources. First, religion is integrally bound up with power relationships in Northern Ireland as churches continue to cooperate with politicians to represent the unionist and nationalist political mainstream. Secondly, religion is the dominant boundary-marker and the basis of widespread social segregation. As such, religion provides a variety of resources to distinguish in-group from out-group members. These include religious rituals which are widely participated in and help construct a sense of community, both practically and cognitively, for many Protestants and especially Catholics. Religious ideology – religiously derived but non-theological concepts of self and other – also informs communal identifications, especially for Protestants. Finally, theology and doctrine help constitute the meanings of group identity and politics for some Protestants. These dimensions of religion overlap with and reinforce one another. So too, they overlap with and reinforce other dimensions of social difference such as ethnicity and inequality. This is why religion is so deeply rooted in political culture and structure in Northern Ireland.

Increasingly, claiming that conflict in Northern Ireland is about religion is seen as a kind of lazy shorthand for deeper divisions. Something of an academic consensus now hangs around the idea that conflict is essentially ethnonational, and that other factors merely reinforce rather than constitute ethnic division. Of course it is clear that political divisions in Northern Ireland for most people do not revolve around doctrinal disputes, and people rarely cite theology as a reason for their political fears. As such, it has become the dominant intellectual view that religion plays only a minor role, if any at all, in helping to structure political relationships. Generally, religion is thought to be merely a social marker, a badge of difference that is unimportant in and of itself. However, most concede that religion still provides the dominant signifier of community membership, more so than economics or nationalism. Therefore we are compelled to ask what meaning does this have? Is there any substantive religious content to ethnic identity?

This book challenges assumptions that conflict is essentially ethnonational and argues that religion gives meaning to group identities in a variety of ways. These processes are different for Protestants and Catholics, for churchgoers and nonchurchgoers, for believers and even for some nonbelievers. I argue that religion does not just mark out the communal boundary in Northern Ireland, but that it gives structures, practices, values and meanings to the boundary. To understand this, we cannot reduce the issue to one of a straightforward link between theology and politics, but instead we need to explore the ways in which religious rituals, ideas, doctrines, values and powerful agencies help construct ideas about self and other in an uncertain and divided political situation.

As a framework of ideas and an organizer of community, the importance of religion cannot be underestimated. This book understands religion as a dynamic of personal and group identification. It maps the top-down connections between the churches and political power, as well as exploring how religion is used by Protestants and Catholics from the bottom up in processes of social identification and community construction. Sometimes religion does simply act as an identity marker. However, religion generally provides substantive meanings to Protestant and Catholic identities. Thus, rather than just marking out ethnic identities, this book argues that religion provides content and meaning to processes of categorization and social comparison in Northern Ireland. Whilst this is social religion that moves beyond the confines of individual religiosity, it is not simply civil religion where a group worships its own groupness without reference to the sacred. On the contrary, in Northern Ireland, specifically religious practices and religious ideas remain socially significant beyond the confines of the devout.

As a consequence, religion continues to pervade political culture and structure in Northern Ireland. Churches and politicians alike are aware of the importance of this relationship and seek to cultivate it in order to promote their own strength. In this way the connection between religion and politics is maintained from the top down. As such, religion remains socially significant and continues to inform political culture as well as social relationships. Because religion continues to help shape social identity, churches retain social influence. So there is a processual two-way relationship between religion and politics, and between ordinary people and religious and political structures. People use religious beliefs and structures for their explanatory and organizational power, whilst churches and politicians work together to explain and indeed organize community relationships. Each tends to reproduce the other.

Another central theme of the book is the responsiveness of religion to context, power and politics. Most people experience religious journeys, where over time theological beliefs and religious practices can deepen, loosen, and change. Groups experience a similar process, and religiosity in a given community can rise and fall over time. Moreover, the importance of religion in social and political life ebbs and flows in response to changing contexts and crises. Secularization is not an inevitable linear trajectory. Religion can come on to, and drop off, the political landscape. At some points it may have higher explanatory power than at others. When political life is stable and predictable, religion may be less politically relevant. However, it may remain beneath the surface of a society, ready to emerge in times of trouble, as has often been the case in Northern Ireland. This is why religion must be examined as a fluid dynamic of social life. Indeed changes in social or political context can often produce changes in religious identity, even religious beliefs. Despite the fact that most religions claim the unchanging truth of their traditions, we must look beyond this and also consider how religious identity responds to the present and to politics.

In the final section of this chapter we elaborate on the dynamics of this two-way relationship between religion and politics. To contextualize this it is necessary to provide a brief discussion of the nature of the conflict in Northern Ireland and the role of religion within it.

The nature of the conflict

Although Northern Ireland is in the midst of a peace process, social relationships and politics continue to be characterized by high levels of conflict. The conflict in Northern Ireland is a meta-conflict. That is to say that there is conflict over what the conflict is about. Many attempts to answer this question have been reductionist, where commentators argue that conflict is in essence about x, y or z, and that all other dimensions are secondary to this. In other words, analysts tend to simplify and reduce the causes of conflict to certain key elements. Literature of this kind includes McGarry and O'Leary (1995) who argue that conflict is essentially ethnonational, MacDonald (1986) who argues that it is basically colonial, Smith and Chambers (1991) who argue that it all boils down to economic inequality; this literature also includes some who argue, like Hickey (1984), that conflict is essentially about religion. These accounts cannot get to the heart of divisions in Northern Ireland, as they all simplify, exaggerate and generalize their preferred causal explanation, and sometimes the competing arguments as well.

A convincing analytical approach to the nature of the conflict is offered by Ruane and Todd (1996). They argue that there is a 'system of relationships' in Northern Ireland, which interlock and mutually reinforce each other. This system of relationships has three interlocking levels: a set of differences, a structure of dominance, dependence and inequality and a tendency towards communal division. This means that people were first divided over a range of differences, such as 'Protestant/Catholic', 'Irish/British' and 'settler/native'. Whilst these differences do not overlap exactly, over centuries of conflict two fairly defined groups have developed in opposition to one another. These differences, for example,

Protestant/Catholic, are rooted in actual experiences of social relationships. Whether one was a Protestant or a Catholic influenced one's position in the economy, demographic strength and access to the means of force. Historically, to be a Protestant settler meant to occupy a more powerful position in society. So group differences became associated with dominance, dependence, inequality and power struggles. This is why the 'system of relationships' has resulted in a tendency towards communal division.

Ruane and Todd highlight the connections between various dimensions of difference in Northern Ireland. Whilst stressing the relative autonomy of religion, ethnicity and colonialism as bases for communal opposition over time, they also trace how the different elements 'intertwined and mutually conditioned each other' (1996, p. 11). So what it meant to have a 'Protestant identity' was conditioned by feelings of Britishness and settler status as well as an attachment to the Reformed Protestant religious tradition. Because differences overlap with each other in this way, it is therefore more difficult to isolate one of them and remove it from the overall equation. So if somebody is a member of the Catholic community, even though they may not practice or believe in their religion anymore, their associations with Catholicism remain. Because of the way Northern Ireland is organized, people's contact with the churches and religious ideas usually continues long after they cease to be active members. This contact is maintained, for example, through education, the role of the churches in family formation and the religious ideas and symbols in everyday life. These arguments are elaborated on later. The important point is that in a deeply divided society, religion is one of the key dimensions of difference. It is not what conflict is all about, but it is very closely tied in to wider structures and experiences of group differences.

Is the conflict religious?

Previous approaches to the question of religion in Northern Ireland have raised more questions than they have answered. Aside from a collection of community studies and surveys,[1] the wider literature has been rather reductionist in its theorization of what religion is and does. How religion is defined makes all the difference to one's analysis of its social significance. Previous studies have allocated religion importance in terms of theological ideas, *or* church structures of power, *or* as a symbolic resource for ethnic difference. This has limited the types of analyses that can follow. Instead, we need a theoretical approach to religion that allows us to take into account all of these dimensions of religion. Any analysis needs to tackle how different aspects of religion can be important for different people and needs to be sensitive to the differing historical and political experiences of the Catholic community and the Protestant community. Before we map out such a theoretical approach, we briefly unpack the types of approaches that have been used up until now to understand religion in Northern Ireland. We assess which aspects of these approaches can be built upon, and what questions have been left unanswered.

Religion as an ethnic marker

The most popular school of thought on religion is encapsulated in McGarry and O'Leary's *Explaining Northern Ireland* (1995), and is echoed by Coulter (1999) and Clayton (1998). The central argument is that religion is an ethnic marker, but that it is not generally politically relevant in and of itself. Instead, ethnonationalism lies at the root of the conflict.[2] Hayes and McAllister (1999a) point out that this represents something of an academic consensus. McGarry and O'Leary criticize other commentators for mistaking the 'markers' of conflict for its real basis. They argue that there is nothing innate about religious or cultural differences which makes people disagree, rather, that these are just signs which could be substituted with anything else, and which exist simply to distinguish group members from non-group members. They point out that whilst there was decline of church attendance and traditional morality since the 1960s, conflict escalated. McGarry and O'Leary also argue that there is no correlation between the areas most affected by conflict and the intensity of religious convictions.

Indeed, in some cases religion is little more than an ethnic marker (see Chapter 4); however, it is McGarry and O'Leary's assumption that this is the general trend that is problematic. This assumption stems from their rather narrow conceptualization of religion, focusing on 'measurable' levels of religiosity, such as church attendance, divorce rate and number of children born outside of marriage. Evidence of the social significance of religion for McGarry and O'Leary, one would imagine, would have to be explicit political battles over doctrine or correlations between high levels of religious devotion and political extremism. Neither of these is the case in Northern Ireland. However, many believe that religion is too complex to be measured by divorce rates or church attendance rates (Davie, 2000). Religious beliefs and ideas do not depend on full pews on Sunday mornings for their survival, nor will people's search to find meaning be eradicated by a rise in the number of divorces. Religion does not have to be understood as merely a traditional type of religion. It can also be experienced outside church buildings and outside of theological confines.

Moreover, too often the assumption is made that ethnic and religious boundaries are fixed and that they converge. Amongst the Protestant community there are a number of ethnic and cultural identities: Ulster, Ulster-Scots, British, Northern Irish, British-Irish and even some Irish. Which one exactly does Protestantism represent? Whilst the dominant *national* identity amongst Protestants is British, its meaning is very ambiguous. Ulster Protestants are not simply British nationalists. If Protestantism is in fact the dominant signifier of difference, and one that includes more of the community than any other banner, then we are compelled to ask what exactly is being signified? Might it not be that difference is partially constructed from religion, rather than just represented by it?

These are issues raised by McGarry and O'Leary's work that need to be addressed. Thus, in Chapter 6, we pay close attention to those nominal Catholics and Protestants who no longer practice their religion, drawing out what religious structures and ideas might also mean to them. We find that religion can help give meaning to ethnicity rather than simply just mark it out.

Cultural religion

Others conceptualize religion not as masking ethnicity, but as exemplifying a different kind of religion. Demerath (2000, 2001) proposes a theory of 'cultural religion', which he defines as 'an identification with a religious heritage without any religious participation or a sense of personal involvement per se' (2001, p. 59). This is similar to Gans's (1994) concept of 'symbolic religiosity' – an attachment to a religious culture that does not entail regular participation in its rituals or organizations. Protestantism and Catholicism are two civil religions that provide the symbols, rituals and labels of identity. Whilst there is little traditional religious content in these religious identifications, Demerath says that there is a sacralization of ethnic group. In Northern Ireland and elsewhere he argues that this qualifies as a distinct type of religion – theologically weak but socially important. Demerath is quite right that theology is not usually the locus of religious significance in modern societies. However, he does not pay much attention to the possible substantive religious content of cultural identities. This book builds on Demerath's idea that religion provides symbols and rituals to support identities, but pushes further in asking how these religious ideas and practices might substantively constitute rather than simply signify difference.

Bruce (1986, 1994) and Fawcett (2000) add some texture to debate on cultural religion in Northern Ireland. Like McGarry and O'Leary, their accounts of ethnic conflict also present religion as pre-modern, hanging on in the present because it symbolizes deeper divisions. Whilst Bruce quite rightly emphasizes the importance of context and power, by treating religion simply as a resource for ethnicity – which changes in ethnic relations cause to rise or fall – he perhaps underestimates the ways in which religion helps constitute ethnicity and reproduce social relationships. This is evidenced by the persistence of religion even after conflict becomes less pronounced.

Bruce is the chief proponent of the cultural religion argument for Protestants, and particularly loyalists, in Northern Ireland. He provides much insight into the role evangelical culture plays in the ethnic identity of Ulster Protestants, and argues that it pervades politics beyond the numbers of the faithful (Bruce 1986, 1994). This is because it defines group belonging, figures large in history, legitimizes the group's advantages and radically distinguishes the group from its traditional enemy (Bruce, 1994). In fact, Bruce feels that this is the dominant theme in politics, and concludes that 'the Northern Ireland conflict is a religious conflict' (1986, p. 249). However, this is misleading as Bruce frequently argues that secularization is the normal course of events, except when religion overlaps with culture in a situation of conflict or change (1996). What he means is that religion has become a mark of belonging to a specific ethnic group. For Bruce (1996, p. 122), 'what matters is not any individual's religiosity, but the individual's incorporation in an ethnic group defined by a particular religion.' So conflict is ethnoreligious.

Fawcett's extremely well-researched analysis of the Presbyterian churches in their 'cosier mainstream variety' (2000, p. 2) is an invaluable contribution to a debate that concentrates mainly on the religious fringes. However, she also ultimately argues for a cultural religion when she maintains that religious worship is a ritual act that flags identity. She focuses on religion as cultural symbolism, ethnonationalism, boundary maintenance and as a power resource rather than examining how religion constructs the boundary itself. Fawcett argues that religion is as visible as skin colour in Northern Ireland. However, whilst nominal religious affiliation may indeed be deduced by a set series of questions about name, school, and so on, these labels tell us very little about what religion actually means to people. This raises questions about the content of religion itself and how people may use doctrine, morality, values and practices to understand social and political relationships.

Cultural religion is a socially real process, particularly in divided societies. Sometimes religious acts and symbols do just flag identity. But we need to go further than this. Indeed by arguing that the primary significance of religion is establishing ethnic belonging, we risk ignoring how religious practices and ideas are used to *constitute* the meanings of ethnicity itself. Ethnicity and cultural identity would have different meanings without their religious dimensions. Furthermore, experiences of ethnic and cultural relationships can help constitute the local meanings of a particular religion. Political experiences may even influence religious beliefs and practices. So these commentators are quite right in highlighting the ethnic dimensions of religion and in arguing that conflict gives cultural religion added political significance. But we need to push further in relation to the content and causality of religion. Religion, ethnicity and conflict are deeply intertwined and mutually conditioning. Ethnicity and conflict can rehabilitate religion, which in turn can sustain its own existence and feed back into social life. In other words, conflict is religiously constituted as well as religiously represented.

Religion as theology

Hickey (1984) is one of the few commentators who focus primarily on the doctrinal aspect of religion and his work is instructive when we come to look at interrelations of theology and politics. His core theme is as follows: the terms 'Protestant' and 'Catholic' are 'religious in meaning and therefore have significance which is based on the beliefs which their adherents hold. Those beliefs, in turn, motivate the lives of the people who are committed to them and this, obviously, means that the beliefs themselves are of fundamental importance in formulating social action' (1984, p. 59). The content of beliefs is what matters. The theoretical stance in this work, that religion is not a mere function of interest situations, is borrowed from Weber. Religious beliefs may change with reference to society or economics, but also in response to religious needs. They are important in and of themselves. Moreover, the specific type of religion can have a far-reaching influence on a given society. What Hickey (1984, p. 63) draws from this is that in Northern Ireland, 'doctrine can, in fact, account for sociological reality.'

Hickey is right that religious beliefs can have 'profound political implications for the manner in which their adherents not only live their daily lives but view society' (1984, p. 58). But he exaggerates religious causality, calling these beliefs a 'total world-view' (1984, p. 68). It is by no means obvious that religious beliefs are a primary basis for social action, even for the theologically convinced. Moreover, Hickey inaccurately reduces the role of religion in Northern Ireland to the direct political implications of *doctrine*. He assumes that official church doctrines correspond with the religious ideas of ordinary believers when this is often not the case. Indeed, a central concern of this book is to examine not just official church doctrines, but also how 'ordinary' believers use them to understand politics. Hickey also criticizes arguments that suggest that religion plays a role in social identification, group belonging and othering, stating that this prevents one from studying the actual content of the beliefs themselves. However, it is exactly the relationships between these that we need to understand.

In the overall literature, the argument that religious beliefs cause political divisions is not that common. Whilst McGarry and O'Leary (1995) are extremely critical of those who prioritize religious explanations of conflict, they do not reference many commentators who do this. In this respect, they cite Rose (1971) who also pays much attention to the political and economic situation in the 1960s, Akenson who refers to the Protestant belief in a chosen people as 'dying embers' (1992) and Cruise O'Brien (1994) who does prioritize cultural and religious explanations of conflict, but who is generally regarded as a nonconformist in Irish political life. Thus, it is important to bear in mind that although it is a popular stereotype, the link between theology and politics is not widely argued for in the literature. It is also highlighted only in the case of evangelical Protestants. However, it is just as unwise to ignore the relationships between doctrine and politics, as it is to over-exaggerate the link. We revisit this question in Chapter 7, highlighting when, how and for whom this link may be important.

Religion and structure

In contrast, Fulton's (1991, 2002) chief concern is the analysis of religious structures. He argues that religion, and in particular the institutional churches, has played a vital role in structuring the power relations of the two dominant 'historical blocs' in Ireland. Fulton is quite right to argue that religion is not the primary or sole cause of division, but that it has overlapped with culture, economics and politics throughout conflict. Moreover, Fulton makes a crucial contribution to the debate in paying careful attention to structure, developing how religion acted as an agent in historical struggles for political power. He places oppositional religious ideas in the context of religious structures (2002). That religion must not be reduced to symbolism or theology, and that we must also analyse how religion has been used to construct opposition from the top down is a crucial point that is sometimes lost in accounts that emphasize the importance of religion and culture as opposed to political structures.

However, Fulton tends to over-emphasize structure at the expense of culture and beliefs. He refers to Catholic-nationalists and Protestant-loyalists as 'the real subjects of the battle for domination' (1991, p. 227). He argues that Roman Catholic bishops are the intellectuals organizing the beliefs of Catholic-nationalists in a conservative way. He focuses on the Catholic ethos of Bunreacht na hEireann (the Irish Constitution), and Catholicism's emphasis on moral issues such as abortion and divorce, understanding theology as official theology. However, whilst bishops may try to organize people's beliefs, they can never quite control how people interpret their religion. Of course people relate to others, and interpret their place in the world, with reference to how powerful ideas and actors have helped structure their lives. But whilst the institutional churches may provide possibilities and constraints to human action, they do not totally direct it. Moreover, there are significant debates within the churches over attitudes to orthodoxy that make it problematic to talk about 'imposed ruling ideas' as Fulton does.

Overall, Fulton's focus on power injects a much-needed element into what often becomes a narrow debate about religio-cultural differences. The attempts of churches and politicians to cooperate in order to promote their authority is of crucial importance. However, it is also important to assess the relationships between structure and culture, institutional power and individuality, rules and interpretations. Therefore, this book seeks to develop Fulton's arguments about religious structures, but within the context of culture, ideas and individualism as well as institutional authority and power.

Religion and ideology

An article written in 1973 by the late Frank Wright provides one of the strongest analytical approaches to religion in Northern Ireland to date. Wright is concerned with the ways in which religious ideas permeate Protestants' common-sense understandings of social relationships. He argues that these ideologies structure many Protestants' ideas about the actual condition of Catholics and Catholicism, that they provide a source of values which give legitimacy to the 'Protestant' cause, and that they may at times be an outward expression of material conflicts. He maintains that people are socialized into a mutual hostility that takes on a life of its own, above and beyond an understanding of the original theoretical origins of the conflict. The greater the amount of physical and spiritual separation between the two communities, the greater the intensity of ideology. He argues (1973, p. 213) that in a deeply divided society, 'knowledge' of the other is 'comprised very largely of indirect experience and socialized teachings rather than of first hand experience'. While the presence of the other is a constant preoccupation, not much is known about them and this gap is bridged by a 'vast body of ideas, theories and mythologies' (1973, p. 218).

For Wright, the relationship between ideology and socio-economics is very important. The key is that 'the socio-economic situations of Protestants undoubtedly affect their estimation of the nature of the political situation in relation to Catholics, but only through the mediation of pre-structured ideological beliefs' (1973, p. 243). So for Protestant fundamentalists, Wright argues that the conflict is essentially religious, but that these issues would never develop the significance they do if they had no deeper socio-economic and political meanings. The argument is not that religious beliefs mask an underlying quest for political power. What Wright is arguing is that religious beliefs are important, but they become even more important in their political context. In turn, these beliefs give meaning to that context. Here we get a sense of religion influencing politics and politics influencing religion in a two-way relationship. This reflects closely the argument followed here. We turn now to elaborate more fully upon the line of argument adopted in this book.

Religion, culture and structure

Thus far we have discussed a variety of forms in which religion relates to politics in Northern Ireland. From this it is clear that there are many different ways to define and measure religion. Whilst some emphasize the importance of doctrines, others argue that religion's significance comes from churches' positions as powerful political actors. Others again hold that religion is more symbolic of group differences than anything else. So it is clear that there is conflict over what exactly counts as religion. This brief literature review in the context of Northern Ireland is a microcosm of the wider debate within the sociology of religion about definitions of religion. It is not within the remit of this book to deal exhaustively with this issue, but a few words are necessary in order to clarify the position taken here on the endlessly debated questions: what is religion and when is it socially significant?

Religion is often defined in a substantive way – as a means of relating man to God, answering 'ultimate questions' or pertaining to the supernatural (Glock and Stark 1965; Wilson 1979; Tillich 1963). When seeking to evaluate religion in this way, commentators generally look to 'measurable' indicators of personal religiosity such as belief in certain doctrines or the supernatural. Others prefer functional definitions – or what social roles religion performs. Durkheim (1915), for example, argues that religious practices, rather than beliefs, are what matters. Through meeting together and practising the same rituals, feelings of group belonging are generated and shared views can be reinforced. A similar approach is exemplified in the ideas of 'civil religion', for example, Bellah's (1970) analysis of Americanism. In other words, religion can be defined as shared feelings and ritual enactments of group belonging. Other theorists such as Marx (in McLellan, 1995) and Gramsci (1994) are more concerned with religion's relationship to power, highlighting how churches and states use religion as a form of social control in an attempt to spread ideological hegemony. Religio-political alliances may form as churches endorse political agencies, and vice versa, to consolidate their social control. Meanwhile, as Marx argued, religion acts as a form of social opium to provide consolation for people in order to distract them from the injustices of the political world.

When faced with this array of definitions of religious meanings and functions, it may be difficult for the analyst to decide what to rule in and rule out. Indeed, most problems arise from an over-clear distinction between what religion *is* and what it *does*. In fact, the substantive dimensions of religion (beliefs, feelings, practices) often overlap with functional dimensions (acting as social cement or social control). They can reinforce each other. So in Northern Ireland the question becomes one not just of looking for correlations between doctrinal positions and political attitudes, but also of the roles religion can play in politics for a community in conflict. The approach taken here follows Wittgenstein's idea of family resemblance. We do not outline the *essence* of religion, or say what religion *really* is, but rather outline some of the family characteristics by which it can be recognized and understood. The most important of these characteristics – power, boundary marking, ritual, ideology and theology – are outlined and elaborated upon in Chapters 3 to 7.

Arguing for an inclusive definition of religion does not mean that everything and anything should be seen in some way as 'religious'. One difficulty with functionalist arguments, for example, is that anything that binds people together, such as football fanaticism or rallying around the American flag, can be interpreted as religious. This is problematic as there are qualitative differences between religion, sport and patriotism. Whilst recognizing the quasi-religious structure of other social rituals, we are primarily interested here in ideas and behaviour that are connected in some way to the institutional Christian churches and other specifically religious organizations in Northern Ireland. In this way membership of the Orange Order, which has a clear religious remit, is deemed to be at least partially religious in nature. Membership of the Gaelic Athletic Association (GAA), a sporting organization that brings people together but has no religious remit, is not included in our analysis of religion. Of course if the GAA were to issue a religious mission statement or finance itself from church coffers, its activities would then have a religious dimension.

The same logic applies to substantive approaches to religion that define it as the search for meaning. Whilst some people may well have spiritual feelings when standing on top of a mountain or when doing yoga, we are not primarily interested in these individualized forms of belief here. These personal encounters may well be classed as religion, but they are not very relevant to an analysis of the social and political dimensions of the religious boundary in Northern Ireland. Rather, we are interested in how people's understandings of the world relate to recognizably Protestant and Catholic traditions. In other words, our concern is the public rather than simply the private significance of religion, although of course in practice it is not always possible to separate these out. However, in the final analysis, this book is concerned with forms of religion that are socially and politically relevant in Northern Ireland, not with the vast spectrum of individualized private beliefs. The question then becomes one of how we may locate, measure and evaluate these types of religious beliefs and behaviour. We turn now to an investigation of the relationship between religion and identification to provide us with useful analytical tools to address these questions.

Religion and identification: belonging, boundaries and beliefs

Social identification and community construction

In order to capture the variety of ways in which religious ideas and structures help people make sense of the world, we need analytical tools to access how people construct meaning, how they understand themselves, others and their place in society. The approach utilized here is social constructionism (also referred to as social constructivism). This is informed by the idea that our 'identity', or our sense of who we are, is not a fixed thing that we are born with. Rather, over our lifetimes we are engaged in a constant process of *identification* (Brubaker and Cooper, 2000). This means that we are constantly drawing on our social relationships and experiences of the world to construct and reconstruct our self-image and our ideas about where we belong. So it is not the case that somebody is simply born feeling he or she is a Catholic, but that over a lifetime of experiences a person comes to feel that Catholicism is a part of who they are. When the term 'religious identity' is used here therefore, it does not imply that there is a fixed 'Catholic identity' that people have or do not have. Rather, it refers to the social-psychological *process* of the construction of our sense of self in society.

Identity is also hybrid. This means that there are different aspects of our self, which are important to how we feel and act. For example, my identity as a woman, as a young person and as a university lecturer may be just as important to me as my communal or ethnic identity. In certain situations, some aspects of my identity will be more prominent than others. For example, giving a sociology seminar, my identity as a university lecturer will probably be most pronounced. However, if I go to a bar in Belfast that evening, depending on its location in the communal geography of Northern Ireland, my identity as a communal Protestant may be much more important than the fact that I teach a sociology by day. This will be the case despite the fact that I do not attend church and am religiously agnostic.

The reason different aspects of our identity are sometimes more important than others is because we take our cues from the people around us. Identification is an intrinsically relational process (Berger and Luckmann, 1967; Jenkins, 1996; Hogg and Abrams, 2001). Our self-images are always formed, in large part, through comparing ourselves to others. It is only in relationship with others, and recognizing what we are not, that we construct our own sense of who we are and where we feel we belong. How other people treat us, and their expectations of us, feeds back into our sense of self. In this way personal identity is very much produced from our experiences of the social and political world.

Social psychologists argue that we are naturally disposed towards social categorization and that this forms the basis of social comparison and therefore identity construction. To create a meaningful order for ourselves, we tend to divide the social world into categories: black/white, friend/enemy, tasteful/tacky. As a result of social categorization and comparison, boundaries are created (Brown, 2000). The boundary does not necessarily refer to a physical line of division like the borders between countries, but rather it is a psychological demarcation (Barth, 1969). We tend to draw boundaries between what is familiar and what is different. The boundary very often becomes entangled with moral evaluations – that difference is threatening, or in some way worse (M.B. Brewer, 2003; Douglas, 1966). Furthermore, we tend to assume that those that we place in the same group as ourselves are more similar than we really are, whilst overestimating the qualities that differentiate us from members of other groups (Tajfel, 1981). So the boundaries we construct between us and them, insiders and outsiders, are not necessarily based on clear differences, but rather our *perceptions* of difference. Of course, boundaries, like identities, are fluid and permeable. Identity categories are not fixed in time. They are often fuzzy and sometimes contradictory. However, categorization appears to be a dominant universal process.

Another concept that is used throughout this book is 'community'. Community is based on social categorizations. Community is a tricky word that can be used to describe small groups of people who know each other (for example, in a local village community) or large groups of people who have never met (for example, the Cornish community, or an on-line community). In each case, community is based on individuals' feelings that they belong to a larger group. People could feel this way because they share certain things with one another, perhaps a language, a location or a regular activity. In all of these cases, however, communities only actually exist because individuals believe them to be real. Communities are not entities in their own right, but rather live in the minds of groups of people who identify with them, talk about them, organize events for them, apply for funding for them, speak on their behalf or campaign to get recognition from official bodies (see for, example, Kertzer and Arel, 2002; Howard, 2004). When the Protestant 'community' and the Catholic 'community' are discussed throughout the book, we are not arguing that these groups exist other than in the minds and actions of individuals who think and behave as if they are real. This also means that the 'Catholic community', for example, is not a fixed, homogenous entity. What it means to be a member of the Catholic community can change over time as individuals adapt what they believe being a member entails. Whilst this might have meant being a mass-going, Irish-passport-carrying Catholic in the past, in the present it might simply mean having Catholic parents and being educated in a Catholic school. Religious attendance and Irish nationality might not be necessary for an individual to feel that they are part of the Catholic community. The point is that communities are what people believe them to be and that this can change over time.

In Cohen's (1985) terms, communities are 'symbolic constructions'. By this he means that we draw psychological lines of division between people like us, and outsiders. Whilst the people on our side of the line may actually be very different from one another, Cohen argues that we cluster around symbols that allow us to imagine our own unity. In our daily lives, the boundary may not seem very pressing and we can freely express our differences with those on our side of the line. However, in times of difficulty or crisis, the boundary may loom larger in our imagination and experiences. At these times, the sense that there is a bigger division in society, and that those on the other side of the line are *more different* than we are from one another, allows us to feel that we are indeed part of a community. So communities, for Cohen, exist cognitively: they are not actually 'things', but symbolic constructions.

However, identities and communities do not just exist in our heads. They are also created by our actions. We cognitively internalize social categories, acting and behaving as if they were intrinsically real. This is what Bourdieu (1990, 1991) means when he talks about the 'habitus'. This refers to a culturally specific way of thinking about the world and acting in it. Bourdieu argues that social life is made up of systems of social classification built upon the logic of inclusion and exclusion. We associate different qualities with insiders and outsiders and intuitively know how an insider, or someone in our group, should behave, dress and speak. The habitus tends to be assimilated into our unconscious, in embodied and entrenched perceptions and reactions. It becomes part of shared group understanding and a basis for social action. In other words, as we cognitively order social life into categories, we 'know' which categories we belong to and tend to act accordingly. This is what makes groups practically, as well as psychologically, a social reality.

But this does not answer the question of why some boundaries are more important than others. Out of the huge number of differences that exist between people, why do only some, like Catholic/Protestant, come to dominate social relationships? This is because individuals do not simply freely select categories and boundaries from the wide range of cultural resources at hand. Whilst one is not born with them, there are very good reasons why everyone develops certain types of identifications and feels themselves part of particular communities over time. Sometimes people may try to leave a community, and others may try to join. But this is easier said than done as pre-existing relationships and structures often limit our ability to change how others see us, and therefore how we are likely to see ourselves. To a large degree, existing historical, institutional and structural relations have already selected what dimensions of our identity are going to be most socially important throughout our lives – whether this be gender, race, religion or nationality. These form the bases of our most salient communal memberships (Jenkins 1996, 2000). Although I, as a communal Protestant from Northern Ireland, may have many different identities and allegiances, only some of these make a difference to my opportunities in life. My identity as a single woman, political liberal and soap opera fan may be extremely important to me, but they are not structurally significant in contemporary Northern Ireland. If I want a job in the police force, it is irrelevant that I like watching soap operas. As regards to the new hiring policies, it is significant that I am a Protestant. It may also be significant that I am a woman. In such a way, the structures of society have determined already which parts of my self will make most difference to my life chances.

In this way, politics and power are crucial factors in the identification process (Castells, 1997). Our social status, access to resources and opportunities are ways of measuring one's value against that of others. And it is often through politics that these opportunities are granted or withheld. As citizens, social practices and knowledge are mediated through the state, for example, through social policies, education or censorship. Political policies can promote or discriminate against groups in the allocation of resources. Even where resources are equally accessible to all, the character and ethos of states may recognize some identities as legitimate, or positive, and others not. To a large extent, group or communal identification is about competition for power (Calhoun, 1994). Groups try to demonstrate that they are more deserving of, or have more right to, representation or redistribution. Politics compels people to compete for resources and influence. As Finlayson argues (1997, p. 92), 'politics is itself constitutive of the sorts of identities that people fight for rather than a simple reflection of something pre-given.' In other words, not only do politics set the context for identity construction, it is also, at least partially, what makes people care about identity and community.

Whilst politics and structure are very important in the identification process, we all of course have free will, or agency. But our agency operates in the context of practices and relationships that are already there, and what has already been experienced. Brubaker and Cooper (2000) argue that identification is a product of social and political action, as well as a basis for further action. This means that we are shaped by the political context we are born into. In turn, we think and act according to ideas that we are familiar with, and therefore tend to reproduce that political context. Of course, it is possible that we can change and transform the way we think and act. However, this depends on our experiences of other people as well as of political structures. If I'm constantly told that I am a Catholic, go to a Catholic school, attend mass at a Catholic Church, am beaten up by Protestants and have been discriminated against in my workplace for being a Catholic, it is unlikely that I will transform my identity to Protestant or even to no religion. This is because Catholicism is so interwoven with my experiences in life. So, we *find* ourselves in situations at least as much as we *choose* them; there is at least as much reification of identity as the *way we are*, as there is renegotiation of boundaries. This is why some identities are more embedded than others in our sense of who we are.

Religion and social identification

Religion plays a crucial role in the identification process, not least in divided societies such as Northern Ireland. First, religious affiliation often determines one's place in the social and political structure. As discussed above, some identifications are more deeply embedded than others because they influence our access to power and resources, our place in the society we find ourselves in and how others perceive us. This is certainly the case in Northern Ireland where Protestant and Catholic identifications impinge on almost every sphere of public life, from school selection to filling in employment monitoring forms, from area of residence to choice of partner. These religious communal binaries have been further reinforced in recent years after the Good Friday Agreement of 1998 as more power-sharing arrangements are made in politics and equality legislation is extended into ever more areas of public life, increasing incentives to identify with one community or another. The point is that Protestant and Catholic identifications in Northern Ireland still matter to one's life chances and place in society. So religious identity continues to be a salient boundary marker.

But religion often plays a much more significant role in social relationships than just providing group labels. In societies with significant religious presence or history, it can form a kind of cultural reservoir from which categorizations of self and other may be derived. Religious traditions provide a wealth of cultural data from different sorts of values, lifestyles, expected behaviour and decorum to different architectural styles, religious paraphernalia, memorials and calendars of sacred events. Since individuals and groups are constantly engaged in a process of categorization of self and other, it is unsurprising that religion, which forms an enormous part of childhood socialization and daily life in Northern Ireland and elsewhere, should become part of the substance of these categorizations (Baston et al., 1993, pp. 26–30). In other words, as well as marking out the boundary, religion can give meaning to it. It can provide the substantive content to differentiate insiders from outsiders. Religious practices and behaviour that are different from ours can seem strange. In the context of conflict, they can also seem threatening. So ideas of religious difference can become embedded in how we perceive ourselves as well as what we think the other group is like. When we think and act in these terms, we reproduce these religious differences. Religious culture and practices can help provide the substance of the boundary.

We are inclined to attribute negative and positive values to perceived out-group and in-group characteristics anyway. Thus in a country with a religious history, it is likely that *theological* beliefs and religiously informed values, which are often intrinsically about good and bad, come into play. Rather than simply helping mark out the boundary, religious beliefs can help people evaluate what the boundary means. If I believe that certain groups go to heaven and others to hell, this may help explain why some groups in society are more antagonistic than others. Not only is there a political boundary between Catholics and Protestants, but religious beliefs can also justify people's feelings that their group is superior to the other. So religious beliefs can help justify and explain social relationships. But it is not simply a one-way relationship where people use religious beliefs to legitimize boundaries that are already there. Sometimes, experiences of the boundary and of politics can influence a person's religious beliefs. If someone experiences political persecution or insecurity, they may have increased needs for reassurance or explanation that religious beliefs may provide. These beliefs may differ sharply from those of the persecutor, thus reinforcing the boundary. However, it is not simply that religious beliefs are a mask for a deeper boundary. Sometimes, they may even encourage believers to forgive or reconcile with their persecutor. The point is that religious beliefs can help provide the meanings of the boundary.

Moreover, religious agencies and institutions are powerful actors that help set the context in which identities and boundaries are formed. They strive to structure and set the tone of social life. On a practical level, churches can play an important role in the structuring of life from birth, marriage and death, to more regular activities such as child care, education, sport or cultural activities. Churches can also provide fault-lines that help structure divisions: teachings or sermons, for example, very often tend not only to view outsiders as different, but also hold them to be in some way 'worse', heathens, heretics, unsaved, damned, and so on. Churches too legislate on certain issues, an important example being the Catholic Church's prohibitions on moral issues such as divorce and abortion, and its interreligious policies such as the infamous 1908 *Ne Temere* decree, which instructed that the children of a mixed religion marriage must be brought up as Catholics (although this stipulation has subsequently been loosened with *Mixta Matrimonia* in 1970). This clearly defines who is inside and outside of the group. Churches have also provided sanctuary and guidance in times of communal crisis; they have negotiated with politicians, governments and paramilitary organizations; they have acted as spokespeople for their communities seeming to articulate nationalist or unionist political views (Morrow et al., 1991). Through this process churches carve out a specialized niche for themselves. They seek to maintain their authority and to influence as many people as possible. In such a way, churches play a very significant role in the identification process. Whilst the churches in Northern Ireland have in fact generally sought to mediate rather than exacerbate political tensions, they are primarily interested in the maintenance of their own power and authority. They are by no means neutral social actors. So it is important to bear in mind how the religious institutional setting of political life in Northern Ireland helps structure social boundaries and their meanings.

To sum up, ideas of identity and difference are shaped by perceptions of both cultural and structural power and powerlessness. Identification develops through experience and choice, but this process is mediated through powerful actors and institutions that structure the context in which social and political relationships take place. Perceptions of self and others often take the form of moral evaluations in a struggle to appropriate the past and to shape the future. The purpose of this book is to examine in depth how people in Northern Ireland draw on religion to identify social differences, similarities, values, place, relation to power, and so on in order to construct their personal and group identifications. Using this approach allows us to see how religion is a lot more significant than just a marker of group difference in Northern Ireland.

Structure of the book

Religion helps give substance and meaning to identity and group membership. This is not to say that the boundary in Northern Ireland is *essentially* religious. Instead, the boundary between communities that has been constructed in Northern Ireland over centuries is best described as 'communal'. This term captures how the boundary encompasses politics, nationalism, inequality and colonialism as well as religious dimensions of difference. Being a Catholic is not simply about having a political preference on the constitution; rather, it describes a person's experience of Northern Ireland in general. People can feel themselves members of the Catholic community without necessarily being a nationalist, ever having experienced inequality or favouring a united Ireland. This is because Catholic group membership is tied into family relationships and social networks as a result of socialization and education. It is also because in a divided society, differences are felt very acutely and are seen to structure access to power and opportunities as well as psychological perceptions of sameness and difference. As Ruane and Todd (1996) argue, although communities are diverse and intangible, they are none the less socially and politically real. Although communities in Northern Ireland are certainly capable of change, for the meantime, they are as divided as ever. Most people still find security in communal membership, and people's empathy and sense of moral responsibility continue to be shaped by communal boundaries (Ruane and Todd, 1996). In this way, Catholic and Protestant remain practical categories of analysis in Northern Ireland.

This does not mean that either the Protestant or the Catholic community is a united, homogenous entity. Although the communities have been by and large constructed in opposition to each other, they each contain huge internal variations of aspirations, identities and resources. British versus Irish, settler versus native, advantaged versus disadvantaged, and indeed Protestant versus Catholic are clumsy ways of identifying a communal division that actually encompasses all of these things, in varying degrees, for various people. Furthermore, these dimensions of difference overlap and mutually reinforce each other. Thus to single out one main division, and hang the others around it, is to deny the complexity of the communities themselves. In such a way, the argument presented here by no means tries to assert the primacy of religion as a cause of conflict, but rather locates religion within the wider structure of communal relationships and politics.

Religion is an important dimension of identity and community in five main ways. It provides institutional support for the boundary, it marks out different identities and underpins social segregation, it offers rituals and practices that reinforce community membership, and it provides religious ideas and theological beliefs that sustain and reproduce divisions. These dimensions of religious significance are developed in Chapters 3–7. To provide background information, up-to-date survey data on religious and political attitudes is presented in Chapter 2. The persistent importance of belonging to a religious community in Northern Ireland is highlighted. This chapter argues that Northern Ireland ranks extremely high along all indicators of religious belief and practice, but that these do not map directly onto political attitudes or voting behaviour. It suggests explanations for this lack of congruence and argues that religion should not be dismissed as socially insignificant on this basis. The various strengths and weaknesses of using survey evidence to measure the social and political dimensions of religion are discussed.

Chapter 3 analyses the institutional connections between the churches and politics. It argues that whilst there is official separation of church and state in Northern Ireland, religion continues to influence the tone of public life and remains deeply involved in a wide variety of semi-state and community activities, particularly for Catholics. It also examines the continuing trend of Protestant cleric-politicians. Data for this section comes from secondary analysis of ethnographies, community studies, media reportage on the links between churches and politicians, official statistics, literature written by clerics and political figures as well as a wealth of academic analyses. It is also informed by the author's interviews with a variety of Protestant and Catholic clergy.

Chapters 4–7 turn to analysis of the bottom-up dimensions of religion. Interviews were conducted with 35 Protestants and Catholics as part of a PhD study, completed in 2001. These interviews are drawn on to elaborate central themes and excerpts are provided to illustrate various points. Details of the background and process of these interviews can be found in the Appendix, along with some demographic information about interviewees. More recent interviews with 30 evangelical Protestants, as well as some who have left their faith, conducted 2001–2003, also inform the analysis, particularly the discussion of religious ideology and theology in Chapters 7 and 8 (see also Appendix for details). All participants are of course anonymous and names have been changed to protect identities. Other data for Chapters 4–7 come from secondary analysis of ethnographies, community relations literature including proceedings of workshops and conferences, and other relevant historical, anthropological, psychological, sociological and political science studies relating to Northern Ireland. At the beginning of each chapter there is some more general discussion of the dimension of religion at hand. This discussion is largely informed by contemporary debates in the sociology of religion and is intended to provide the reader with a broader theoretical background to the more specific discussion on Northern Ireland.

Chapter 4 outlines the significance of religion as an identity marker and as the basis for social segregation in Northern Ireland. It argues that religion is a central dimension of social difference and is maintained through segregated education, residential patterns, endogamy and social networks. Religion, more than any other dimension of difference, underpins organizational and relational segregation, particularly for those who cannot afford to live or be educated somewhere more neutral. This chapter provides examples of how deeply religion becomes entangled with communal identities because of people's experiences of social relationships and structures. It points to cases where religion simply flags difference and gives no substantive meaning or content to identity and community.

Chapters 5–7 on the other hand explore the ways in which religion actually helps constitute the boundary by providing practices and meanings to support it. Chapter 5 examines the role of rituals and practices in the construction of community and identity in Northern Ireland. It argues that, although less pronounced than at the beginning of conflict in the early 1970s, the churches continue to play a central role in organizing community life. Moreover, extremely high levels of religious practice add to perceptions of social difference by giving communities practical as well as ideological resources with which to identify in-group and out-group members. Religious rituals regularly bring groups of people together. This helps construct feelings of belonging and helps community members 'recognize' other group members. It also means that they partake in common activities that can lead to perceptions that they share certain understandings of social life. This is particularly the case when social and political issues are addressed from the pulpit. Of course, people do not agree with everything that the churches say; however, the institutional context in terms of transmitting messages is significant. Finally, the chapter argues that the ritual dimensions of religion are particularly significant for Catholics in Northern Ireland.

While Chapter 5 deals with practices, Chapter 6 explores the importance of religious ideas. It argues that often religion takes the form of ideology. This is where religiously informed concepts help construct identity and imagine community. Whilst these ideas are not concerned with answering existential questions or relating man to God, they have religious origins and features. They constitute narratives of morality and help individuals recognize which social groups are familiar or unfamiliar, better or worse. Moreover, religious ideology is significant because it keeps religious ideas of difference alive. In times of political stability, these ideas of difference are for the most part fairly benign and may resemble any other cultural identity categories. However, in times of personal or political crisis, ideology may emerge and have more substantively religious implications. Religious ideology is most likely to construct identity and community for Protestants, but plays an interesting part in Catholics' identification processes as well. This is an underdeveloped theme in the sociology of religion and is possibly the most widespread way in which religion is socially significant in Northern Ireland.

Religious ideology is related to the political significance of theology, which is elaborated on in Chapter 7. As people strive to find sense in life and explain the social world, theology is often politically meaningful. It can offer explanation, justification and comfort in otherwise uncertain social situations. Like religious ideology, theology is more important for Protestants than Catholics. In fact theology probably only has political importance for some groups of evangelical Protestants. However, to use Davie's (2000) term, if theology is the 'tip of the iceberg', religious ideology is the mass of meaning that lies beneath the surface of the water. That is to say that whilst theology is the most noticeable form of religion, it is closely related to a wealth of ideological concepts that are less visible, but just as important.

These six chapters that follow can be read in a variety of ways. Each chapter elaborates a different aspect of religious significance in Northern Ireland, and an understanding of each component part is needed in order to appreciate the full extent of the relationship between religion, identity and politics. However, the chapters may also be read as essays on related themes. Those seeking contemporary survey analysis about religious trends will find what they are looking for in Chapter 2. Historical institutionalists and perhaps practitioners will be most interested in the connections between religious and political institutions over time and should turn first to Chapter 3. Sociologists of religion who are interested in public/private distinctions, implicit religion and alternative forms of religious significance in an ostensibly secular world will be most interested in Chapters 5 and 6 on religious ritual and ideology. Scholars and students interested in specific religious groups, in particular, evangelicals, will find relevant information in Chapter 7 which relates to theology and politics.

The central argument of this book, however, is that religion cannot be reduced to any one of these dimensions. Just as conflict in Northern Ireland must be understood as multifaceted, so too the significance of religion in the conflict must be seen as comprising a variety of different dimensions. Each one of these dimensions reinforces the others. This is why the relationship between religion, politics and conflict in Northern Ireland is so strong and has remained for such a long time. If one dimension of religion declines in significance, the others will not necessarily follow suit. This is why religion in Northern Ireland remains socially and politically important despite falling church attendance and secularization along some measures such as attitudes to the Sabbath. Religion is much more widely and deeply rooted than this. It forms an integral part of social relationships. These social relationships are practically constructed through religious segregation and religious rituals. These relationships are cognitively constructed through ideologies and theologies that define self and other. Furthermore, these relationships are institutionalized as religious and political elites work together on a variety of levels to extend their influence. Each dimension of religious power, practice and ideas has implications for the others.

Religion then, is partially constitutive of ethnic, communal, national and political identity in Northern Ireland. Indeed, what is identity if not constituted by the resources at hand in a particular society? For some, religion is a very strong dimension in communal identity, for others it is weaker, but we find that it is seldom absent. Moreover, the salience of religion is not limited to the devout or the practising, as it provides meanings that are social at least as much as they are spiritual. As such, the political and social importance of religion must be analysed in terms of the meanings it gives to identity, community and politics. Furthermore, there is a two-way causal relationship between religion and politics. Religion is responsive to political change. A large part of what religion does in Northern Ireland is to make sense of what is going on politically. Religion is not passive; it actively produces, reproduces and transforms social relationships. It is constitutive of political context and possibilities.

2
The 'sectarian headcount'

Key points

- *There is a very strong relationship between religious identity and political attitudes.*

- *Only a tiny minority of people cross over the community divide in party preference, political and national identity.*

- *The relationship between churchgoing/strength of theological beliefs and political attitudes is weak.*

- *A survey-based approach to measuring religious meanings and significance is limited.*

Based mainly on analysis of recent survey material, this chapter examines the 'measurable' relationships between religion and politics. It begins by charting the changing religious landscape of Northern Ireland, assessing the extent to which secularization has occurred in the region and asking how far we can talk about the persistence of religion. Following this, an up-to-date analysis of political attitudes and identity in Northern Ireland is presented. The chapter also examines the relationship between religious and political attitudes and behaviour. It finds that religion is a very good predictor of national identity, political identity and voting behaviour. Protestants are fairly homogenous in that they see themselves as not Irish and not nationalist. Similarly (although to a somewhat lesser extent), the vast majority of Catholics see themselves as not British and not unionist. This is why demography in Northern Ireland has often been termed a 'sectarian headcount'. There are mixed views within communities about the possibility of united Ireland and maintenance of the union with Britain, although there are clear trends for Protestants preferring the union with Britain and Catholics preferring Irish unity. However, whilst religious affiliation is central to political attitudes, religious behaviour and beliefs are not. Churchgoing and strength of religious beliefs do not actually seem to tell us very much about wider social and political attitudes. Fervent religious views do not correlate with fervent political views. The chapter concludes by suggesting possible reasons for this disjuncture and argues for the importance of looking beyond statistical analysis, outlining a rationale for approaching the relationship more qualitatively.

Most of the data in this chapter comes from the Northern Ireland Life and Times Surveys, unless otherwise stated. It is referenced as NILTS and the year of the survey is given. The Young Northern Ireland Life and Times Survey is also used. Both sets of data are publicly available at <http://www.ark.ac.uk/nilt> and <http://www.ark.ac.uk/ylt> respectively.

Religion and secularization

Northern Ireland continues to be a very religious society along almost all indicators of beliefs and practices (Mitchell, 2004a). Whilst it has experienced some secularization over the last 30 years, it still ranks amongst the most religious societies in western Europe and indeed the world (Fahey et al., 2004) Whilst in later chapters we explore different ways of assessing the social and political significance of religion, here we simply map out recent trends in religious affiliation, practices and beliefs.

Religious belonging

First of all, Northern Ireland has an extremely high rate of religious belonging, as measured by religious affiliations. In the 2001 census, 46 per cent of the population identified as Protestants and 40 per cent as Catholics (see Table 2.1). The breakdown was reported in the media as 44 per cent Catholics and 53 per cent Protestants, because it included those who now identify as having no religion with the religion that they were brought up in. If we take the former figures relating to self-identifications, we can see that Protestants are no longer in an absolute majority in Northern Ireland. They do however remain the predominant group. The number of individuals who self-identify as Catholics has slowly but steadily grown from 35 per cent in the 1961 census. However, predictions that Catholics would rapidly outnumber Protestants, on account of higher levels of Protestant emigration and higher Catholic birth rates, have proved to be overstated. Demographic change is best described as gradual.

Table 2.1 Religious affiliation in Northern Ireland

Religious denomination	Population (%)
Catholic	40
Presbyterian Church in Ireland	21
Church of Ireland	15
Methodist Church in Ireland	4
Other Christian (and Christian related)	6
Other religion and philosophies	>1
No religion or religion not stated	14

Source: Census Office for Northern Ireland, Key Statistics Tables 2001, KS07a

Of these 'other Christian' denominations, the vast majority might be described as Protestant variations and can be grouped into the larger Protestant category. These include just over 1 per cent of Baptists, and under 1 per cent of Free Presbyterians and of Brethrens. There are over eighty additional smaller denominations that can be classed as Protestant, all of which number less than 0.5 per cent of the population and a number of which have membership of less than a hundred people (Northern Ireland Census, 2001, Key Statistics Tables, KS07c). Whilst mainstream Protestant denominations have been declining in numbers in recent years, this has been coupled with some growth of conservative evangelical churches, such as the Baptists and Free Presbyterians, as well as an increase in more liberal charismatic and independent house churches (Brewer, 2004). Thus the category of Protestant encompasses a wide variety of denominations and solitary congregations. As we shall see below, this picture is complicated further by the fact that within even singular Protestant denominations there can be a variety of theological perspectives.

Whilst 96 per cent of the population have been raised a Catholic or a Protestant (NILTS, 2003), the number of people reporting that they now have no religion has been steadily climbing over the last 15 years.[1] In the 1961 Northern Ireland census, only 384 persons out of one and a half million identified themselves as atheists, free-thinkers or humanists (Rose, 1971, p. 248), whereas in the present period around 8–10 per cent claim to have no religion (not to be confused with religion 'not stated' where people refuse to answer the question) (NILTS 2002, 2003). This figure has been fairly consistent since the mid-1990s and represents a significant new grouping in Northern Ireland (Hayes and McAllister, 2004). The Protestant grouping have lost more numbers to the no religion group than has the Catholic grouping. The retention rate for Catholics is 93 per cent as opposed to 74 and 79 per cent for the Anglican and Presbyterian churches respectively (Hayes and McAllister, 2004, p. 6). In what Hayes and McAllister describe as 'fundamentalist Protestant' churches, the retention rate is only 65 per cent. We compare the beliefs and behaviour of those with no religion to Protestants and Catholics below.

Despite the growth of the no religion group, religious belonging remains strong amongst the young. In a 2003 survey of 15–17 year olds, 88 per cent regarded themselves as belonging to a particular religion. When asked a slightly different question, 'Do you see yourself as part of a religious community?', 91 per cent of Catholics and 88 per cent of Protestants agreed (YNILTS, 2003). Seventy per cent of Catholic and 59 per cent of Protestant teenagers felt that their *religious identity* is important to them, more than national identity in both cases. When asked a slightly different 'How important is your religion to you?', 71 per cent of Catholic and 59 per cent of Protestant teenagers answered that it was important. Eighty-six per cent think that religion will always make a difference to the way people feel about each other in Northern Ireland. This certainly indicates that religious belonging is just as important to young people as is to their elders, albeit probably in different ways.

Another important aspect of belonging to point out is that rates of mobility between Catholics and Protestants in Northern Ireland are extremely marginal. Hayes and McAllister found (2004, p. 6), based on the 2002 Northern Ireland Life and Times Survey, that less than 1 per cent of those raised Catholic became Protestants, and less than 2 per cent of (mostly Anglican) Protestants became Catholics. Overall then, there is small but significant movement towards disaffiliation, particularly amongst Protestants, practically no movement back to affiliation amongst those with no religion, and very little crossing of the religious communal divide.

A final point of interest is the geographical spread of religious belonging. Catholics number over 60 per cent of the population in much of the west of Northern Ireland, and over 70 per cent in Derry as well in Newry and Mourne. In the northeast of the region, for example, in local government districts of Ards, Ballymena, Ballymoney and Larne, Presbyterians number almost twice their national average. Church of Ireland membership is highest in the southwest, often inching ahead of Presbyterians and in Fermanagh outnumbering Presbyterians by nearly eight times. Out of 26 local government districts, only three have over 20 per cent of people in the no religion/religion not stated grouping. These are the wealthier satellites of Belfast: North Down, Ards and Carrickfergus. Belfast comes eighth with almost 17 per cent in this category. In practically all areas with a small no religion/religion not stated group (less than 10 per cent), there is a Catholic majority (Census Office for Northern Ireland, Key Statistics Tables, KS07a). It is therefore significant to consider that religious belonging in Northern Ireland is uneven, with the west being mainly Catholic, the north being disproportionately Protestant and urban areas having the highest rates of disaffiliation.

Overall, despite the recent rise of a significant no religion grouping, it is much too soon to talk of religious decline in Northern Ireland. Religious belonging today is extremely high, and is still very much structured along traditional Catholic–Protestant lines.

Religious practices

Another way religion can be measured is in terms of church attendance. Northern Ireland has experienced some decline in religious practice in recent years. However, comparatively speaking, Northern Ireland is more notable because of the persistence of participation.[2] Figure 2.1 shows the change in weekly church attendance over time. As we can see, church attendance amongst Catholics has dropped considerably since 1968 when 95 per cent went to mass every week. However, as shown in Table 2.2, attendance remains high with three out of five Catholics going to mass weekly or more, a further 17 per cent attending at least monthly and only 8 per cent never at all. Amongst Protestants, the rate of decline is somewhat less dramatic – although Protestants overall remain almost half as likely to attend church weekly as Catholics. In 1968, 46 per cent of Protestants attended weekly, whereas this figure had fallen to 34 per cent in 2003. A further 14 per cent attend at least monthly, and 19 per cent never attend at all outside of special occasions such as weddings, funerals and baptisms. Some Protestant denominations such as the Brethren and Free Presbyterian Church have attendance rates over 60 per cent. Although their numbers are small, 87 per cent of members of the Elim Pentecostal Church attend church at least weekly. So, in some sections of Protestantism at least, religious practices are thriving.

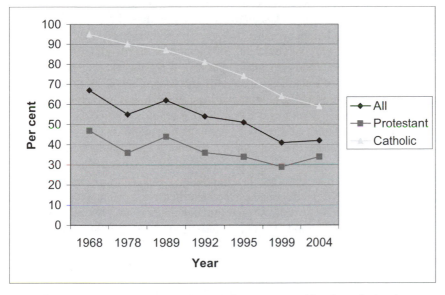

Figure 2.1 Trends in weekly church attendance rates in Northern Ireland

Sources: Adapted from Fahey et al. (2004) based on Northern Ireland Loyalty Survey, 1968; Social Attitudes Survey, 1978; Northern Ireland Social Attitudes Survey, 1989 and 1995; Northern Ireland Life and Times Survey, 1999 and 2003.

Table 2.2 Church attendance by religion (%)

Religion	1+ times per week	2/3 times per month	Once a month	Several times a year	Less frequently	Never
Catholic	60	11	6	6	10	8
Protestant	34	8	6	14	18	19
No religion	4	—	3	8	14	70

Question: How often do you attend services or meetings connected with your religion?

Source: Northern Ireland Life and Times Survey, 2003 (N=1738)

NB figures may not add up to 100 because of rounding.

Although church attendance rates remain relatively high overall, it is important to take into account the effect of age. The under-35s practise less regularly than their elders. In fact, those aged 18 to 35 are about half as likely as those over 55 to attend church once a week or more – 42 per cent of Catholics under 35 compared to 79 per cent of Catholics over 55, and 16 per cent of Protestants under 35 compared to 44 per cent of Protestants over 55 (NILTS, 2003). However, amongst some Protestant denominations, attendance amongst the young is much higher than this. Very strikingly, amongst evangelicals, teenage church attendance is high – 85 per cent claim frequent or regular attendance (Bruce and Alderdice, 1993, p. 15). There are also indications churchgoing remains strong amongst teenagers under 18. Sixty-five per cent of 16-year-olds surveyed in 2003 claimed to attend religious services regularly (once a month or more), and 44 per cent at least weekly. Regular attenders included 73 per cent of Catholic 16-year-olds and 54 per cent of Protestant 16-year-olds (52 per cent and 34 per cent attend at least weekly, respectively). Therefore it appears that whilst religious practices are lowest amongst the young overall, they may remain an important aspect of socialization before adulthood.

These figures indicate that religious practices are declining considerably in Northern Ireland. However, comparison with British trends helps put this into perspective. Overall, if we class regular churchgoing as monthly or more, 57 per cent of the population of Northern Ireland can be identified as regular attenders. This is far higher than in Britain as a whole, where regular attendance in 1999 was 13 per cent, and 54 per cent never attend (De Graaf and Need, 2000, p. 124). Moreover, the British figures are slightly influenced by the fact that religious minorities there are much more religiously active, with nearly three quarters of Sikhs, Muslims and 'New Protestant' Caribbeans, and over half of Hindus attending services, prayer meetings or a place or worship every week (Modood, 1997, p. 303). In any case, a huge number of families in Britain have absolutely no contact whatsoever with a church. In contrast, in Northern Ireland, experience of the church is more universal. Only 18 per cent of the entire population never attend church and even amongst this group, there is often familiarity with religious rituals and behaviour as a result of religious socialization and education.

Comparison with church attendance figures in the Republic of Ireland is also revealing. Whereas church attendance in the Republic of Ireland stood at 94 per cent in 1973, this had fallen to 84 per cent by 1992 and to 64 per cent in 1999 (Fahey et al., 2004). Although not strictly comparable methodologically speaking, the most recent TNS/MRBI survey in 2003 found that attendance had dropped to 44 per cent (Stevens, 2003). This shows a steady decline in attendance amongst Catholics in the Republic of Ireland that is not reflected to the same degree in Northern Ireland. Indeed, it indicates that religious practices are deeply embedded in Northern Ireland – a theme that is developed in Chapter 5.

In sum, we can say that whilst churchgoing in Northern Ireland has declined since the 1960s, it continues to be a thriving practice in comparison with many other western European states. Nearly three out of five members of the population can be classed as regular churchgoers. Churchgoing is particularly strong amongst Catholics and in some smaller evangelical Protestant denominations. Moreover, it is the exception rather than the rule that a person has no contact whatsoever with religious practice.

Religious beliefs

We have seen the extent to which churchgoing continues to pervade Northern Ireland. The next question must be 'What do people believe?'. Over three-quarters of the population believe in God, and of these, 51 per cent have 'no doubts' whatever that God exists. Only 4 per cent do not believe in God. Three-quarters of the population also believe in heaven, Catholics slightly more so than Protestants. Fifty-three per cent believe in miracles, again more Catholics than Protestants. However, the 62 per cent that believe in hell are rather more evenly spread between Catholics and Protestants. Overall, 70 per cent of the population pray at least once a month (NILTS, 1998).

With regard to specific theological beliefs in Northern Ireland, by far the best means we have of measuring these is Boal, Keane and Livingstone's 1997 survey of Belfast churchgoers. Amongst Catholic churchgoers, Boal et al. observe both continuity and change in the 1990s. They found a high degree of orthodoxy and obedience to the church, alongside significant generational changes in patterns of beliefs. In particular, young Catholics display a more 'a la carte' attitude to church teachings. Overall, 48 per cent of Catholic churchgoers are found to be of high orthodoxy, 38 per cent of moderate, and 14 per cent of low orthodoxy. This classification was made in relation to respondents' levels of belief in a range of church teachings, for example, the resurrection of Christ, the concept of sin, the immaculate conception, papal infallibility and the Catholic Church as the 'one true church'. Whilst this seems to indicate that Catholic churchgoers are rather legalistic, Boal et al. point out how, post-Vatican Two, ostensible obedience to rules camouflages growing liberalization, a sense of individualism and disobedience of formal religious requirements. This change must also be seen in the light of the recent domestic problems of the Catholic Church in Ireland including sexual abuse as well as the increased questioning of authority in secular Irish society. The large decline in numbers attending confession throughout Ireland is well documented (Inglis, 1998), and almost half of those surveyed by Boal et al. considered individual conscience, rather than church teaching, to be the most important guide to their decision-making.

In terms of Belfast's Protestant churchgoers, Boal et al. find more continuity than change in religious beliefs. Amidst the denominational mosaic of Protestantism in Northern Ireland, a system of theological classification was devised based on commitment to biblical inerrancy and the centrality of a conversion experience. Conservatives were so categorized for their firm beliefs in each and represented half the sample. One-quarter of liberals adopted neither of these commitments, whilst a further quarter of 'liberal-conservatives' espoused one or other of them (1997, p. 95). In comparison with their similar 1983 survey, Boal et al. found that theological conservatism was continuing to thrive, and had even made marginal gains over the decade. As such, they argue that 'theories assuming the decline of either fundamentalism or evangelicalism with the progress of industrial modernism must seriously be questioned' (1997, p. 96). Interestingly, this data shows a higher level of doctrinal conservatism within younger age groups. Nearly three-quarters of those between the ages of 25 and 34 fall into the conservative category compared with just over half ten years previously (1997, p. 98). So although young Protestants are less likely to attend church overall, many of those who still go appear to be very conservative. Overall then, for the Protestant churchgoing community in Belfast, it is difficult to make the argument that any substantial decline or liberalization of religious beliefs is taking place.

But what of those who rarely or never practise their religion and those who claim to have no religion? Here, Davie's (1994) thesis of 'believing without belonging' becomes salient in relation to Northern Ireland. People who do not go to church often define themselves as religious persons, pray regularly and rarely describe themselves as convinced atheists. Davie rightly concludes that many people in Britain are still interested in belief and religion, but feel less of a need to give this institutional expression, and as such, 'unchurched' is a better description of these people than secular (2000). Likewise, Casanova (1994, pp. 38–9) argues that in America, 'both religious "fundamentalists" and fundamentalist "secular humanists" are cognitive minorities' and that 'the majority of Americans tend to be humanists, who are simultaneously religious and secular'.

A similar trend is at work in Northern Ireland. Those who cite no religious identification cannot be described simply as secularists. In fact, 40 per cent of them believe in God and a further 26 per cent believe in some kind of higher power. Nearly two-thirds believe that there is truth in one or in many religions. Nearly one-fifth feel they are religious persons and pray at least every day (NILTS, 1998). As Brewer (2002) points out, some of those who claim no religion share many beliefs with Christians, such as in life after death. Although these beliefs may be more unstructured and individualistic, it is not possible to argue that the no religion group are convinced secularists. Of course Hayes and McAllister (1995) are right to point out that there are significant differences in belief between those with and without religious affiliations; however, it is also clear that there are shades of grey inside and outside the churches in Northern Ireland.

In conclusion, along these three main indicators of religiosity – affiliation, practice and belief – Northern Ireland continues to rank very highly. Although there has been a slight decline in affiliation, a significant decline in attendance and reorganization of religious beliefs in different directions, Northern Ireland can by no means be described as a secularized society. Nor is it likely to become as secularized, or at least as religiously privatized, as the rest of Britain in the immediate future. Religious practices remain more deeply embedded in Northern Ireland than in the Republic of Ireland. Whilst indicators of religiosity are lower amongst the young, they are still significant and it is unclear whether or not generational factors will encourage their re-entry into religious life in later years. In Chapters 4–7 we explore how these religious affiliations, practices and beliefs are important to people's understanding of politics. Before that, the next two sections provide an introduction to recent survey material on the relationship between religion and political attitudes.

Religion and political attitudes

Three themes are immediately striking upon analysis of the connections between religion and political attitudes. The first is the strong relationship between religious affiliation and communal politics. For the majority of people in Northern Ireland their political identity and their religious affiliation are almost coterminous. Whilst there is internal variation within communities, there is almost no crossing over the boundary to the other side. Political preferences are sharply differentiated between

Protestants and Catholics, while the absence of a religious affiliation is associated with the lack of a political identity (Breen and Hayes, 1997, p. 228). Secondly, variations in religious beliefs and practice within communities do not make a significant difference to political attitudes. Strong religious beliefs or regular churchgoing do not mark out the political extremes in any way. And thirdly, those who identify with no religion often follow the political attitudinal patterns of their religious community of origin. Again, whilst those with no religion are more likely to opt out of communal politics, there is very little crossing of the divide. We conclude that association with religious community, rather than theological position, continues to form the strongest basis for political preferences.

Religious affiliation and national identity

There is a reasonably stable relationship between a Protestant affiliation and British identity, and a Catholic affiliation and Irish identity over time. Since a 'Northern Irish' identification has been introduced to questionnaires in 1989, it has been selected by almost a quarter of Catholics and of those with no religion, and almost one-fifth of Protestants. A Northern Irish identification is often seen as more 'neutral', and is chosen more by the under-45s than their elders.[3] The category 'Ulster' is selected more frequently by Protestants than Catholics, probably because of its historical associations with Protestant dominance. The general trend since conflict restarted in the late 1960s is the strengthening of both Irish and British identities amongst Catholics and Protestants respectively, at the expense of the alternatives. Just less than two out of five of the no religion group identify themselves as something other than Irish or British. Overall, the trend is one of stability, with nearly a third of the population opting out of Irish/British national identifications (see Table 2.3).

Table 2.3 National identity by religion (%)

Religion	Irish	British	Northern Irish	Ulster	Other / Don't know
Catholic	63	8	25	2	4
Protestant	2	66	22	8	2
No religion	27	41	23	4	11

Question: Which of these best describes the way you think of yourself?

Source: Northern Ireland Life and Times Survey, 2003 (N=1783)

NB figures may not add up to 100 because of rounding.

Religious affiliation and political identity

There are similar trends in political identification, with strong Protestant-unionist and Catholic-nationalist correlations (see Table 2.4). Over a quarter of the population profess neither a nationalist nor a unionist political identity; however, there are extremely small movements across the communal boundary. Significantly, 66 per cent of those with no religion espouse neither a nationalist nor a unionist political identity. Amongst this group there is more likely to be a unionist, than a nationalist, identification as more Protestants than Catholics disaffiliate with their religion of origin. Like Irish national identity, nationalist political identity has strengthened somewhat along communal lines after the Good Friday Agreement. After the cease-fires in 1994 and the subsequent growth of respectability of Sinn Féin it became more acceptable to identify with nationalism in Northern Ireland. Amongst Catholics, a nationalist identification rose by over 30 per cent between 1989 and 1999 (it has since fallen slightly).[4] The numbers of Protestants identifying as unionist has been more or less stable over time.[5]

Table 2.4 Political identity by religion (%)

Religion	Nationalist	Unionist	Neither	Other
Catholic	60	—	36	1
Protestant	1	69	29	2
No religion	9	22	66	3

Question: Do you think of yourself as a unionist, a nationalist or neither?

Source: Northern Ireland Life and Times Survey, 2003 (N=1782)

NB figures may not add up to 100 because of rounding.

Religious affiliation and party preference

The relationship between religious affiliation and party preference is also strong (see Table 2.5). Over six out of ten Protestants vote for unionist parties, and over six out of ten Catholics vote for nationalist parties. Just over a quarter of Catholics and just under a quarter of Protestants say they do not know who to vote for or support no party. However, there is very little crossing of the political divide. A mere 2 per cent of Protestants identify with the SDLP, whilst no Catholics identify with any unionist political party. Nearly half of those with no religion are also politically disaffiliated, whilst the rest of this group is divided between unionist, nationalist and other party preferences. So, there is strong evidence that mobility into the no religion group leads to less communal voting.[6] However, if we analyse the number of people professing no religion by their religion of origin, and remember this is about one in ten people overall, there remains scarcely any *crossing* of the communal political divide (see Table 2.6). Thus, whilst it is possible to loosen communal political ties, 'betraying' one's community of origin is extremely rare.

Table 2.5 Religious affiliation and expressed party preference (%)

Party*	Protestant	Catholic	No religion
UUP	34	—	9
DUP	28	—	8
PUP	1	—	1
SDLP	2	39	10
Sinn Féin	—	23	9
APNI	5	2	12
Women's Coalition	1	2	4
Other party/answer	6	5	6
No party	20	24	39
Don't know	4	4	3

*UUP – Ulster Unionist Party; DUP – Democratic Unionist Party; PUP – Progressive Unionist Party; SDLP – Social Democratic and Labour Party; APNI – Alliance Party of Northern Ireland.

Question: Which Northern Ireland political party would you support?

Source: Northern Ireland Life and Times Survey, 2003 (N=1782)

NB figures may not add up to 100 because of rounding.

Table 2.6 Party preference of 'nones' (no religion) according to religion of origin (%)

Party	Protestant	Catholic	None	All
DUP	11	2	17	10
UUP	31	—	17	23
SDLP	2	29	—	9
Sinn Féin	—	15	—	3
APNI	22	12	8	19
No Party	33	42	58	37
[N]	[123]	[41]	[12]	[176]

Source: reproduced from Breen and Hayes, 1997, p. 231; based on 1991 and 1994 Northern Ireland Social Attitudes Surveys.

Religious affiliation and constitutional preference

Finally, preferences for the future of Northern Ireland are also structured along lines of religious affiliation, although there is a stronger relationship for Protestants than Catholics (see Table 2.7). Currently, less than half of Catholics express a preference for a united Ireland.[7] Interestingly, when the question is turned around and people are asked what would they do if there *was* a united Ireland, a very different picture emerges with only 19 per cent of Protestants saying they would find this almost impossible to accept, another 54 per cent saying they could live with it, and 24 per cent saying they would happily accept the wishes of the majority. If there was *never* a united Ireland, only 2 per cent of Catholics say they would find this almost impossible to accept with 65 per cent saying they would happily accept the wishes of the majority (NILTS, 2003). This leads us to suggest that although constitutional preferences may seem oppositional, other political attitudes concerning identity may now be more significant than those related to territory.

Table 2.7 Religious affiliation and constitutional preference (%)

Religion	Remain part of the UK	Reunify with Ireland	Independent state	Other	Don't know
Catholic	21	49	10	1	19
Protestant	82	5	5	2	7
No religion	45	27	10	4	15

Question: What do you think the long-term policy for Northern Ireland should be?

Source: Northern Ireland Life and Times Survey, 2003 (N=1783)

NB figures may not add up to 100 because of rounding.

Religion and the Good Friday Agreement

Not surprisingly, there is a striking relationship between religious affiliation and perceptions of the Good Friday Agreement of 1998. At the time of the referendum in 1998, the Protestant community was divided almost down the middle over support and opposition, whereas the Catholic community were almost unanimous in voting yes.[8] Table 2.8 shows how attitudes have changed since 1998 with just over a quarter of Protestants expressing that they would vote yes for the Agreement if there were a rerun of the referendum (see Mitchell, 2003a). This is very much in keeping with the political mood of the Protestant community, as demonstrated for example in the June 2001 general election and the 2003 Assembly election results, which showed a significant swing away from UUP to DUP. Amongst Catholics, Sinn Féin have overtaken the SDLP as the largest nationalist party.

Overall in 2003, practically no Protestants thought that unionists had gained more than nationalists from the Good Friday Agreement, 18 per cent believed that both communities had benefited equally and over two-thirds thought that nationalists had benefited more than unionists (see Table 2.9). On the other hand, nationalists were much more likely to perceive equal benefit in the Good Friday Agreement. Unsurprisingly then, just as religious affiliation is a dominant signifier of communal

Table 2.8 Support for the Good Friday Agreement and religious affiliation (%)

Religion	Yes	No	Wouldn't vote	Don't know	Other answer
Catholic	74	4	13	8	2
Protestant	28	42	17	10	3
No religion	50	14	23	8	5

Question: How would you vote if Good Friday Referendum was held again?

Source: Northern Ireland Life and Times Survey, 2003 (N=1782)

NB figures may not add up to 100 because of rounding.

Table 2.9 Perceptions of gain and loss from the Good Friday Agreement by religion (%)

Religion	Unionists benefited a lot	Unionists benefited a little	Equal benefit	Nationalists benefited a little	Nationalists benefited a lot	Neither benefited	Don't know
Catholic	3	2	50	14	8	11	13
Protestant	–	–	18	17	53	4	8
No religion	2	1	36	19	23	6	13

Question: Has Good Friday Agreement benefited unionists and nationalists equally?

Source: Northern Ireland Life and Times Survey, 2003 (N=1784)

NB figures may not add up to 100 because of rounding.

membership, it is a significant determinant of perceptions of gain and loss in the Agreement.

In all the main indicators of political attitudes, religious affiliation continues to provide the dominant cleavage. Both Protestants and Catholics can be broken down internally in terms of class, status and gender – but none of these variations produce anything close to the strength of the religious cleavage. Amongst those without a religious affiliation, there is an increased tendency to also feel politically detached. However, there is also a significant secondary trend towards reflecting the politics of one's religious community of origin, and there is virtually no crossing of the political divide. The chapter turns now to examine the relationship between religious beliefs and practices, and political attitudes.

Religious beliefs and political attitudes

Religious affiliation is still the dominant cleavage in Northern Ireland. However, there is no significant relationship between strength of theological beliefs, church attendance and strength of political position. This does not mean that religion is simply a marker for what is really an ethnonational divide. However, it does mean that religious beliefs cannot be viewed as the *cause* of conflict.

Even though it is often supposed that there is a strong relationship between evangelicalism and strong forms of unionism and loyalism (Bruce, 1986; Todd, 1987; Akenson, 1992), this should not be over-exaggerated. While some strong unionists and loyalists may indeed be influenced by religion, there is no clear-cut causal connection and many are nonreligious (Bruce, 2003). Evans and Duffy (1997) found that some Protestant denominations such as the Presbyterians and Free Presbyterians are more likely to support the DUP than those in the Church of Ireland. However, it must be borne in mind that even within mainline Protestant denominations there are wide variations in religious and political attitudes. Mitchell and Tilley's (2004) findings indicate that there are no differences in political attitudes between evangelicals and other Protestants. Attitudinal differences between evangelical and non-evangelical Protestants concern views on morality and lifestyle rather than political identity and attitudes. Analysis of the Northern Ireland Life and Times Survey 2003 shows that churchgoing amongst Protestants makes little difference to political attitudes. In fact Evans and Duffy (1997) found that those who attended church least were most likely to support the DUP. In line with this, those Protestants who attend church more regularly are slightly more likely to favour the Good Friday Agreement.

Amongst Catholics, it is those who never go to church who are more likely to be anti-Agreement. This may comprise republicans who are alienated from the Church, although the sample is much too small to draw any conclusions. Evans and Duffy (1997) found that religiosity, as defined by church attendance, does not discriminate between supporters of Sinn Féin and the SDLP. In sum, religious practice is not significantly related to strength of political attitudes for Catholics or Protestants.

However, there is a stronger relationship between religious beliefs and the question of social mixing – attitudes to social relationships with the 'other'. Boal et al.'s (1997) study highlights the trend, within both Catholicism and Protestantism, for liberal personal theology and beliefs to have an important effect on one's attitudes to having neighbours of the other religion, willingness to participate in ecumenical services, and openness to mixed marriage. The survey shows that around 20 per cent more Catholic theological liberals than conservatives were happy to mix with Protestants at work and in their neighbourhoods, and 30 per cent more liberals were open to the idea of a mixed marriage to a Northern Ireland Protestant. Overall, only 28 per cent of Catholic churchgoers in Belfast said they would be happy to marry a Northern Ireland Protestant, but those of a younger age, and a higher level of education, were significantly more open to the idea.[9] The same trends are apparent amongst Belfast's Protestant churchgoers. Only 7 per cent of conservatives were open to mixed marriage, as opposed to 28 per cent of liberals – however, it must be noted that even the latter figure is low (Boal et al., 1997, p. 104). Differentials are also higher between theological liberals and conservatives on the issues of exclusive school ethos and school type, and just slightly less for mixing in the neighbourhood and at work (Boal et al., 1997, p. 105). Overall, the most theologically conservative

Catholic and Protestant churchgoers in Northern Ireland are the least willing to mix with the other community. We shall explore the relationship between religion and lack of social contact in later chapters. However, before this, it is necessary to reflect in more depth upon the seeming lack of relationship between religious beliefs and practices on the one hand, and attitudes to politics on the other.

Behind the statistics

From the analysis presented above, we can see that religious *affiliation* is politically very important in Northern Ireland. Although individually, Catholics and Protestants have different views on political questions, there is very little crossing over to the 'other side'. However, we have also seen that, statistically speaking, religious belief and behaviour do not seem to make much difference to political attitudes. Does this mean that religion is simply an empty communal marker in Northern Ireland, providing the labels but not the substance of political identity?

The answer to this question is no. Religion does provide much substance and depth of meaning to social and political relationships. However, in order to proceed with this argument, it is necessary to explain why it seems at face value that this may not be the case. The question is a methodological and theoretical, as much as an empirical, one.

One reason for lack of correlation between religious beliefs and behaviour and political attitudes is the depth of the communal divide itself. The sections above have shown how non-porous the boundary is. Boal et al. (1997) found that despite much internal theological diversity within both Protestant and Catholic churchgoing communities, each presented a very united front on political questions. Catholic churchgoers in Belfast were almost unanimously non-British, non-Ulster and non-unionist, and Protestant churchgoers, predictably, non-Irish and non-nationalist (1997, pp. 67, 164). They argue (1997, p. 111) that in light of this high degree of consensus, especially for Protestants, 'theological conviction, it seems, has little bearing on political identity.' Indeed, this is the point that Rose (1971) argued at the beginning of recent conflict: that the strength of opposition between communities has papered over great variations within them. This applies to theological perspectives, just as much as class and gender differences, all of which have been engulfed by a deeper communal cleavage. Rose argued (1971, p. 265) that religiosity did not make a difference to Catholics' political attitudes through the civil rights period because Catholics shared similar political grievances anyway. Similarly, it is possible that high rates of religiosity overall mask the specific social roles of religion. If only 8 per cent of Catholics never attend mass, it is less likely that churchgoing will mark out any specific attitudes.

Second, it is well documented that moderate views are always over-emphasized in surveys in Northern Ireland due to the social unacceptability of extreme views. Whyte has argued (1990, p. 91) that there are problems with the reliability of information given by respondents in Northern Ireland because of the tendency to play down or deny non-mainstream views. This is evidenced by the consistent over-representation of moderate attitudes in survey and interview material – attitudes that are not reflected in the privacy of close social circles or in the polling booth. Bruce (1994) outlines similar concerns, arguing that views expressed in public can differ quite sharply to views expressed in private. Indeed, as Millar (1999, p. 18) has asked, what church attender is going to present his or her religious beliefs as a source of conflict?

This gets to the heart of the purpose of this book. To a large extent, we need to take people at 'face value'. We need to take seriously how they see themselves and other people. Surveys that place religion lower down the rank of causality than other factors are important.[10] But instead of concluding that therefore religion is insignificant, it may also be interesting to ask why religion might be downplayed. Identities are multi-layered, even contradictory. It is the 'some of my best friends are Catholics' phenomenon. Readers in Britain or the United States may be more familiar with 'some of my best friends are black' – heartfelt disclaimers, and often cordial personal relationships, that coexist with other quite hostile feelings towards a relevant out-group. In-depth interviews, for example, often find people expressing different opinions about themselves and others, depending on the issues and the context. It is not unusual to find statements denying that religious differences hold any importance, juxtaposed further down the transcript with quite hostile pronouncements about the beliefs, morality or behaviour of those of another faith (Millar, 1999; Mitchell, 2001). This book does not seek to claim that although people say one thing, they *really* mean something else. However, people's presentation of themselves must be subjected to analysis and their contradictions explored.

But there is an even more compelling reason why it is premature to dismiss religion on the basis of such findings. This is, third, the issue of definition and measurement. What survey evidence that exists primarily measures theological beliefs or church attendance. The way that we measure religion determines what results we find regarding its social and political significance. Following the discussion of what religion is in Chapter 1, it is clear that there are many different ways that one could define and measure it. Some feel that religion is a substantive, spiritual thing, measured by beliefs and doctrines. To measure this we can use survey items on prayer, belief in heaven and hell or in the Bible. For other analysts, practices are much more important and we can measure this using items on church attendance.

Other facets of the relationship between religion and politics, however, such as the impact of religion on political power relationships, cannot be measured by survey data. Whilst we can count up the numbers of clergy involved in politics, and politicians who consult with clergy, we are unable to statistically evaluate the impact of this on ordinary people. Similarly, general surveys do not allow us to measure the significance of religious symbolism and ideas in establishing the meaning of communal identity. We can only access these meanings by asking people and in this regard qualitative approaches are more suitable. Unless specifically designed, surveys cannot tell us much about processes of social categorization, social comparison and stereotyping that we argued in Chapter 1 are integral to social and political behaviour and relationships. Only a social psychological approach, either experimental or interpretative, can throw light upon these processes. Moreover, surveys can only tell us what people say, not why they say it or what their responses mean. Surveys also do not tell us what people actually do. Methods utilized in anthropology, such as participant observation, are much more useful in this respect. So whilst it is vitally important to evaluate statistically the relationship between religious beliefs, practices and political attitudes, this methodological approach can only take us part of the way to an understanding of the relationship between religion, identity and politics. The purpose of the remainder of this book is to use a variety of different methods and approaches, drawing on original primary, as well as a wide range of secondary, material to explore this relationship in more depth.

Conclusion

From analysis of recent survey material we see that by and large, differing religious beliefs and practices are not the *cause* of oppositional political attitudes in Northern Ireland. However, we should not dismiss the glaringly obvious way in which attitudes correlate with religious affiliation. This prompts us to ask, what then is the nature of the relationship between religion and politics? At this point, many commentators conclude, based on this kind of data, that religion may be important for a group of evangelical Protestants but must be merely an ethnic marker for everybody else. But this is just one way to look at the data, and perhaps a rather superficial way. On the other hand, we can clearly see the existence of two relatively separate communities, politically divided, with virtually no going over to the other side. The fact that these communities are religiously differentiated is highly significant. Continuing high attendance rates mean that they inhabit different social spaces – at least some of the time. The fact that Protestants and Catholics often express their willingness to come together, but seldom do so as the issues become more personal in shared worship and marriage, adds another layer of estrangement from one another. The religious and often moral language of each community is unfamiliar to the other. Whilst they in fact share many similar values such as conservatism in the moral sphere (Fahey et al., 2004), Protestants and Catholics do not share the same symbols or codes with which to express these values. Many of these symbols and codes stem from religious traditions. The fact that churches and clergy play a key role in the provision of education and social structure to everyday life underlines the difference. Whilst of course the beliefs and practices of people in Northern Ireland may be in all likelihood *more* different from those of Romanians, Iranians and even the English than they are from one another, this is not the point. It is the boundaries that we experience every day that are the most pressing, echoing Freud's 'narcissism of minor differences'.

The communal boundary has evolved over generations in Northern Ireland. It probably would still have existed if conflict had historically been British atheists versus Irish atheists. But if this were the case, the boundary would have different meanings. Social practices would be structured differently and political debates would have a different tone. Bearing in mind how intricately religion is still woven throughout daily life in Northern Ireland, it is imperative to explore the meanings it provides to the political boundary in a deeply divided society, and how this in turn perpetuates division.

3
The churches and politics

Key points

- *Church and state are separate, but churches remain politically influential.*

- *The Catholic Church plays a significant role in structuring community and social life, more so than in party politics.*

- *Protestant churches have many representatives within unionist political parties, but play a less important role in the organization of community life.*

- *Both Catholic and Protestant churches are involved in political consultation, mediation and representation of their members' interests.*

- *Neither Catholic nor Protestant churches have been significantly involved in radical politics or violence.*

In television coverage of major events and crises in Northern Ireland it is common to see Catholic priests and Protestant clergy moving in the background and making statements to the camera. In most local newspapers there are regular slots for articles and comments by religious figures. The churches are usually asked to send delegations to key processes of political consultation and they can be seen to-ing and fro-ing from parliament buildings in full clerical dress. When victims of violence are buried, it usually falls upon religious ministers to publicly interpret and try to make sense of the situation. In civil disturbances clerics have often been in the foreground of protest, for example, during civil rights marches[1] or at Drumcree.[2] Other clerics are regularly found attempting to foster conciliation and non-violence. These are not unusual sights. The presence of the churches in political and cultural life is a constant. It is the purpose of this chapter to establish exactly what kind of roles the churches play in politics and how significant these roles are.

The separation of church and state is the least controversial form of secularization in the modern world (Casanova, 1994). This dynamic is clearly at work in Northern Ireland. Churches are not significant economic actors, political authority is articulated in secular terms and citizenship is political. However, despite this official separation, churches continue to heavily influence the tone, and often the substance, of political life. They play a crucial role in civil society and are deeply involved in a wide variety of semi-state and community activities. The Catholic Church in particular plays a very important role in the organization of social and cultural life. Its continuing involvement in the education system continues to be of extraordinary significance. Amongst the Protestant churches, there is no equivalent provision of education; however, there is a strong tradition of clerical participation in party politics. Although most clergy tend not to involve themselves in the big constitutional questions, they do speak up on cultural issues such as parades and policing. Whilst politicians and civil servants do not officially negotiate with religious figures, they are usually consulted about important policies. There is an important distinction between actual involvement in decision making, and the more secondary role of part-time consultation and pronouncement.

It may at first glance seem problematic to argue that the churches play a role in the politics of conflict in Northern Ireland. Throughout conflict, churches and clerics articulated messages of peace and reconciliation, almost without exception. Violence has been continually denounced from Catholic and Protestant pulpits. With only a few exceptions, discussed below, clergy have not been involved in radical political movements. Whilst churches have sometimes been ambiguous about previous political settlements, the present period after the Good Friday Agreement of 1998 has seen unprecedented support for the political order from religious institutions. There may be internal clerical debate on the matter, but public statements tend to endorse many of the new political developments.

And this is precisely the nature of the churches' role in politics: the attempt to represent and lead the views of their community. Throughout conflict, the main concern of all the churches was to locate themselves in the political mainstream of their respective communities, providing comfort, support and often political empathy for their members. As Catholics in the 1970s struggled to obtain equal rights, clergy led prayers for justice from the pulpit and gave practical support to families in difficulty, for example, through their influence in credit unions. As Protestants in the 1980s reeled against the 'sell-out' of the Anglo-Irish Agreement, renditions of the hymn 'Oh God Our Help in Ages Past' were led at mass protest rallies outside Belfast City Hall. The religious mainstream has been closely allied to the political mainstream in both communities. And this relationship has been mutually beneficial. Unionist and nationalist parties and policies have gained extra legitimacy from clerical endorsements and the churches have benefited not only from the friendliness of politicians but also the way in which they have seemed to have their finger on the pulse of the concerns of the communities they represent.

Religion is often used from the top down, by influential groups trying to force their ideology onto society. Indeed, churches are powerful actors that seek to stamp their meanings upon social and political relations. Marx and Engels (in Tucker, 1978; Turner, 1991), in particular, focused on religion as the dominant ideology of the state. They argued that churches and dominant classes worked together to monopolize 'mental production' through education to protect their material interests by ensuring that the subordinate classes experienced the world in passive religious terms. This, combined with the capacity of religion to explain and take people's attention away from political hardships, worked to suppress class conflict. Fulton

(1991) draws on the work of Gramsci to elaborate on dominant ideology in Northern Ireland. He argues that Roman Catholic bishops are the intellectuals organizing the beliefs of Catholic-nationalists in a conservative way (1991, p. 170). However, it is simplistic to view religion merely as a form of social control. High orthodoxy and elite activity are not necessarily the best indicators to establish the influence of religion. Individuals are not helpless subordinates who think what they are told to think by elites. Moreover, religion's hold on education has weakened throughout the modern world, and dominant classes now use many other mechanisms, such as the media, to influence social relationships.

With these qualifications in mind, the discussion that follows is informed by perspectives on the power of religious institutions, especially when working in tandem with political actors. It concludes that the relationship between churches and people is better described as co-dependent rather than top down. People use religious structures and ideas, just as religious structures attempt to use people. This argument is fleshed out throughout this chapter, and in the conclusion. The sections that follow explore the political character of the Catholic and Protestant churches. They provide discussion of clerical contribution to party politics, their role in radical politics, their involvement in political mediation, consultation and representation, and their provision of structure to social and cultural and sometimes economic life. A combination of these factors ensures their place at the heart of their respective communities' experiences.

The Catholic Church and politics

The Catholic Church in Northern Ireland has been much more than just an interest group to be consulted in nationalist politics. Whilst there has been consistent clerical condemnation of secret societies and republican violence, the Church has always been at the heart of the nationalist political mainstream. The Catholic Church has no parallel with Protestant clerical politicians, but it has continually articulated opinions and interpretations of the political situation in Northern Ireland. It is rare for priests to consciously promote party politics of one kind or another (McElroy, 1991), but they have been consistent in their representations of the Catholic community, and mediations with those outside. This does not mean that the Catholic Church's *raison d'être* is to engender ideological monopoly in Northern Ireland. However, their location in the political nationalist mainstream has given them a unique position from which to promote Catholic values and teachings. Similarly, its support has lent added legitimacy to nationalist politics – so the relationship is mutually beneficial.

The Church has frequently been thrust into playing a political role in Ireland because it has been the institution best placed to provide stability and coherence for the Catholic community. Whilst this role was unofficial throughout most of the seventeenth and eighteenth centuries, the Church became a permanent participant in the political sphere in the nineteenth century as it threw its weight behind campaigns for Catholic Emancipation and Home Rule. Throughout the late nineteenth and early twentieth centuries, at a formative time in Irish politics, the Church was extremely close to Irish nationalism in general, and the emerging northern Catholic community in particular. Harris (1993) argues that the Church soon became an integral part of nationalist politics in the newly established Northern Ireland and maintains that it was responsible in no small way for the delay of northern nationalists in recognizing the legitimacy of the Northern Ireland state. Throughout the Stormont years of devolved government in Northern Ireland (1922–71), the Catholic Church continued to identify itself with the struggles and desires of the community.

Indeed, throughout the recent phase of conflict, and indeed in the present, the Catholic Church in Northern Ireland continued to play a variety of important political and pseudo-political roles. These are now discussed in turn.

Party politics

The involvement of the Catholic Church in nationalist party politics in Northern Ireland is minimal. There is no tradition of the clerical-politician equivalent to that amongst Protestants. Furthermore, evidence suggests that clergy do not use their position to promote one party or another. Although an overwhelming majority of clergy favoured Irish unity in the late 1980s, McElroy (1991, pp. 66–78) found clergy were reluctant to advise people how to vote. Only 4 per cent of clergy surveyed said they had ever promoted any kind of party politics. However, these facts belie the close and mutually beneficial relationships between the Church and the political parties. Whilst the Church is formally removed from party politics, there is a degree of enthusiasm on all sides to nurture and protect the relationships between them.

The Catholic Church is ideologically and practically closest to the SDLP. It has enjoyed a close (although unofficial) relationship with the SDLP since their establishment in 1970, finding themselves involved in similar organizations and supporting the same issues. The SDLP have however made efforts to widen the scope of their appeal, to act as a secular party, and have rejected any formal relationship with the Church. But the circumstances of Northern Ireland politics have often meant that they have been seen to be voicing a similar message and working together on certain issues or in certain areas. Their relationship is not one of ideological unity, but often of practical cooperation.[3] Whilst some in the SDLP would prefer that the relationship was not so close, others know that closeness to the Church does them no harm. As O'Connor (1993, p. 290) remarks, 'it would be difficult not to notice how nice they are about each other.' This is for two reasons. First, both sets of actors share a communal background, and may be close anyway in terms of what they feel is best for the community. And secondly, cultivation of the nationalist political consensus helps safeguard the position of both actors.

Sinn Féin's relationship with the Church has been more volatile, but despite frequent mutual antagonism, there have been continual attempts at cooperation. A long-standing tension exists between republicans and the Catholic Church, and many have felt let down by the hierarchy's lack of support, and even scorn, for them.[4] This tension has been further exacerbated where Sinn Féin and the Catholic Church have competed against each other to obtain government funding and grants, such as through the ACE schemes (Action for Community Employment) in the late 1980s and early 1990s.[5] It is not surprising that in this context many modern republicans distance themselves from religion. Many, such as Martin McGuinness and Mitchel McLaughlin, claim that their political beliefs are the sole product of Protestant discrimination during the Stormont years and British misrule after 1969 and that an historical mystical republican tradition and Catholic religion have influenced them in no way (McIntyre, 2000; see also Juergensmeyer 2000, pp. 36–43).

Having said this, others in Sinn Féin seem keen to cultivate the relationship with the Church. O'Connor (1993, p. 293) describes Gerry Adams, for example, as 'republicanism's most public Catholic: an assiduous mass-goer, conspicuously prayerful'. She argues that for Adams, the constant republican emphasis on membership of the Church is a clear response to what they know their supporters want to hear, and an attempt to locate Sinn Féin within the mainstream of northern Catholic identity (see also Bishop and Mallie, 1988). Indeed Sinn Féin were to be found trying to patch up their historically uneasy relationship with the Catholic Church in the wake of the peace process in the 1990s. Gerry Adams said he appreciated the radical efforts being made by the Church for peace, whilst Cardinal Cahal Daly argued that Sinn Féin had an important political contribution to make and should be admitted into talks. The renewed relationship was highly significant, as it has helped Sinn Féin locate themselves within the mainstream of the Catholic community. Through nurturing this relationship, the Church's symbolic power is emphasized and Sinn Féin is given added legitimacy. As in the past, religious endorsements of political actors could be swapped for Church-friendly policies such as the maintenance of denominational education, which nationalists and republicans rarely raise as a priority area for policy change.

Thus, the Church's relationship with nationalist politics has been close. Whilst this closeness is in a sense organic – priests, politicians and nationalists after all share a communal background – it is hard to deny that the relationship has been mutually beneficial. Political actors can sustain credibility by nurturing the ideological link whilst the Church can appear to be at the heart of the nationalist community.

Radical politics

Whilst the Catholic Church has always been close to the political mainstream, it is a myth that it has made any significant contribution to radical republican politics or IRA activities. The Church has historically balanced on a tightrope between nationalist groups and the British establishment. Although it had been persecuted, by the early nineteenth century Catholicism in Ulster was remarkable in its loyalty to the British crown and constitution, having supported the Act of Union (between Ireland and Britain) in 1800 (Rafferty, 1994). Naturally conservative, it has often been reluctant to assume an anti-state position. As such, the institutional Church has always tended to distrust radical political movements, and has consistently opposed armed republicanism. The Catholic Church has continually denounced the modern IRA, banning membership in 1935 and making frequent references to the sinfulness of the organization (Gallagher and Worrall, 1982).

Another myth is that the Catholic doctrine of 'just war' has been widely used both by clergy and republicans to justify armed struggle in Northern Ireland. This doctrine has been given some credibility by radical clergy, and has occasionally been used by some republicans to legitimize their actions. However, the Church hierarchy maintains that the doctrine of 'just war' does not apply in Northern Ireland. Former archbishop Cahal Daly (1991, p. 62) has argued that 'every single condition for the just war ... is violated in the Irish situation.' 'Just war', or just revolution, claims that violence and the killing of innocents are immoral. Violence is only legitimized when it is used as a last resort, and self-defensively, against an unjust aggressor who has forfeited his or her innocence on account of serious abuses of the fundamental human rights of others. A 'just war' should also have a proper mandate and chance of success – neither of which the Catholic Church thought applied to Northern Ireland. However, some protest this point. Father Joe McVeigh has argued (1989) that the Catholic community should have a deeper understanding of violence – from the perspective of the poor and oppressed (see also Wilson, 1985 for more flexible interpretations of the 'just war' doctrine). Overall, whilst the concept of just war is debated, it has not been a central part of republicans' own justifications for violence.

There are, however, two caveats to the Church's disassociation with radical politics. First, whilst tough on republicanism, it has retained a certain amount of ambiguity regarding republicans. Radical movements have been condemned, but their members have rarely been totally isolated from the religious community. Some lower clergy have maintained links with republicans and paramilitaries have not been excommunicated. Secondly, the Church participates in politics symbolically. The vast majority of republican paramilitaries have received conventional Catholic funerals, which are not universally approved of, but which can create an illusion of unity of purpose between the Church and 'the struggle'. In addition, when the political situation has been at its darkest for Catholics, there has been a small degree of clerical ambivalence about IRA activities. In the early 1970s, some priests became involved in the Central Citizen's Defence Committee (CCDC), which included members of the IRA (O'Connor, 1993). Indeed, until the ceasefire in 1994, some lower clergy did appear to empathize with the IRA's campaign (Buckley, 1994; McVeigh, 1989). But this is not the norm. In 1991 McElroy (1991, pp. 66,75) found that whilst 91 per cent of Catholic clergy surveyed were in favour of Irish unity, 88 per cent said they would be most likely to vote for the SDLP at the next election and just 4 per cent for Sinn Féin. Thus the idea of a large body of dissident priests giving support to radical republicanism is fiction.

Political mediation

Whilst the Church has seldom been involved in party or dissident politics, it plays a much more prominent role through political mediation. Church deputations and negotiations with governments, parties and paramilitary organizations are commonplace in Northern Ireland. Mediation occurs at the grassroots in local communities as well as at elite level. Clerics are well equipped to carry out such negotiations because of their unique place within the mainstream of the Catholic community. Similarly, their ability to successfully involve themselves in political mediation reinforces their social influence.

Attempts at political mediation have taken place at the level of public protest as well as formal negotiation. In the late 1960s, Bishop Edward Daly and his fellow clerics attended civil rights demonstrations in Derry. McElroy (1991) argues that, given the unique position of priests within the Catholic community, this encouraged participation in civil rights activities, and also added respectability to the campaign as a whole. Amongst some of the most effective human rights campaigners in Northern Ireland have been priests – for example, Fr Denis Faul of Dungannon and Fr Raymond Murray of Armagh – during the 1970s and 1980s, priests (although not the hierarchy) made pronouncements on the inhumanity and immorality of internment, the use of plastic bullets, interrogation in depth and the supergrass system (McElroy, 1991).

At various junctures, Church leaders have tried to act as intermediaries between the community and the state. For example, Cardinal O'Fiaich and Bishop Edward Daly tried to defuse the hunger strikes in the early 1980s; Fr Alex Reid mediated with the IRA in the late 1980s and 1990s to encourage them in from the political cold. Catholic clergy were also engaged in a consultation process with the Ulster Unionist Party (UUP) in 1997. This was an important gesture on behalf of the UUP, but also excellent PR for the Catholic Church, whose members saw Dr Sean Brady, the Archbishop of Armagh, shaking hands with David Trimble after exchanging views. This creates an image of the Church as having something to say about politics, and being influential enough to get their voice heard. More recently, a former Derry-based priest, Fr Denis Bradley, who in the past has acted as an intermediary between the IRA and the British and Irish governments, has encouraged the IRA to disarm for the benefit of nationalists. Fr Denis Faul, generally associated with more radical political views, has urged Catholics to join the new police service (editorial, *Irish News*, 29 November 2000). Thus, whilst in contemporary Northern Irish politics the Church's input may not be one of critical political or policy significance, it remains important at a practical level, keeping open channels of communication with politicians and the state and through its attempts to agitate on behalf of Catholic community.

Church personnel have been involved in political mediation at grassroots as well as elite level. In the early 1990s, a group of Jesuit priests influenced by liberation theology picked a Catholic housing estate in Portadown, County Armagh, to live and work amongst the local community. Coincidentally, this area became entangled in a lengthy and bitter dispute between Orangemen and Catholic residents over the right to march down the Garvaghy Road, a now-predominantly Catholic part of mainly Protestant Portadown. The Jesuits became involved with the Garvaghy Road Residents' Association, who held their meetings in the Jesuit house there.[6] So too, priests have been at the forefront of community relations in interface areas of Belfast, for example, Fr Aiden Troy's negotiations amidst the Holy Cross School disputes in 2001 and 2002. Fr Troy walked every day for three months with 225 schoolgirls to Holy Cross Primary in the Ardoyne, escorted by the security forces as loyalists tried to block their path. In this way, Catholic figures are seen to be at the heart of the community's struggles, their pastoral roles deepened and widened by the necessities of dealing with conflict.

Representation and pronouncement

As well as proactively negotiating with politicians and state actors, the Catholic Church also tries to provide leadership to their community through interpreting the political situation. On key issues the Church tries not only to reflect the views of its members but also to provide leadership and direction to them.

Indeed, one of the most important roles the Catholic Church has played is in their interpretation of the relationship between Catholics and the Northern Irish state. Harris argues (1993) that in the 1920s, the Church's public statements took on a propaganda significance against the Northern Ireland state and its government. Cardinal Thomas O'Fiaich in 1978 expressed his view that the British should withdraw from Ireland (as opposed to advocating reform, which had been the norm up until that point). This came under much criticism from loyalists, adding to tensions, and from then on statements from the Church hierarchy tended to be more vague (McElroy, 1991). But again, after the New Ireland Forum Report in 1984, the Church criticized the attitude of the British government. In more recent times, the Church has tried to stay on more neutral territory, balancing condemnation of violence with their role as a voice of the Catholic community.

The Catholic Church's tendency to provide political guidance in Northern Ireland after the Good Friday Agreement of 1998 is less prominent than during the eras of civil rights demonstrations and the hunger strikes. But it is by no means absent. The Church continues to make political pronouncements, speak up for its people, negotiate on their behalf and provide political direction. Dr Sean Brady, still Archbishop of Armagh, is perceived as an active figure in political life, and has been criticized by unionists for 'interfering' in the peace process. Whilst strongly supportive of the Agreement, the Church continually seeks to locate itself in the nationalist mainstream underlining Catholics' concerns about policing, decommissioning and demilitarization.

Thus the Church has showed a constant willingness to identify itself with the struggles and desires of the community (Morrow, 1995). Whilst in the past, the Church used this platform to speak out against the injustices that the Catholic community were subjected to, its brief in the present has shifted. Much of the heat and urgency has gone out of the political situation in Northern Ireland and most clergy now prefer to play a more secondary role interpreting politics, supporting the Good Friday Agreement and not being drawn into controversy. None the less, these representations and pronouncements are symbolically important, maintaining the impression that the Church is a central spokesperson for its people.

Social organization

Whilst the role of the Church in politicking could be described as symbolic and secondary, the role it plays in social organization continues to be a primary source of strength. Morrow et al. argue (1991, p. 122) that institutionally, the political profile of the Catholic Church is much higher than that of any Protestant Church, and 'in the absence of a State to which many Catholics owe their unconditional allegiance, the Church has become the main institutional organizer.' To a minority in a state run by the majority, to which they were largely denied access, the Church became the key facilitator of what Phoenix terms (1994, p. 196) as a 'state within a state', or a 'society within a society' (Ruane and Todd, 1996, p. 52). Alternative networks of business, media, hospitals, sport and, importantly, education for Catholics were established, and soon became the focus for an alternative political identity. From partition to the late 1950s at least, the parish was the main civic unit (O'Connor, 1993). Morrow et al. argue (1991, p. 119) that

> Catholicism is clearly political in a different way to Protestantism. There are no leading politicians who stake their position on a defence of Catholicism. Nevertheless the Catholic Church has a much higher profile as a social, political and economic actor than the Protestant institutions who are content to hand over most of this activity to 'their state'. In this sense it has a political reality to be attacked in a far more concrete sense than Protestantism.

The Catholic Church still has a strong presence in the educational system in Northern Ireland, as indeed it does in Scotland and other parts of Britain. Most Catholic children are educated denominationally and only 4 per cent of children overall are educated in integrated schools (<www.nicie.org> 7 August 2003). Catholic Maintained Schools receive public funding and are represented by the Catholic Council for Maintained Schools (CCMS). Whilst there are less clerical teachers in schools than in the past, clerical management and influence is still substantial. Catholic doctrines are taught through religious education and teachers prepare children for the sacrament of First Communion and Confirmation. Concerns that these aspects of education would not be provided for adequately in integrated schools lies in large part behind the Church's continued insistence on segregated education (Fraser and Morgan, 1999).

In addition to education, the Church continues to be involved with charities, such as Trocaire or St Vincent de Paul. It runs preparatory marriage courses and offers marriage guidance and pregnancy counselling. Its Council for Social Welfare concerns itself with emerging social problems – the nature of which differ from rural to urban areas and in specific areas of conflict in Northern Ireland. It is involved in youth work and runs many other social clubs and cultural activities.

The Churches' resources are utilized in other arenas of state administration. For example, some social services are run through the Catholic Church (Morrow et al., 1991). The Catholic Church was involved in administrating government job-creation through the ACE (Action for Community Employment) schemes in the 1990s (see discussion of Party politics above). Given the scale of unemployment amongst the Catholic community at that time, this brought more people than usual into contact with the Church. Often people had to attend religious services to hear about vacancies. With the demise of the ACE schemes, the Church is now less involved in the administration of economic life in the community; however, it continues to look after the social and economic needs of its members in less official contexts.

The Catholic Church then has assumed a vitally important role, by default and by design, in the social organization of the community. This has added to the perception, on all sides, that the Catholic Church is very deeply entangled with everyday social life and politics (see also Chapter 5).

In summary, the Catholic Church is less politicized than at the height of the Troubles, when priests joined civil rights protests and visited the hunger strikers. But the Church is still politically interested, and it is occasionally interventionist. It interprets and advises on political issues and represents the Catholic community through political mediations. It does not get involved in paramilitary politics nor does it have direct influence on state policy. In terms of providing alternative social organization to the state, its role continues to be strong, and highly significant at the level of structuring daily life. The Church's influence is not at the level of structure or policy, but of seeming to articulate mainstream Catholic views, reinforcing ideas of its solidarity with the community.

The Protestant churches and politics

The Protestant churches too play an extremely significant, if quite different, role in the politics of Northern Ireland. Although the Protestant churches have had some involvement in the organization of social life, their most striking public role is their actual involvement in political organizations. Overlap of religious and political personnel is found amongst all the Protestant churches, and has encompassed political opinion forming, leadership and community activism as well as participation in unionist and loyalist party politics. Although there is a small minority of religious personnel active within loyalist paramilitary circles, by and large Protestant clergy have been orientated towards the mainstream unionist UUP and the more hardline, yet constitutional, DUP. In addition to political activism, Protestant churches, like the Catholic Church, have been involved in political mediation, consultation and representation of their community.

However, in contrast to the religious monopoly of the Catholic Church, the Protestant market is highly fragmented. There are nearly a hundred denominations, of different sizes, that house a variety of religious as well as political outlooks. Some denominations are highly politicized whereas others are more pietistic and apolitical. Denominations such as the Free Presbyterian Church, set up by the Revd Ian Paisley, are well known for their political activism. Others, such as the Church of Ireland, are notoriously entangled with politics through their association with the Orange Order. Others again, such as the Baptists, tend not to engage with political issues. Politically integrationist strands also exist within most of the bigger Protestant churches (Church of Ireland, Presbyterian and Methodist). Historically, the dominant trend has been for the Protestant churches to rally behind the unionist political mainstream. There have been moments of progressive and radical political involvement, such as Presbyterian involvement in the United Irish movement, known as the Dissenters, in the late eighteenth century. But this is not the norm. In more recent times, the landscape of Protestantism has been usefully described as a 'mosaic' (Boal et al., 1991). The following sections tease out in more detail the facets of the relationship between the various Protestant institutional churches and politics.

Party politics

In contemporary Northern Ireland, as in the past, there is a high degree of involvement by Protestant clerics in political institutions and parties. Brewer (1998) points to the Protestant cleric as a familiar type in Ireland, who has skilfully woven together theological arguments against Catholicism and defence of Protestant political and economic interests since the sixteenth century. Indeed, although the roles that clerics play in politics have proven to be adaptable to new political contexts, their input has been a constant.

A variety of clerical-politicians such as Revd Ian Paisley are active in politics. In 2005, Paisley was joined by nine DUP MPs at Westminster – all of whom gave the credit for their victories to God on being elected. Overall, three out of 57 unionist MLAs are clergymen.[7] An additional two DUP MLAs, George Dawson in East Antrim and Mervyn Storey in North Antrim are members of the Caleb Foundation, a conservative evangelical pressure group. Dawson is also a director of the Evangelical Protestant Society. Nelson McCausland, DUP representative for North Belfast, is one-time secretary of the Northern Ireland Lord's Day Observance Society. David Simpson (Upper Bann) and Willie McCrea (South Antrim), both DUP MPs, are gospel singers. Andrew Hunter of Lagan Valley was vice-president of the National Prayer Book Society until 1997. Many more DUP members are involved in the Orange Order, the Black Preceptory and similar organizations. Many more unionist figures are active in lay roles in churches.

Ian Paisley, the son of an evangelical Protestant minister, is the most famous as well as an archetypal example of the Protestant clerical-politician. He traces his lineage back to figures such as Henry Cooke in the nineteenth century who used his dominance as a church leader to try to influence political affairs (Holmes, 1981). His message has been a mixture of evangelical religious orthodoxy, political conservatism and a strong defence of the union. At the heart of this position is a strong opposition to Catholicism which he sees as heretical and opposed to freedom (Brewer, 1998). In contemporary Northern Ireland, not all clerical-politicians are as forthright, conservative and controversial as Ian Paisley. However, those clerics that do get involved in politics tend not to come from the liberal strands within the Protestant churches. Despite the efforts of evangelical organizations such as Evangelical Contribution on Northern Ireland (ECONI) to encourage clergy as well as ordinary Protestants to engage in the politics of reconciliation and reform, this remains a minority position.

One of the key ways in which the relationship between churches and political parties has been maintained is through the Orange Order. Since its inception in 1795 the Order has played a key role in the institutional interaction of unionism and Protestantism. The Orange Order is committed to a classic brand of Reformed Protestantism, opposed to biblical error and concerned with promoting scriptural truth. Whilst the Order stresses religious tolerance for all creeds, Orangeism is explicitly 'Christ-centred, Bible-based and Church-grounded', and opposed to the 'tyranny of a soulless state [and] of an authoritarian church' (Long, 2004, p. 4). It forbids members to marry a Catholic or attend Catholic religious services. Many prominent political figures have made no secret of their Orange affiliations: the most well known of the many politically active past Grand Masters include the Revd Martin Smyth, UUP MP until 2005 and J. M. Andrews, former prime minister of Northern Ireland. The Orange Order was linked to the UUP since the founding of the latter but, as Long points out (n.d., p. 7), Orangemen are not required to be party members, and it has always had members in a variety of unionist political parties.[8]

Indeed, the influence of Orangeism extends far beyond its actual membership. From the 1790s to the 1970s, the Order represented an important network in informing the opinions of ordinary Protestants at key moments – exerting pressure on senior unionist party officials, formulating opinions at local lodge meetings and then transmitting these to the local MP (Buckley and Kenny, 1995). Until the early 1970s, no unionist party politician, in Westminster or Stormont, could regularly oppose the opinions of their local Orange Order and expect to be re-elected (Buckley and Kenny, 1995). In the early 1980s Gallagher and Worral argued (1982) that Protestant sensitivity to Orangeism continued to be very strong and highlighted the difficulty of non-Orange clergy in standing up to them. As such, the nature in which the Orange Order has been able to foster a link between religion and politics has been unique and extremely powerful.

There are, however, indications in the present that the role of the Orange Order is waning. Although the Order claims to have 100,000 members, one estimate was that this has fallen nearer to 40,000 by the mid-1990s (Jarman, 1997, p. 94). Violence and disruption surrounding controversial parades during the late 1990s and early 2000s have further sullied its reputation and popularity. The loyalist riots of autumn 2005 were very damaging with images of Orangemen clashing with the PSNI broadcast on television screens around Northern Ireland.

The Orange Order's linkages with the UUP are also less straightforward than in the past. Historically, the Orange Order and the UUP consistently cultivated the link with one another. The image of David Trimble appearing hand in hand with Revd Ian Paisley in 1995 at the annual Drumcree parade before hundreds of Orangemen is an abiding one. However, in 2005, the Orange Order decided to sever its formal linkages with the UUP. Many in the Order felt that they were losing their influencce in the UUP and felt increasingly unwelcome at meetings. But it would be naïve to assume that the link has been permanently lost. Orange Order Grand Master Robert Saulters has said that 'The loyal Orange Institution will continue to lobby for the unionist cause as events require', whilst Reg Empey, UUP leader from June 2005, intimated that the two organizations would remain close – 'I think we have to keep focused on what continues to bind us together' (BBC News 2005).[9] Support for the Order also remains strong within other sections of political unionism. Overall, whilst all Parliamentary and Assembly unionists are certainly not members of the Orange Order or similar institutions, it is estimated that about half of them are.[10]

A second, extremely well-known, facet of clerical involvement in party politics is the close relationship between the conservative evangelical Free Presbyterian Church and the DUP, formed in 1951 and 1971 respectively by Revd Ian Paisley. These two organizations are not synonymous and many individuals belong to one and not the other (Bruce, 1986). The DUP have a constituency of non-Free Presbyterian working-class voters who try to ignore the religious overtones of their message and are attracted to the DUP's robust defence of the union. This explains their continuing political strength despite the relatively small number of Free Presbyterians.[11] However, whilst not synonymous, there is a clear overlap between the organizations. As Bruce points out (1994, p. 23) from 1972 to 1980, 64 per cent of DUP activists belonged to the Free Presbyterian Church, and even more to other Protestant conservative or evangelical congregations. Overall, of the current DUP

MLAs, seventeen belong to Paisley's Free Presbyterian Church, six to other conservative Protestant denominations (three Elim, two Baptist and one Free Methodist), six to the Presbyterian Church and one to the Church of Ireland. Therefore, the personnel of the DUP continue to be predominantly composed of conservative evangelicals.

The DUP has in recent years tried to present itself as a party with more secular policies, no longer, for example, having Sabbatarianism at the heart of its agenda. They clearly acknowledge the limits of social acceptability of a conservative evangelical message and appear to have something of a PR drive to cut down religious references in the political sphere. However, there are limitations on how far the DUP can transform. Current political issues such as the right of gay couples to marry or adopt have seen them assume a strict morally conservative stance. As Smith (1998) argues in the context of the US, evangelicalism easily adapts to political change and engages with whatever issues modernity throws up. Playing down Sabbatariansim does not necessarily make the DUP more secular. In fact, it would seem likely that the DUP will continue to advocate for morally and socially conservative policies, influenced in no small part by their religious beliefs.

Radical politics

A persistent issue is the ambiguity surrounding Revd Ian Paisley's commitment to solely peaceful constitutional politics and the extent of his contribution to the loyalist struggle. Bruce (2001) works through a series of arguments linking Paisley to violence and concludes that whilst Paisley has tended to keep bad company and has twice worked with paramilitaries in civil disobediences (during the Ulster Workers' Council Strike in 1974 and an attempt to repeat it in 1977), there is no evidence that he himself was ever involved directly in terrorism. Similarly, Bruce finds few examples of Free Presbyterians being involved in violence and only six DUP activists ever implicated in serious crimes such as arson (see also Bruce, 1986).

There are a few other examples of clerical involvement in radical loyalist politics. Bruce argues (2001) that whilst many UVF and UDA members have become born-again Christians inside prison, loyalists were rarely committed Christians *before* their paramilitary involvement. However, there are some exceptions. After the UDA and UVF ceasefires in 1994, a number of dissident loyalist groups emerged to continue the campaign of violence. One of these, the Orange Volunteers, was led by Clifford Peeples who went on to become a Pentecostal pastor and defended the Volunteers' attacks on various Catholic churches on the basis that they were bastions of the Antichrist. Another loyalist, Billy Wright, also took a sabbatical from leadership of the Portadown UVF to become a gospel preacher for five years. He said that Ian Paisley was one of his heroes and a great defender of the Protestant faith (Juergensmeyer, 2000, p. 41). Tara was a paramilitary organization that came out of William McGrath's Christian Fellowship, and conceived of the conflict in Northern Ireland as a holy war (Garland, 1997). Bruce (2001) gives a few other examples and concludes that what these figures have in common is that they are independent evangelicals, self-appointed leaders with small followings. They are not sanctioned by any of the official evangelical churches.

So, the extent of Protestant clerical involvement in radical loyalism has been minimal. There is a difference, however, in actually being involved in violence and in creating the conditions in which violence occurs. This point is discussed further below under 'Representation and pronouncement'.

Political mediation

Like the Catholic Church, Protestant churches have played an active role in political mediation. During the years after partition, throughout the Troubles and after the Good Friday Agreement, church figures have been consulted about and have interjected on key political issues. They have sought to intervene and represent the Protestant community's point of view on successive political settlements (generally, to express opposition to them). However, due to the fragmented nature of the Protestant churches, a variety of negotiating positions have been put forward. These range from the peacemaking efforts of many Anglicans, Presbyterians and Methodists to the virulent political dissent amongst the Free Presbyterians and other small conservative Protestant churches, many of whom put out anti-Agreement literature in 1998. The relatively democratic nature of most Protestant churches' internal structures has meant that conflicting political views have been expressed by clergy, even within single denominations. A good example is the internal dispute over the use of Anglican Church buildings for Orange Order services in the height of marching season tensions – some clergy advocated their use whilst others were deeply opposed (see below). This makes the notion of a Protestant clerical political delegation problematic. Such fragmentation also means that there is no clearly defined source from which political mediation is expected to come. There is competition in terms of who is seen to speak for the Protestant community.

None the less, the 'big three' Protestant churches in particular (Presbyterian, Church of Ireland and Methodist) continue to make a significant contribution to political consultations. Following the 1994 ceasefires and the acceptance of the Good Friday Agreement in 1998, there was noticeable clerical traffic to and from Stormont, as Protestant church delegations sought assurances from politicians and, in turn, began to throw their weight behind change. After the first IRA ceasefire in 1994, the political profile of the Presbyterian Church was significantly raised. They held meetings with the government, lobbying on particular issues of unionist interest, and received assurances from the British and Irish governments that no secret deals had been done and that there would be no 'sell-out' of unionists (Fawcett, 2000). This contact has been important in various ways: it located the churches within the political mainstream and highlighted the importance of their support. For example, it was implied by one former Presbyterian Moderator that the British government would have liked the Presbyterian Church to be 'persuaders', selling political change to their congregations (Fawcett, 2000, pp. 119–20). Contact between government and the churches is important in and of itself, as the failure to consult Protestant representatives about the Anglo-Irish Agreement of 1985 was one of the main reasons for its failure. Clergy can also make a significant contribution to political debates. Some, such as the Archbishop of the Church of Ireland, Dr Robin Eames, have played an active moderating role, stressing peacemaking and reconciliation during the present process.

In terms of mediation at the grassroots level, the Protestant churches have not been as successful as their Catholic counterparts. This is partially due to the fact that the Protestant churches are primarily frequented by, and appeal to, the middle classes. Most of the flashpoints of conflict occur in deprived areas in Northern Ireland and the Protestant churches are not very well-equipped to reach these groups. This is also because they are not as embedded in the infrastructure of daily life as the Catholic Church. Similarly, there is a perception that apart from figures such as Revd Ian Paisley, Protestant ministers do not use their influence effectively in the political sphere. Fawcett found in her interviews that there was a desire on the part of 'ordinary' Protestants for their church to speak up for them: one states, 'I think it's very difficult for the ordinary people like myself to have their voice heard ... I really think the Presbyterian Church should be looking after the interests of the Protestant people. The ministers are able to speak out' (2000, p. 120). Indeed, this speaking-out is perceived as something that the Catholic Church is much better at than the Protestant churches.

Representation and pronouncement

If the Protestant churches are somewhat weaker than the Catholic Church in political mediation, they do try to maintain their reputation as representatives of Protestant community by speaking out on issues that affect unionists and maintaining links with traditional Protestant 'cultural politics'.

One of the ways in which they do this is through sermons. McBride argues (1998, p. 6), that in the eighteenth century the Presbyterian pulpit was 'a vehicle for the dissemination of radical propaganda' and that '[m]inisters saw themselves not only as spiritual leaders, but as tribunes of the people.' Today, by no means all sermons are political in nature, but the pulpit remains an important medium for speaking out on certain political issues. Fawcett (2000, p. 133), for example, found that 40 per cent of Presbyterian clergy had addressed political and economic issues at least four times in the last six months, and only 11 per cent not at all.[12] It is very much the personality and ideas of a particular minister which dictate the frequency and content of political advice and prayers in church services – and there are no official church positions on this. Portadown Orange Order figure, Revd Harold Gracie frequently preaches politics from the pulpit, inviting people to march outside the church. Others, such as the 2004 Presbyterian Moderator Rev Ken Newell, are heavily involved in ecumenism and the politics of reconciliation and promote this message from their pulpits.

The churches also played a vital role throughout conflict offering a place of sanctuary and hope, and helping Protestants imagine a sense of community in times of stress. A poignant example is the use of funeral orations to establish political principles and beliefs. Morrow et al. argue (1991) that the role clergy are expected to play in burying the victims of violence is inherently political, in that they must direct their calls to political sources – claiming that the murder was unjustified, that there should be more security, or that the IRA must be punished. This results in a blurring of the division between unionism and Protestantism as churches help individuals to imagine their community exclusively. Of course, as the political climate changes so too does the brief of the clergy. The less there are victims of violence, the less churches are required by their flocks to be a place of sanctuary and the less clergy are expected to address such sensitive political issues.

The churches also represent the Protestant community in the sense that they have maintained many of their links with unionist culture. For example, in September 1998, the Presbyterian Church presented a cheque to the RUC benevolent fund – which was seen as the territory of Protestant unionism. The churches are often reluctant to place too much distance between themselves and these powerful historical and symbolic issues. This sends out a strong signal: that the churches still want to locate themselves within, and be seen to represent, the unionist political mainstream.

Protestant church reactions to marching have been more difficult to decipher. For example, the Church of Ireland strongly disassociates itself from events at Drumcree, making clear they respect the state and the law, and that they condemn any violence. It also says it welcomes those with any political persuasion and none. However, it continues to allow its church buildings to be used for Orange Order services in the height of marching season tensions.[13] From the Orange Order's 300-member Grand Lodge of Ireland, Martin Smyth estimates there are 35 Presbyterian ministers and a similar number from the Church of Ireland (cited in Fawcett, 2000, p. 106). In a postal survey of Presbyterian clergy, Fawcett (2000, p. 105) found that three-quarters of Presbyterian ministers allowed their church to be used for Orange Order services: 72 per cent of ministers said they also preached at these services (this was, however, often on an occasional basis, and the ministers were not always pro-Orange Order). So there is a tendency for clergy, although they might not support the Orange Order, to not actively oppose this bastion of Protestant-unionist domination. However, as the popularity of the Orange Order wanes and it is seen less as a barometer of mainstream Protestant opinion, the position of the clergy is slowly following suit. Storey (2002, p. 126) characterizes the relationship between the Church of Ireland and the Orange Order as 'progressive disengagement'. He argues that whilst the Church of Ireland is becoming uncoupled from unionist politics and Orangeism, that the transition risks exacerbating Protestant insecurity and must be handled sensitively.[14] Once again, we see that the churches' role in representation and pronouncement is contextual: they do not seek to set the 'Protestant position' on political issues as much as speak up on behalf of what they perceive to be mainstream opinion in their community.

Social organization

The Protestant churches have also played an important part in the social and economic life of the community. They have helped organize social life – church choirs, mothers' groups, and various recreational, sporting and fund-raising events (Brewer, 2004; Morrow et al., 1991; see also Chapter 5). Many Protestants have had links with their church in these more informal ways, for example, through a crèche rather than through attendance at Sunday services. The tendency for children to be sent to Sunday School in a church without the parents' attendance was documented by Wright in 1973 and also emerged in interviews conducted by this author in the early 2000s. The Protestant churches have been less active as regards to the ACE schemes that played such an important role in the social and economic profile of the Catholic Church. The Presbyterian Church did run some government-funded work experience schemes for the unemployed in the 1990s; however, Fawcett (2000, p. 57) found that no individual congregation ran any specific scheme targeted at the unemployed. Since then, the ACE schemes have been even less important in economic and communal life.

With regards to the education system, there are no 'Protestant' schools run by Protestant churches to parallel Catholic educational provision. After partition, the national schools that had been run by the Protestant churches were transferred to the state, becoming legally non-denominational 'controlled' schools. However, in practice these schools were Protestant and unionist in ethos, and Protestant clergy retained a considerable role in their management (Fraser and Morgan, 1999). Today, Protestant clergy often sit on schools' Boards of Governors, and are represented in the Education and Library Boards. They may also be employed for the provision of religious education, in full-time or visiting capacities.

Whilst the activities that Morrow et al. (1991) highlighted persist, these are mainly at the level of social activities rather than paralleling state structures. It is widely recognized that the Protestant churches do not play as active a role in social and economic life as does the Catholic Church.

Overall, how can the political involvement of Protestant churches be characterized? The churches have little participation in political structures, administration and decision making, but play a continued role in tone setting, consultation and diagnosis of the political situation. Their role in social organization, although less significant than the Catholic Church, persists. There is a slow disengagement from Protestant cultural politics amongst the mainstream churches, if not amongst smaller conservative evangelical denominations. This is coupled with a widespread recognition amongst the mainstream churches' hierarchies of the value (or inevitability) of change, and this has caused discourse to shift to conciliation and toleration. In the years since 1998, it is more difficult (but by no means impossible) to find clerical dissent from the new political order or strong opposition to the Good Friday Agreement. This is the case amongst Presbyterian, Church of Ireland and Methodist denominations alike. How far this has taken root ideologically amongst church members is another question. Obviously religious support for political change has a backlash, with conservative evangelicals (within as well as outside these main three denominations) denouncing more liberal clergy. Notably, the Free Presbyterian Church maintains a firm anti-Agreement stance, as do many other smaller conservative evangelical churches. But overall, there is a gradual adaptation to the political mainstream by the main churches, and a tendency to take a more secondary role in politics. In the political field, a very significant number of unionist politicians continue have close links with the churches. Some are ministers and others are involved in religious societies and activities. Whilst Revd Ian Paisley's religious anti-Catholicism is less representative of even conservative unionist politicians than it was during the Stormont years, he is by no means a political anomaly in Northern Ireland. Although its power is waning, the Orange Order continues to provide a bridge between religious and political actors.

Conclusion

The Catholic Church and the Protestant churches differ in some respects in the nature of their political involvement. The Catholic Church plays a much stronger role in structuring the social life of Catholics, particularly through education. On the other hand, Protestant clergy are much more likely to be involved in unionist party politics than Catholic clergy are in nationalist party politics. Where the churches are similar is in their lack of involvement in radical republican and loyalist paramilitary campaigns and organizations. They also share a desire to represent the political mainstream of their communities. Moreover, both Catholic and Protestant churches have been involved in political mediation, negotiation and consultation. Whilst their input may not be of critical policy significance, their representation and sometimes leadership of 'the views of the community' is socially important and strengthens their public roles. Despite some secularization of Northern Irish society, the churches continue to play these roles. However, their involvement in politics is undoubtedly less intense in the present because of the changing political situation. Although communities are still polarized, a reduction in levels of violence and numbers of victims as well as progress on fundamental issues such as civil rights has meant that there is less immediacy in the churches' involvement in politics. They now play a supporting rather than a leading role.

However, the churches continue to be much more important than other interest groups in Northern Ireland because of their central role in the organization and representation of the two main communities. These roles were deepened and widened by the politics of conflict. As churches comforted and serviced Protestants and Catholics through troubled times they became more embedded in community structures. In turn, they capitalized upon their central social position to maintain their influence in other areas of life, not least in politics. By occupying this position at the heart of the community, the churches are still in a unique position to argue for their own ideological agendas. Indeed, the churches are powerful agencies in society, not just neutral communal mediators. They are organizations with beliefs, goals and strategies. Churches have clear ideas on the difference between right and wrong, and the meaning of the good life. Their purpose is to influence people. It is not necessarily that priests and clergy tell people how to vote, but rather, by addressing the issues that affect Protestant and Catholic communities, the churches have a platform from which to promote their own perspectives and values.

Politicians recognize that the churches play a unique social role in their respective communities and have an ability to reach a wide audience. Thus, most politicians have prioritized their relationship with the churches, remaining on friendly terms, consulting with them on political and cultural issues and often working in partnership with them. This adds legitimacy to political actors who in return often shy away from introducing policies that would incur the churches' opposition. In addition to politicians in Northern Ireland, the British and Irish states also know that the churches are influential. They have courted conciliatory strands within Protestant and Catholic religious establishments in order to promote political stability. This has reinforced the impression that churches are important and respected social actors. In such ways, it is clear that there is a two-way, and mutually beneficial, relationship between the churches and politics.

However, a Marxist interpretation, of a power-bloc alliance of the churches and politicians attempting to gain social control by spreading ideological hegemony, does not explain the complexity of the relationship between the churches and people. It is not simply the case that people are, as Fulton argues (1991, p. 227), 'the real subjects of the battle for domination' – pawns in a religio-political power struggle. Of course, analysis of structures and politics is integral to an understanding of religion in Northern Ireland. But whilst politics provides possibilities and constraints to human action, it does not control these. In fact, the relationship between the churches and the people is better described as co-dependent. Religious institutions do not just use people – people also use them. We turn to the bottom-up dimensions of the link between religion and politics in the following four chapters.

4

Religion as a boundary marker

Key points

- *Religious identity is the key boundary marker in Northern Ireland.*

- *The religious boundary is maintained through segregated education, marriage, housing patterns and social networks.*

- *The religious boundary is breaking down through employment and consumption.*

- *Sometimes religious labels have no substantive religious meaning or content and are merely identity markers, especially amongst nonchurchgoers and non-believers.*

> Politics and religion are so confused in Northern Ireland …
> someone who plays rugby or hockey by nature is stereotyped as a
> Protestant, and that is a religion, whereas someone who plays
> Gaelic is a Catholic, and that is a religion. Now what those two
> people believe is their own personal belief. But they play those
> sports. I suppose that comes from divided communities.
> (Vinny, Catholic, Co. Down)

Whilst communities in Northern Ireland are divided along many lines such as ethnic, national and political, the dominant cleavage since the seventeenth century has been religious. Although it was not inevitable that this would be the case, over subsequent centuries Catholicism and Protestantism became closely associated with wider power struggles within society. As argued in Chapter 2, religious affiliation, more than any other social difference, provided a stable source of identity and belonging. However, neither religious 'bloc' has ever been internally homogeneous. In fact, each grouping has contained significant differences in religious as well as political attitudes. But what is significant is that religion, whilst never universally practised or doctrinally coherent, has over time come to be the most entrenched signifier of the communal boundary in Northern Ireland.

Religious labels are deeply persistent in Northern Ireland, even amongst those who have no strong religious beliefs or regular practices. As Tonge points out (2002, p. 98), 'labelling by religious denomination remains the most convenient method of identifying the division between the communities.' Unlike political labels, religious labels embrace the vast majority of the population. Religion acts as a boundary marker both in terms of personal identities and social structures. The first section of this chapter analyses the extent of segregation between groups and the role of religious structures in maintaining the boundary. The second section shows how this boundary is internalized and reproduced by many ordinary Protestants and Catholics. Whilst subsequent chapters explore the ways in which religion is more substantively meaningful than just a group label, the aim of this chapter is to examine the extent to which communal identities are in fact bound up with religion. In other words, this chapter asks how religion helps *signify* the boundary in Northern Ireland whilst subsequent chapters ask how religion helps *construct* the meanings of the boundary.

Religion and structures of the boundary

Protestant and Catholic communities in Northern Ireland continue to be largely segregated according to religious background. Schools attended, marriage partners chosen, areas of residence and social networks are all influenced by religion. Whilst the situation has slowly been changing over the 1990s and early 2000s, segregation remains the rule rather than the exception in many areas of life. Social class is also a central source of social division; however, it tends to be interwoven with, rather than eclipsed by, the dominant religious cleavage.

Most children in Northern Ireland go to what are essentially Protestant or Catholic schools. The first integrated school, Lagan College, opened in 1981 and there are now 46 such schools at secondary level or below (by third level, institutional segregation is filtered out). Fourteen thousand pupils attend integrated schools, just 4 per cent of the total school age population (<www.nicie.org> 7 August 2003). The bulk of the remainder of Protestant children go to state-maintained schools that are predominantly Protestant in intake, whilst the vast majority of the remainder of Catholic children attend Catholic-maintained schools. As discussed in Chapter 3, the Catholic Church is still involved in education, as are Protestant churches, if not in such an official capacity as in the past.

The main charge levelled against segregated education is that it enhances perceptions of social difference and, as a result, causes intolerance through lack of understanding of other traditions (Murray, 1985). Some go further and suggest that segregated education reinforces antagonism through offering different school curricula that are slanted towards the teaching of particular British or Irish histories that help legitimize difference. In fact, Gallagher (1989) finds that there is little difference in school curricula, but Darby and Dunn (1987) suggest that the difference is in 'school ethos' and the 'hidden curriculum'. Whereas wreaths are laid in Remembrance Day services in Protestant schools and assemblies often involve singing traditional Protestant hymns, Catholic schools concentrate on Irish historical commemorations and Catholic religious rituals.

Recent research by Lambkin (1996) confirms that segregated education impacts deeply upon schoolchildren. Despite the widespread Education for Mutual Understanding (EMU) scheme's promotion of joint activities between Protestant and

Catholic schoolchildren, Lambkin's report shows that knowledge of the other community's religion is weak, and that many religious and historical myths fill in gaps of knowledge about the 'other side'. In fact, Lambkin found that schoolchildren thought that religion was very important and, unlike adults, believed that the conflict was caused by religion. As such, segregated education is one of the most important ways in which the boundary is maintained in Northern Ireland. Not only does it deprive schoolchildren of significant social contact with those of a different religion, but it can also add to the perception that the divide is religious in nature.

Indeed, increasing communal polarization in Northern Ireland, especially amongst the young, is a pressing issue. Contrary to assumptions that young people may be less prejudiced than their elders, Hayes and MacAllister (1999b) found that ethnic stereotyping and political attitudes are at least as strongly entrenched among the young as the old. Data from the Young Northern Ireland Life and Times Survey 2003 indicates a high awareness of communal belonging amongst young people, and in particular religious belonging (Devine and Schubotz, 2004).

Furthermore, separate education is significant because it is connected to other forms of social segregation. Hornsby-Smith (1987) has outlined the importance of separate schooling for the Catholic minority in Britain in maintaining endogamy – the tendency to marry within one's own religious group. Similarly, O'Leary and Finnas (2002) found that shared educational networks and leisure facilities facilitated the maintenance of religious intermarriages in the Republic of Ireland and Finland. They relate this to class, and argue that more middle-class groups have better access to these kinds of networks. Whilst there is also a class factor at work in Northern Ireland, there is no doubt that separate educational networks influence the lack of intermarriage that has been fairly consistent over time. At the beginning of recent conflict, Rose (1971) reported that only 5 per cent of marriages were mixed, and this figure remained constant throughout the early 1980s and 1990s (Moxon-Brown, 1983, 1991). More recent survey evidence finds that 10 per cent of partnerships are now between people of differing religious identifications (NILTS, 2003). Whilst this figure has increased since the early 1990s, 94 per cent of Catholics and 88 per cent of Protestants have a partner of the same religion. Although a growing percentage of people now say that they would not mind if one of their very close relatives were to marry a partner of the other religion (Wigfall-Williams and Robinson, 2001), high rates of endogamy persist.

This has led Moxon-Brown (1991) to argue that in Northern Ireland, endogamy both reflects and causes strong communal identities and is the single most important factor in maintaining group boundaries. This point was also made by Harris (1972) in her study of Ballybeg, where she found that endogamy was at the heart of the community divide because of the enormous importance of kinship ties. Having kinship networks solely within one's own community means that it is difficult to get to know people from another community intimately. She also found that when intermarriage happened it did not bridge the community divide because the husband tended to cut off contact with his community of origin. The conservatizing role of the Catholic Church in seeking to place limitations on mixed marriage couples has been noted already in Chapter 1. Although restrictions were lifted in the 1970s, for many Protestants this indicated the monopolistic nature of the Catholic Church and may help explain their reluctance to intermarry (Fulton, 1991). This perhaps is related to Wigfall-Williams and Robinson's (2001) finding that Catholics have been consistently more likely than Protestants to say that they would not mind a mixed marriage within their own family.

Not surprisingly, segregation also extends to where people live. On the eve of the outbreak of recent troubles in 1969, Poole and Boal (1973, p. 14) found that only 32 per cent of the population of Belfast lived in streets that had some degree of mixing between Catholics and Protestants. This figure has since fallen, due in no small part to the enforced population movements between 1969 and 1972 where many people were intimidated out of their homes. Intimidation and forced migration still occurs in Northern Ireland, albeit to a lesser extent than during the height of conflict. Although some of the more prosperous areas of Belfast contain a mixture of Catholics and Protestants, most electoral wards in the city are segregated, in that fewer than 10 per cent of the inhabitants in a given area belong to the 'other' religion (Tonge 2002, p. 109). In Belfast, and in many towns around Northern Ireland, it is relatively easy to work out if one is in a Protestant or Catholic area on account of the flags, murals, graffiti and painted kerbstones as well as the names of shops and pubs. However, it must be underlined that Belfast is segregated to greater degree than anywhere else in Northern Ireland (Whyte 1990, p. 34). It is also the case that working-class areas are more segregated than middle-class areas. However, whilst one is more likely to see museums than murals in leafy south Belfast, most people are priced out of this neutral territory and usually choose to buy property in 'their own' areas.

Residential segregation in the most deprived housing estates in Belfast has continued to increase despite the Agreement and the peace process, and there is a perception that in these areas community relations have worsened (Shirlow, 2001). Contact has often been cut off by the presence of physical barriers such as concrete 'peace' walls that separate one community from another. Indeed, Shirlow's findings are sobering: 68 per cent of 18 to 25-year-olds living in certain parts of Belfast reported they had never had a meaningful conversation with anyone from the other community; 72 per cent of all age groups refuse to use health centres located in communities dominated by the other religion; only 22 per cent will shop in areas dominated by the other religion; 62 per cent have been the victims of physical or verbal abuse since 1994. Although this is not representative of the situation throughout Northern Ireland, it is none the less of crucial significance that the religious boundary in certain housing estates in Belfast is becoming more, rather than less, entrenched over time.

Whyte (1990) noted that in his experience of Northern Ireland the middle classes had plenty of cross-community friendships. Other trends such as the urban regeneration of Belfast and the creation of new social spaces have led to increased mixing between Catholics and Protestants in some spheres of life. Murtagh (2002) argues that patterns of selective consumption in the city centre with riverside cafes and bars, tickets to expensive ice hockey games and multimedia events have loosened religious identity boundaries and are reconstructing identities around lifestyle, income and consumption. However, Murtagh bases this on the fact that most people who go out for a meal or go to a concert do so away from their own localities. This is certainly the case and does begin to break down contact barriers.

But it is also important to remember that people have to go home afterwards. They must return to neighbourhoods and families that are more often than not segregated and, in turn, they are reminded of the boundary and the nature of their belonging. This is borne out in survey data with only two out of five teenagers saying that they felt safe in an area predominated by people of the other religion (YNILTS, 2003).

One field where there is now a significant degree of mixing is in the workplace. Of course, in predominantly Catholic or Protestant neighbourhoods it is likely that locals are employed to service the community in local shops and businesses (Barritt and Carter, 1962). Smith and Chambers (1987, pp. 101–103) found that 80 per cent of the workforces they surveyed were described by respondents as mostly one religion or another: 57 per cent as majority Protestant and 23 per cent as majority Catholic. In about two in five cases, the majorities were very large with 95–100 per cent Catholic or Protestant employees. However, there is much less segregation in large than in small workforces. Whyte's (1990, p. 37) conclusion, that 'segregation at work is one of the least acute forms of segregation in Northern Ireland', is still pertinent today and is due in no small part to the extensive equality legislation that has been in force since the 1980s. Since then, the Equality Commission (2000) reports that, although some degree of segregation remains, there has been 'significant' improvement in the situation in recent years. In addition, 83 per cent of the population of Northern Ireland now say that they would prefer a religiously mixed workplace (NILTS, 2003).

Overall, the religious boundary in Northern Ireland continues to pervade many areas of life. However, the situation is changing, albeit in a variety of contradictory directions. In some cases, there is growing polarization as communities, particularly in interface areas of Belfast, have less contact with one another than ever before. On the other hand, for those who can afford it, there are more social spaces, cosmopolitan activities and meeting places opening up in 'neutral' territory. At the same time, there has been a slow increase in openness to mixed marriage and integrated education, particularly amongst younger people. However, whilst these have chipped away at the religious boundary in Northern Ireland, they have yet not significantly eroded it. Most people are very aware on what side of the boundary they belong. We turn now to reflect on how the boundary is experienced by ordinary Protestants and Catholics.

Religion, personal identity and the boundary

Nearly 90 per cent of the population of Northern Ireland identify themselves as Protestant or Catholic. And we have seen in the previous section the ways in which Protestant and Catholic groups are segregated by religious background. But there are many levels at which these religious identities have meaning. For some, a Protestant or Catholic identity has very little spiritual content and entails infrequent or no form of religious practice. It is therefore problematic to speak of communal identity simply as religious. In this section we explore these types of identities. We examine how religion psychologically, as well as structurally, marks out the boundary. We then look at cases where this is the full extent of religious identification. This is where the religious boundary is acknowledged and experienced, but has little religious content or meaning. In contrast, the next three chapters will be devoted to the ways in which religion gives meanings to the boundary.

First of all, as is argued in Chapter 1, identity is intrinsically relational. People recognize who they are by comparing themselves to other people and establishing what they are not. Consider some answers to a question asked in interviews 'do you remember first becoming aware that you were a Protestant?':

> No, because when I was growing up, I lived in a street with lots of Catholics, so I was brought up with Catholics you know? (Betty, Belfast)

> I remember being dragged along to the July demonstrations, and they were quite good. Around that time there was a Catholic across the street and he didn't go and I did go, and I sort of realized then that there was a difference. (Jonathan, Co. Down)

> I remember the first time that really sticks out in my mind – we had Roman Catholics who lived on the Shankill those days, we all lived together. (Helen, Co. Down)

And, on the other hand, answers to the question 'do you remember becoming first aware that you were a Catholic?':

> I'll tell you exactly when it was, it was seeing a lot of people around me wearing things like Glasgow Celtic tops, lots of Republican paraphernalia all over the place, graffiti and tricolours and things like that. I knew certainly when I was able to tell the difference, I knew that there was differentiation in society and I knew that I wasn't supposed to support Rangers. (Fred, Co. Down)

> It was all Catholics where I lived, there was no other religion. It was only when I came to the town that I found out that there were Protestants. I would have been older, eleven or twelve when I went to school, when I found out I was a Catholic. (Catherine, Co. Down)

> Being brought up in a mixed community, I would have been hugely aware of different identities. Because I lived on the road from Lurgan and it would be Catholic houses, Protestant houses then Catholic then Protestant, so we would have grown up with 12th of July marches and we would just have known not to go up the road then. (Brian, Co. Down)

The reference point for self is other. These Protestants learned 'who they were' when they encountered difference and realized that they were not Catholics, and Catholics, when they realized they were not Protestants. As Jenkins argues, ethnicity or communal identity, 'depends on similarity rubbing up against difference' (1996, p. 65). People arrive at self-awareness by observing difference – whether this is football tops, school uniforms, cultural traditions such as going to watch Orange Order marches or not going.

It is important to note that relational does not necessarily mean antagonistic. Just because we define ourselves by what we are not, does not necessarily mean that we must dislike or fear the other. Sometimes we may even envy what we think we do not have. However, this kind of boundary maintenance often results in our seeing others, who we feel we have little in common with, as strangers. Moreover, very often when we do not know much about other groups, we tend to think about their difference from us in terms of stereotypes. It is not surprising that in the context of deeply divided society such as Northern Ireland, these stereotypes are often associated with fear and threat.

As one Protestant woman from Co. Down, Helen, says of the Irish, 'they don't feel like they are my people'. She states,

> I don't feel anything in common with my Irish counterparts – they feel like strangers to me. And yet if I talk to them, if I meet them, you know I'm as fine as I am with anybody … when I go to Dublin, it actually feels like a foreign city to me, and when I come back up to Northern Ireland, it's such a relief to get home.

Another young Protestant man, John, says 'it just seems strange, they're very, some of them are quite different.' Some Protestant interviewees spoke of Ireland as a foreign country with a foreign government. One woman, Betty from Belfast, offered a poignant example when she compared nationalist desires to fly the Irish flag in Northern Ireland with a hypothetical equivalent demand from Russia. Another, Jane from Belfast, says that the Irish language is just like another foreign language to her: 'It's like if someone is speaking in Chinese and you don't speak it, you're going to think "they're talking about me".' Here again we see the tendency to locate oneself with relation to others and how the strangers' intentions frequently seem suspicious. Often it is the lack of knowledge of the other, as much as any fixed quality, which makes them appear strange. As Fiona, a Protestant woman from Belfast, says, before she participated in a cross-community programme when she was eleven, she had never met a Catholic and had the impression that they were 'ginger-haired squinty-eyed aliens'. Perceptions of difference are very deeply entrenched in Northern Ireland and the Protestant/Catholic boundary looms large in most people's consciousness.

For some people, a religious identification is expressed as a positive sense of belonging. One woman from Newry, Niamh, says 'I am a Catholic, but I don't believe in all that stuff.' She says she does not believe in God, does not attend mass and is not interested in any aspect of the Church. However, she also says that she would have her children christened into the Catholic Church. She gives two reasons: the first that it is better for children to have something to rebel against, and the second that it is necessary to get her children into a Catholic school. She says this is not for religious reasons but for cultural reasons. She does not want her children to be in a minority in a state (and predominantly Protestant) school, but rather to learn Irish, play Gaelic sport and have a 'confident identity'. Although she continually underlines that the content of Catholicism is unimportant to her, she is happy to participate in certain religious rituals, such as the christening of her children in church, to maintain her family's cultural identity. So for many people there is a sense in which communal identity can be best handed down in a Catholic institutional context – not in integrated schools, or through language clubs, or in the home. In such a way, religion is a vital part of cultural identity and important for boundary maintenance. However, this has little to do with spirituality or religious practices. There is very little *religious* content in these identifications and, in some cases, religion does merely mark out a deeper sense of belonging.

Religion can also be a social boundary marker even when group membership is not perceived in a positive light. One Catholic man from Belfast, Joe, spoke about the difficulty of changing one's identity. Whilst Joe identifies himself as Catholic, he has no links at all with the Church and instead attends a self-help group that he refers to as his church. He presents himself as religiously agnostic, and says he cannot stomach religious people, religious structures and the type of 'extreme' Catholicism with which he was raised. In addition, he says he is not interested in voting, does not identify with either nationalism or unionism and does not like to spend time with opinionated people. Despite this, he maintains a Catholic identity. He struggles with this, and says that in application forms he refuses to fill in the boxes relating to religious and national identity. However, Joe also describes how having the label of Catholic has made a difference to his life because of the structure of Northern Ireland, and that this has 'angered him to the core'. He describes being beaten up, not getting job interviews, losing a job and a subsequent court battle. The point for Joe is that, 'unfortunately my life has been influenced by the fact that I am a Catholic, of course it has, without a question or a doubt.' This helps explain why he still identifies with Catholicism. It is a label which has impacted upon his opportunities and how he has been treated – he has had to fight for his personal rights because of it:

> I guess when you spend 18 or 19 years in your youth, your teenage years when you are extremely impressionable, being told you are a Catholic, it's hard to remove it. And it is, it's hard to take it away and say I'm not. I have that on my birth certificate – born Roman Catholic. It's very difficult to remove. If you wanted to sort of look at it, why am I Roman Catholic? I was born in a regular hospital, but immediately went to a church and was baptized by a priest who said you are a Roman Catholic, that's about it. I don't know. I don't know. I mean, it's of no importance to me, none at all. If it was my choice, which I guess it is, I don't know if you have to go through a process of deed poll, like you change your name, can you change your religion?

Joe goes on to explain that others will 'seek out what [he is] anyway'. Here, the idea of changing one's religion seems unthinkable, not necessarily because it is a political statement, but because communal membership has been so interwoven with an individual's experiences in life. Even when an individual does not want to identify with a specific community, the structures of Northern Ireland make it almost impossible not to. However, in cases like this, whilst people may feel they belong to a community that is religiously demarcated, there are no traces of religious depth or meaning.

A final example underlines this point well. Simon, a Belfast man, a nonchurchgoer and SDLP member, says he is 'probably a Protestant'. He says that he very occasionally attends the local Church of Ireland, but imagines that going to the local Catholic Church would be no more or less meaningful. However, he also says that if he went to the local chapel: 'I would be making some kind of conscious decision to change who I was.' Simon's self-presentation is of a 'middle-class Protestant', and he says the 'harmless bunch' which are the SDLP are 'really, the same as me'. Overall though, his narrative is not one of an Irish nationalist, but of a person who cannot find a political home in any Northern Ireland party (he says 'the SDLP are the ones that offended me least'). During his student years he was on the fringes of the civil rights movement, but says he was not sure how far Catholics accepted him, as he did not have the 'war stories' and was essentially a middle-class Protestant who had not given up his privileges. Simon talks of his attempts to find a political cause, which have confused him because although he 'would really like to contribute to nationalism' – even republicanism – he does not think he is really welcomed, and feels that he does not really understand Catholics' experiences of Northern Ireland (as he perceives them to be).

This is a good example of how identity is constructed reflexively, and is shaped by the acceptance or not of others. Although this man says that Protestant religion does not have much meaning for him, in the context of feeling that he had not shared in the experiences of the Catholic community, he maintains that the label of his community background is 'who I am'. This is a weak, even reluctant, form of communal identity that has been thrust upon him. This mode of Protestant identity makes no use of any substantive religious content, and is another example of religion as a boundary marker.

Conclusion

Religion sometimes does act, as McGarry and O'Leary (1995) suggest, simply as a badge of identity. Certainly, in the cases outlined above, there is very little religious content or meaning to Protestant and Catholic identities. Religious belonging is closely related to cultural identity for some, whilst for others awareness of religious identity has been shaped by their experiences in life and is therefore difficult to change. This is due in no small part to boundary-maintaining processes in education, housing and relationships that break down along religious lines. This heavily influences the types of relationships people develop in their formative years, as well as in later life. However, religious identities are often held reluctantly. In fact many people would happily not be identified as Protestant or Catholic and are not very attached to their own group. Moreover, religious identities do not necessarily correlate with ethnic and political positions. They have more to do with lived experiences than political attitudes. This is not a civil religion where people appropriate symbols and rituals of national identity as if they were religious. Individuals' feelings about their group membership are often ambiguous. However, drawing away from one's religious identity is easier said than done. This is because religious identifications carry associations of acceptance/non-acceptance, inclusion/exclusion. Moreover, other community members are often unforgiving of those who try to leave the fold and this can place a strain on family and other social relationships. Thus, the religious boundary has become entrenched, but is not necessarily 'religious' in meaning.

However, the analysis must not stop here. It does not follow that religion is nothing more than an empty boundary marker for most people. Whilst the content of religious identifications may not always be religious *per se*, they are very seldom completely empty labels. In fact, there is rarely such a thing as 'just a label'. Instead political, cultural and religious ideas overlap to various degrees to give labels meaning. Group labels, like fashion labels, often come with assumptions about what the wearers of this label are like and how they are likely to treat us. In Northern Ireland, some of these assumptions are in fact informed in various ways by religious beliefs and practices. As is hinted at above, sometimes the maintenance of a Catholic cultural identity requires involvement by Church structures, for example, through the education system. This is examined in depth in the next chapter. Often, cultural differences are perceived to be religious in some way, for example, where Protestants feel that Catholics are controlled by the Church, or Catholics feel that Protestants are uncompromising by nature. In other cases, the boundary is infused with theological meanings. In these ways, religion can be used as an interpretive framework for understanding community relationships and politics in Northern Ireland. It provides some of the content with which inclusion/exclusion and acceptance/non-acceptance are conceived. The following three chapters explore the ways that religion gives substantive meanings to the boundary.

5

Religious practice and community construction

Key points

- *Religion helps build community when people attend church or use the church for other social activities.*

- *Religious rituals physically bring groups of people together.*

- *Religious rituals psychologically create a sense of group membership.*

- *Religious rituals are more important for Catholics in Northern Ireland than they are for Protestants, with the exception of some evangelical Protestant groups.*

- *Sometimes religious rituals appear social rather than spiritual, but they maintain individuals' familiarity with the religious field.*

Taken from the Latin, *religio* means to 'bind together'. This chapter explores how religious rituals create social bonds, and how this feeds into politics and conflict in Northern Ireland. Our concern is how the practices of Protestantism and Catholicism have been utilized to construct a sense of community and have excluded the other group. We focus on attendance, religious rituals, celebrations and other activities that take place in the context of the churches. We also explore how the churches provide the social structures that facilitate community building.

The argument here is informed by Durkheim's functionalism. He argued (1915) that religion works as a kind of social cement, something that binds members of a society together with a common purpose and belief system. For Durkheim, the content of religious beliefs is much less important than the fact that people share common practices. Through meeting up together and practising the same rituals, Durkheim argued that a collective conscience is created. For Durkheim, society exerts a moral authority that is most keenly felt when practising public rites and rituals. Therefore, through collective religious rituals, society upholds its own values.

Whilst Durkheim and other functionalists do overemphasize the power of society over individuals, and the idea of collective conscience is problematic, his ideas are extremely useful when analysing the relationship between religious practices and community construction. Sometimes it does not really matter what the specific religious teachings of a tradition are. Religion can be socially important simply where people come together in groups and participate in the same activities. Not only does this create shared feelings of belonging, it also helps group members to recognize those who do not belong. Outsiders are excluded from the moral community. Whilst this does not mean that society is all-powerful, it is important to bear in mind the role religion can play in gelling communities together and providing some of the codes and meanings of group membership.

Warner usefully elaborates on the role of religious activities in creating community. He argues (1997, p. 217) that religion creates 'embodied ritual'. By this he means that through participating in activities such as singing, chanting, bodily motion or eating, a certain amount of social solidarity is produced. This solidarity is not based on a collective conscience, where people all think the same thing. Indeed, he feels that the best kind of rituals are ambiguous enough to unite the community whilst individual members can provide their own interpretation of them. This is similar to Cohen's (1985) symbolic construction of community. Rituals create an atmosphere where people feel bonded to one another through sharing certain sounds, motions and tastes. Warner gives an example where he attended a Korean Presbyterian Church service in New Jersey. Whilst he did not understand a single word that was said, the rituals were familiar. He recognized the music, he knew when to bow his head for prayer and when to say amen. Warner goes on to argue that religious rituals are actually rather accessible to outsiders and can be utilized to build bridges between communities (for his purposes, immigrant and ethnic communities in the United States). Whilst religion in Northern Ireland may well have the potential to work in such a way, in the context of a deeply divided society, we can easily see how this might not generally be the case.

Warner's emphasis on the ways in which rituals can create, not simply express, social solidarity is extremely important (1997, p. 224). In other words, religious rituals are more than just boundary markers, they actually help produce the boundary and give it meaning. Warner cites Rambo's work on conversion (1993, p. 115), where he argues that 'ritual actions consolidate the community through singing, recitation, and gestures in unison ... ritual helps people to learn to act differently ... [f]rom the details of when to bow, kneel, and stand, to how to carry a Bible or address the minister, priest, rabbi, to more profound truth and teachings.' Kertzer (1988) also argues that relationships and identities are constructed, not just expressed, through rituals. According to Kertzer (1988, p. 68) 'socially and politically speaking, we are what we do, not what we think.'

The next step in analysing the relationship between religious rituals and the creation of community is to define exactly what is meant by religious behaviour and practice. We must avoid falling into the functionalist trap whereby any shared activities that create common sentiments are thought to be sacred. A commonly given example is avid football supporters, who participate in habitual attendance and shared euphoria at games. These are not the kind of activities that we are concerned with in this chapter. Here, our purpose is to explore rituals that are connected in some way to churches. That is not to say, however, that only activities that make reference to the supernatural count as religious practices. Religious practices may or may not do this. The important point is that they centre around what is recognizably the terrain of Protestantism and Catholicism. This may be churchgoing itself or other activities that are related to the churches.

Ammerman's (1997) work helps us focus this debate, broadening concepts of religious commitment, membership and practice in the context of voluntaristic societies. She argues that in modern mobile societies everyday practices are redefining our notions of what counts as religious involvement. The complexity of our lives and our multiple institutional entanglements mean that some contradictions of beliefs and practices are to be expected, and that we should take into account whatever plural or temporary bonds and practices actually exist. For Ammerman, a variety of practices bring modern citizens into contact with the churches. Voluntary organizations, choirs and heritage societies in church congregations are forums where relationships are formed and belonging is nurtured. Most churches are involved in providing some kind of human service activity, whether this is work with the homeless, women's shelters, social benefit programmes, human rights work or supporting cultural and educational programmes. The material and personnel resources of religion then provide a framework for doing the work of the community. In such a way, Ammerman argues that religious organizations, mainly congregations, provide the social space for the development of fellowship, civic skills and charitable practices that are often carried into other areas of life. Whilst these skills are not specifically religious, she points out (1997, p. 212), that 'organizations that claim to be religious turn out to be social spaces in which the rhetoric and sanction of religious good surrounds certain practices – practices which in turn affect the shape of society.'

In the context of Northern Ireland, Morrow et al. (1991, p. 10) explore the central problematic of 'defining the boundaries of where churches begin and end'. Their study, *The Churches and Inter-community Relationships*, draws on interviews with clergy and communities in a variety of regional contexts to answer this question. They find three significant areas of overlap between religion and community life: social/recreational activities, social action and civic involvement. Morrow et al. argue that the wide variety of church-based social activities offered – sports, uniformed organizations, study and prayer groups, youth clubs, women's and men's groups, choirs, bowling clubs, charity work – embrace activities for all age groups, genders and interests. Furthermore, they found that these social activities involve people who have no other links with the churches. The churches in Northern Ireland are also significantly involved in social action, for example, through summer play schemes or the Samaritans, the use of church buildings as meeting places for community politics and credit unions. Moreover, Morrow et al. detail many forms of participation by clergy in civic activities, such as participation in local festivals, Remembrance Day services, social services councils, school management boards and committees, voluntary organizations and events organized by the Orange Order. On the basis of this, they argue that the clergy are important figures in integrating public and private life in Northern Ireland (1991, p. 22). This impacts not only upon the ways in which life is structured, but also on the meanings given to difference.

Of course, in divided societies such as Northern Ireland, these types of interactions have largely taken place on segregated lines. Most civic, recreational and pastoral activities run by churches remain more or less religiously exclusive. On the issue of inter-church contact, Morrow et al. point out that activity tends to be congregational, denominational or inter-faith, but is rarely ecumenical, thus reinforcing distinctions between groups. Although there are noticeable exceptions, Morrow et al. (1991, p. 20) were struck by Protestant and Catholic 'mutual exclusion from acts of worship'. They argue that this 'becomes an act of social and theological significance simultaneously', and that it is perhaps here that 'the extent of the churches' involvement with the politics of the conflict is most visible' (1991, p. 20). These kinds of social and civic activities that take place within a religious forum have played an important role in Northern Ireland, not just in the intra-communal ways that Ammerman has outlined, but also in terms of inter-communal relationships. Social networks have been limited, and the content and meaning of the boundary between Catholics and Protestants is nuanced by separation of church structures and separate religious practices.

This chapter deals with two types of processes, each which interacts with politics in different ways. The first process is where religious rituals foster a sense of communal togetherness. The second is where churches facilitate community-building activities. Religious rituals are politically important because they help create a kind of moral community. Whilst members may not necessarily think 'the same thing' or share specific political attitudes, rituals distinguish insiders from outsiders. By doing 'the same thing', socially and politically salient categories of insiders and outsiders are constructed. The churches' role in community building reinforces a sense of political community. In fact, these elements of religion are much more socially and politically significant for Catholics than for Protestants. Amongst Protestants, religious rituals do play a role in fostering togetherness; however, because of the fragmented nature of Protestantism in Northern Ireland, Protestant churches have not played a community-building role to the same degree as the Catholic Church. This has caused insecurity amongst some Protestants who tend to interpret the seeming unity of the Catholic community as organized political threat. These ideas are fleshed out in the following discussion of the different ways that religious practice and community construction operate for Catholics and for Protestants in Northern Ireland.

Religious practice and community construction amongst Catholics

Community is central concept in Catholic theology and practice. As Crilly points out (1998, p. 41):

> The sense of church is at the core of the experience of Catholic Christianity. That is why the Catholic Church has always been so adamant about the duty of each member to attend mass every week … It is in the midst of his disciples that the Lord Jesus is to be found. Religion is not just a private affair, but is rooted in the experience of a faith community … the individual Catholic does not seek God alone, but by drawing close to God's people.

This is significant at a variety of levels. First, the theological emphasis on togetherness ensures that the practice of Catholicism plays an important social, as well as spiritual, role for its members. Secondly, by creating familiarity with the actual ritual of the mass, certain codes are shared by attenders who know when to sit, stand, kneel, when to participate and went to stay silent. The mass involves common prayers where participants seek forgiveness in the Penitential Rite (Lord Have Mercy), offer praise and prayers together in the Gloria, the Creed and Prayers of the Faithful. It also involves sharing Holy Communion, or the Eucharist, where the priest consecrates the bread, the 'body of Christ' and then offers this to the congregation. In every Catholic Church in Northern Ireland these rituals are the same. By 'doing the same thing', an awareness of the in-group, or at least a mechanism by which to recognize outsiders, is created.

Reflecting on what Catholics should wear to mass, Revd Jonathan S. Toborowsky (2000) expresses this sense of common understanding poignantly:

> The truth is we should not need any piece of paper to tell us what is appropriate to wear to Mass. Mass is not some foreign thing in a strange place; it is a 'family reunion' on our home turf. We know what happens at every Mass, and we know how God wants us to spend his day. How we dress should be obvious.

This captures well how groups of people that regularly participate in the same rituals instinctively know where they are and know what to do. It almost feels like a family. Richstatter (1999) gives the analogy of 'the structure of the Mass as like Thanksgiving dinner at Grandmother's house'. At mass, like Thanksgiving, Richstatter argues, people gather as a family, tell their stories, say grace, pass the food, eat and drink before returning home. It is significant that mass is compared to family gatherings – occasions that are generally associated with an understanding of members' shared history, familiar patterns of behaviour and communication and a sense of belonging. This resonates strongly with Bourdieu's (1990) idea of the 'habitus' – internalized and embodied systems of meaning that help us know who we are and how to behave.

In Catholic theology, community can seen more as an optimistic aspiration to unity, rather than a drive for uniformity.[1] A sense of belonging is important, faith is to be found in communion with others, and all strands of Catholicism emphasize the relational context of religion. The Church has been given a pastoral role to encourage the togetherness of followers of Christ: it sees Christianity as a wide body of believers, and therefore has room for some theological interpretation. However, theology is always mediated through cultural context, and in Ireland, conflict and power struggles encouraged not the unity of all Christians, but oppositional notions of community. Catholicism strayed away from its theoretical optimism of inclusion, and came to represent a more rigidly defined sense of community.[2]

Catholicism's theological emphasis on community combined with specific historical conditions in Ireland, and later Northern Ireland, to produce an ever stronger sense of belonging. Over centuries of conflict in Ireland, access to power became largely determined by religious background. As communal boundaries were drawn, the role of the churches in social and political life was enhanced. In the nineteenth century, the Catholic Church became part of a nationalist political movement with mass membership. They gave their support to Daniel O'Connell, Catholic Emancipation and the Repeal movement in an attempt to redress Catholic social and political inequality. Clergy joined the Catholic Association, served on committees, canvassed voters and agitated for the cause from the pulpit. O'Connell repaid the efforts of the Church by throwing the weight of the Repeal movement behind explicitly Catholic causes, in particular, behind the demand for denominational education. Connolly (1985, p. 29) argues that O'Connell 'explicitly linked religious, political and economic grievances' to create a mass movement with popular appeal. Although internal tensions existed, the impact of ideology and class, which was so important throughout the rest of western Europe, was blunted in Ireland by the developing religio-political consensus.

The construction of community as Catholic was furthered by Charles Stewart Parnell. Parnell led the Land League and Home Rule Movements from 1879 to 1886 in Ireland, during which time he deepened, but ironically (being himself a Protestant) did not broaden, ideas of Catholic Irishness. Originally an agrarian agitator, Parnell realized that to create a powerful grassroots movement he needed to make a wider appeal to people's sense of belonging, and also enlist the help of the clergy. He succeeded in winning the loyalty of even conservative clerics and built up his new image of a 'politician firmly committed to constitutional methods and devoted to denominational education' (Connolly 1985, p. 111). And so the mutually beneficial clerical-nationalist alliance continued to evolve. In such a way, Catholic community became simultaneously political and religious.

However, this attachment to Catholicism and its centrality in community construction has not been a permanent fixture of Irish, or Northern Irish, life. It continually responded to wider social and political developments. Rafferty argues (1994, p. 1) that the new attachment to Catholicism in the nineteenth century was not based in homogeneity, high levels of practice or recognizable post-Tridentine beliefs. Rather it was a sense of belonging to a wider religious community that gave Catholics cohesion. The construction of Catholic Irishness was strengthened by the disaster of famine from 1845 to 1849. Whelan argues that (1998, pp. 87–8), in post-famine Ireland 'religious affiliation became increasingly a surrogate for national identity as the effective agent for communal solidarity.' He goes on to say that:

> Linked to a shared historic experience of marginalisation, this clerical-nationalist alliance could also transcend and neutralise class division as a basis for political action … Given the failure of post-Famine Ireland to industrialise generally, the Irish church, armed with formidable new ideological arsenal designed by Rome to combat modernism, had an easy victory over its essentially phantom enemies. Only the weakened republican tradition could offer even a token challenge to versions of community and nation based exclusively on religious identity.

Indeed, the Catholic Church 'derived great advantage' from the psychological impact of the famine, says Larkin (1976, p. 72), who points to the growing awareness of a sense of sin amongst Catholics in the 1840s. This was deepened by their conviction that the famine was a manifestation of God's wrath on their community. The tragedy of famine occurred at the very time when fear of losing one's identity, amidst the rapid Anglicization of language, culture and way of life, was paramount. The 'devotional revolution' that followed the famine represented a sea change in how ordinary Catholics practised their religion. Church attendance that had been sporadic became a weekly, even daily ritual. Again it was the Catholic Church, rather than class politics or any other 'ism', which was offering a solution. Larkin argues (1976, p. 83):

> Irishmen who were aware of being Irish were losing their identity, and this accounts in large part for their becoming practising Catholics. The devotional revolution provided the Irish with a substitute symbolic language and offered them a new cultural heritage with which they could identify with one another. This is why … Irish and Catholic have become almost interchangeable terms in Ireland, despite the attempts of nationalists to make Irish rather than Catholic the inclusive term.

Furthermore, in the mid-eighteenth century, not only famine, but also increasing hostility from Protestantism, blended together to deepen the idea of religious community. As Protestantism became more evangelical, and unionism more politically threatening, the Catholic elements of community became more poignant. This indicates the capacity for religious ideas and practices to swell in times where structural conditions cause uncertainty and hardship.

We can trace this theme through to the establishment of Northern Ireland in 1921 and the evolution of a separate northern Catholic community. Partition, which was interpreted as abandonment by their southern patriots, caused an identity crisis for Ulster Catholics who had to make the transition from a fractured to a self-reliant community. Ruane and Todd argue (1996, p. 52) that northern Catholics did become a community, 'but slowly, painfully and ambivalently, with their communal organisation stretching out to the island as a whole'. Partition brought with it the emasculation of the Irish Nationalist Party. Sinn Féin too was poorly organized and had not made significant political gains. As a result, the Catholic Church came forward almost by default to fill the power vacuum. The Church saw itself as the spokesperson and defender of the Catholic community. Harris points out (1993, p. 263), that the cumulative effect of so many clerical protests against the northern government provided 'a rallying point for Catholics and increased their consciousness of a distinct identity'.

Thus, after partition the Church was the most significant integrating force in the Catholic community, engendering positive feelings of belonging and a certain amount of security. Todd argues (1990, p. 35) that 'for Northern Catholics, nationalism was simply an extension of Catholic communalism', and cites McEvoy (1986, p. 31), that their 'way of being Irish was predominantly to be Catholic, for the Irishness of the Church and its calendar of saints meant incomparably more to them than the Irish language, the republic, or even constitutional nationalism, in which they placed little hope after the 1930s.'

Because of the theological importance of community, and its strong structural position, the Catholic Church was very suited to assuming the mantle of chief communal organizer. This position at the heart of the community, in turn, gave the Church a platform of authority to try to transmit its values. Through using Church structures to solidify Catholic identity in a time of political upheaval in Northern Ireland, the substantive content of Catholicism continued to infuse the meaning of communal belonging and the practice of Catholicism reinforced it. Catholicism also became a resource that could be drawn upon to strengthen identity in times of trouble. For example, Fox argues (1997, p. 90) that for northern Catholics in Derry, 'religion became the defining factor of national identity to distinguish themselves from the Protestant majority. This led to a heightening of religious awareness and sensitivity, and inevitably gave more influence to the Catholic hierarchy.' In Derry, Fox argues that the revival of the Columban tradition compounded the intertwining of religion and national identity. So politics was not only responsible for maintaining religious significance, it actually encouraged religious growth at certain junctures.

Harris argues (1993, p. 264) that the fact that religion formed the basis for so much of the infrastructure of the Catholic community made it difficult for nationalists to convert anyone from outside the community to their political views, and that social problems were addressed within the framework of church rather than state. Distrust of outsiders merged with an exclusive Catholic ethos to create this sense of community. This process clearly demarcated who was 'in' and who was 'out' of the group. Despite the relative ineffectiveness of the Church in improving the political condition of the Catholic community in Northern Ireland, its activism aided their psychological condition. Communal life had a focus – the cultural centrality of the Church provided leadership and coherence that even the nonreligious could identify with. Inclusion in, versus exclusion from, the community was the central issue, rather than any theological unity or devotional practice.

The ability of Catholicism to provide practical as well as imagined community, has strikingly differentiated it from Protestantism. As outlined in Chapter 3, the Catholic Church has provided an alternative infrastructure for education, social and cultural life and political organization. Ruane and Todd (1996, p. 74) point out that the Church's role in religious, social and educational life, has been reinforced by cross-cutting linkages with Irish language, music, dance and games organizations – all of which give Catholics a 'heightened sense of their own distinctiveness and shared interests' in an all-Ireland context, as well as in Northern Ireland. Morrow et al. argued in 1991 that the Catholic Church was still central to community life in Northern Ireland, and that virtually the entire community was baptized in, and still had regular links to, the Church (especially outside Belfast). As we saw in Chapter 2, although religious beliefs are now loosening amongst Northern Ireland Catholics, the disaffiliation rate is marginal. Experience of the Church has been universal at some level, and is one that, unlike political outlook, tends to unite the bulk of the Catholic community. For example, in Morrow et al.'s (1991) study of the Drumglass estate in Belfast, they found that because one of the two local pubs was controlled by Sinn Féin and the other by the Worker's Party, the pubs were not accessible by all. In contrast 'the Church is probably the one building on the estate where every resident has been'; as one resident put it, 'the Church is the hub of everything on this estate and the priest is the centre of the hub' (1991, p. 50).

O'Connor's 1993 *In Search of a State* contains many accounts of the entanglement of the Catholic Church with daily lives. One of O'Connor's Derry interviewees explains (1993, p. 278):

> I was part of a majority community within a very small area, a tiny enclave of the town, but surrounding it were all these Protestant places, bigger and more powerful. You thought of yourself as a Catholic first, of course, because in a small town, everything happened through the parish. Going to mass, to the chapel, that was your social life.

> Everybody around was Catholic – for most of my young life I never met anybody who wasn't, all the points of reference came from the Church: Catholic schools, the parochial hall, ceilidhs, carnivals to raise money for this and that, variety concerts, plays – a priest ran the drama society.

She paints a colourful picture of the Church's role in the community and its importance as an agent of socialization. Her formative experience has been one of isolation from 'more powerful' Protestants, and of positive identification with the cultural activities organized by the Catholic Church. She does not talk of Catholic theology, but rather, constructs a sense of belonging with those around her focused on Catholicism.

Today, the political situation for Catholics in Northern Ireland has significantly altered. It is no longer the case that the Church is the only agency able to unite and represent the community. The community-building practices of mass attendance and participation in Church-run activities have declined. People are less likely to structure their social lives around solely parish activities. For the still large proportion of mass-attenders, the Church may only be one of many agencies competing for their loyalty. Having said this, for many Catholics the Church is still a focal point for a sense of community. The local church is still considered to be a meeting point. Consider this debate between three friends who have grown up together in Co. Down – all are under 30 and are professionals:

> Interviewer: Why do you go to mass?
>
> Vinny: It's like smoking a cigarette or having a pint, it's the same kind of repetitive action.
>
> Barry: I suppose I go out of habit as well … I go to catch up with people.
>
> Vinny: Because it clears your head. Because we usually go for a drink on a Sunday, straight after mass, me and my da, and meet my brother and leave my ma to cook the dinner. But we go to mass, and my brother's brother-in-law, we would meet him every Sunday at the bottom of the corner before we go into mass, to get the gossip and all from home.
>
> Mark: The way you're saying it, the Church is nothing more than a community centre.
>
> Vinny: Well it is in a way.
>
> Mark: But you haven't mentioned anything yet about the spiritual aspect of it.
>
> Vinny: You don't have to go to mass to be spiritual, it's an individual thing like, you know?
>
> Barry: You say your prayers and all.
>
> Mark: But what you're saying is that it's a place to look at the talent, catch up on the craic, and maybe say a few prayers. That's ridiculous like.
>
> Barry: But I still say my prayers like.

Vinny describes the facets of his personal faith and says that one does not have to go to mass to have faith. He can also talk to God when he is driving to work, for example. He also describes how he did not attend mass when he spent a summer in America: once he went because of a personal crisis, but left in the middle as the sermon was too long. So we can see that although Vinny says faith plays a big role in his life, going to mass is not principally how he expresses this. Yet he still goes. This leads us to suggest that, as he indicates himself, going to mass plays a more significant social role than spiritual role for him. In contrast, he feels that Protestants are 'much more reverential'. Barry also says that going to mass for him is 'more social than anything', and when asked if he does any church-related activities, he replies, 'going to the pub!' It is interesting that nonchurchgoing Mark challenges their presentation of the Church as 'nothing more than a community centre', which they do not deny. Indeed, these Sunday rituals are a vital aspect of communal life. They provide a meeting point, act as a community-maintaining exercise, and whilst the spiritual significance of mass attendance may be questioned for some, its social significance is more easily demonstrable. Here we get a glimpse of how a sense of community is constituted for many Catholics in Northern Ireland.

Another interviewee, Eamon, a churchgoing teacher from Co. Down, also feels that attendance at mass is generally a very routine thing, 'sometimes I think too routine', and worries that it does not play a significant enough role in his life, coming into play mainly 'in times of tension and whatever when you really need something to hang onto'. Referring to the recent scandals in the Catholic Church and the declining number of priests, Eamon says that he has revised some aspects of his faith, arguing that confession should not be made through another person, but is a very personal thing between God and the individual. (As Inglis (1998) points out, this is a growing trend in Ireland.) Like Vinny above, Eamon presents his spirituality as private, but continues to actively practise his faith. In fact, for years he has helped out in church on Sundays, ushering and doing readings. He says he does not like doing this because he feels it makes him stand out, but still he says he feels a sense of duty towards it. So, his is a private faith with public duties. Furthermore, Eamon feels that the Church plays an important role in the community. Describing the clergy, he says:

> I think that they are fishers of men, in terms of looking out for souls, preaching, and I think that they are social workers – they say that themselves manys a time – much of their time is spent with their parishioners wrestling with problems, day-to-day problems in life – talking them through and helping them through them, and that I think is a lovely role.

The positive analogy of Catholic clergy as 'social workers' is extremely important. Like the exchange above about the Catholic Church being a 'community centre', it creates a positive association of the Church with public service. It is not so much called upon for spiritual sustenance, as it is utilized as a communal resource. With this language of public service, it is as if the Church parallels the state in the provision of these 'services' – a trend based on Catholics' non-participation in state structures after partition. In short, although spirituality is becoming individualized for many Catholics, the traditional social-structural role of the Church continues to be important.

The Church as the centrepiece of strong community has both pastoral and political implications. As long as the Church is perceived as a social actor it is also in certain situations a political actor. This is not in a party political sense, but rather it is because the Church as a powerful agency continues to be entangled with people's lives. This not only keeps communities structurally separate in a practical sense, but also continues to invest this difference with meaning. It keeps salient ideas of difference with Protestant practices of faith (and thus Protestants), and it delimits a 'we'. However, it must be asked, can or does the Catholic Church continue to play the same type of roles amongst the section of the community who no longer actively practise their faith?

A young couple from Co. Down, David and Aine, demonstrate this point extremely well as they discuss their decisions to marry in the Catholic Church and later, to prepare their children for the sacrament of Holy Communion. These have not been easy decisions for them, as neither attends mass nor adheres to traditional Catholic theology. In fact they, half-jokingly, describe their personal belief system as 'Murphyism', 'based on our experiences and our questions'. This is reminiscent of Bellah's (1985) highly individualized 'Sheilaism'. Essentially the point they both make is that faith is very important to them, but not necessarily Catholicism. However, Murphyism's principal expression is through Catholic Church structures. Although David says that he would have got married anywhere, Aine feels that there were political reasons why they chose to get married in the Catholic Church:

> It's different because you live in Northern Ireland, to move to a different religion, I mean I'm sure if you lived in England people chop and change, but you're making a political statement, aren't you also? If you decide if you're going to change your faith, or if you decide you are going to go to a Protestant church or whatever, politics comes into it as well.

When it comes to the issue of christening their children into the Catholic Church, and later deciding to prepare them for Holy Communion, David too expresses the importance of religious identity as distinguished from personal beliefs:

> The other thing that would sway me towards 'let's let them attend the sacraments, let them prepare for Holy Communion and Reconciliation', would be, I think it's important, especially in Northern Ireland, for people to have some sort of understanding as to where they belong. That maybe sounds against what we were saying against the Catholic religion and our views on it, but at least, giving our children some sort of structure to start with ... I think what I'm saying is personally, I don't think I would have a problem with saying no, don't put them through Communion, or don't label them as a Catholic, but what I'm also trying to think of, is if we don't do that, does that make it difficult for the children in this society when they're saying 'am I a Catholic, or am I a Protestant, what am I?', you know.

In talking about their children, this couple are also saying something important about themselves. They may not go to mass regularly and may disagree fundamentally with some of the teachings of the Church, but they feel they need to belong somewhere. This in effect draws them closer to the Catholic Church. Aine says that in order to provide children with a sense of Catholic identity, they as parents will need to start bringing them to mass so that they understand what rituals such as Holy Communion are all about. So to give a child a sense of Catholic identity the Church's involvement is still required. In this way, it is very difficult to abstract communal identity from its religious components. The child is to define itself in terms of Catholic belonging. Even if they rebel and become anti-clerical, this takes places within a bounded space. Anti-clericalism is an exclusively Catholic identity option (see also O'Connor, 1993).

This brings us back to Warner's point that religious rituals do not just express group belonging; they also help to construct it. Maintaining links with the Church does not just mark out identity; it also provides some of the content of Catholic identity. The Catholic Church has clear ideas on what the good life is and its aim is to influence people. When individuals come into contact with the Church, they do so within the bounded space of Catholic discourse and meaning. Of course people are sophisticated enough not to agree with everything the Church says – the couple above are a case in point – but it is significant that the Church maintains its platform and that a wide variety of people regularly come into contact with its teachings. As we shall see in Chapter 6, this has the effect not only of physically segregating communities, but also of creating a specific habitus. This is an assimilated, naturalized way of thinking about, and acting in, the world based on shared, recognized codes and meanings. Catholicism is a key element of this habitus.

At a basic level, the role of Catholicism in community-building distinguishes a significant social other. In general, Protestants do not attend mass and do not participate in other activities organized by the Catholic Church. In the context of a deeply divided society, this has clear implications. Whilst not opposed to the state, the Catholic Church continues to act as an alternative agency to structure social and cultural life. Its continuing strength is perhaps an indication that many Catholics still feel that the state, and Protestants, cannot yet be fully trusted. Although conditions have improved for the Catholic community politically and culturally, there is still a sense in which it needs its own guardians and safeguards.

Differing models of community are often used to construct images of two alternate types of groups, which in turn inform political attitudes. There is a widespread perception amongst Catholics that the Protestant community is fragmented whereas the Catholic community is united in strength. As one Catholic interviewee put it, 'Maybe unionists are too fragmented whereas nationalists have seemed to come together because when it comes down to it, apart from the class difference, there's very little to separate Sinn Féin and the SDLP once you remove, you know, people being killed.'

Although the irony in this statement is clear, Catholics are deeply divided by class and attitudes to violence, the important point is the perception of Catholic unity *vis-à-vis* Protestant fragmentation. Indeed, the religious dimension of Protestant fragmentation is often part of an analysis of unionism. There is an awareness of the large, competing elements within Protestantism and their tendency to schism. In contrast to this, Catholicism was generally presented by interviewees as 'more of a bloc'. One Catholic man poignantly talked about the unity of his community in the context of 'the Holy Trinity of the Church, state and de Valera in government in Ireland'. This supports Millar's finding that 'Negative identification gives the Catholic community the illusion of wholeness – they have got it together unlike Protestants' (1999, p. 355). In other words, the concept of Catholic community continues to be constructed contextually, and relationally *vis-à-vis* Protestants.

Where religion is entangled with practices and structures of community building, it is much more than the empty boundary marker outlined in the previous chapter. Those who go to mass actively reproduce community through performing rituals that are at least as social as they are spiritual. Acting out religion brings one into contact with people in the locale who share certain interests and practices that can affirm belonging. It also helps imagine community in a wider Northern Ireland context. Many non-mass-goers also want to retain some links with Catholicism. These links carry meaning. Whilst this is not theological meaning, there is a sense in which

Catholicism is positively associated with belonging, and its structures are deemed necessary in order to pass in-group membership on to Catholic children. And in passing on community membership, people utilize the structures of the Catholic Church. This may not convince individuals on finer points of Catholic theology, but it has important social implications. It familiarizes people with Catholic liturgy; it exposes people to the Catholic Church's opinion on issues like morality and politics; it underlines the role of clergy in the community; it ensures that people continue to participate in rituals, common prayers and chants; it gets people 'to do the same thing'. It is not just a passive label. Whilst we can find theological bases for the concept of community within Catholicism, for most Catholics it is the practical expression and performance of community that counts. In such a way Catholicism is not just an ethnic marker, it is constitutive of what community means. It continues to play an integral role in defining and supporting community at an imaginative and practical level.

Religious practice and community construction amongst Protestants

There are some similarities, but also important differences, in the way that religious practices help construct community for Protestants in Northern Ireland. Churchgoing amongst Protestants since the 1960s has consistently been about half the rate it has been amongst Catholics (see Chapter 2). So Protestant community is less practised than Catholic community. Certainly, for those groups who do worship together, a sense of religious belonging is significant. Evangelical Protestantism in particular is a busy faith that requires attendance at many meetings and other social occasions that bring the religious community together. However, with up to a hundred different Protestant denominations in existence, some of which have serious doctrinal disagreements with one another, it is difficult to see how the practice of Protestantism could bring together a wider imagined community in Northern Ireland. Even within a specific Protestant denomination, depending on the views of the congregational leader, different messages may come from the pulpit. The next chapter examines Protestant ideas of individualism and how these impact on identifications, whilst this chapter focuses in particular on the connection between individualism and religious practices. Before elaborating upon the variety of ways in which practices *do* matter in the construction of Protestant community, it is worthwhile examining this fragmentation in more depth.

Protestantism in Northern Ireland has always been a broad coalition of conservatives and liberals, ruling, middle and working classes, and a plethora of large and small denominations. Throughout history what they lacked in internal cohesion, they have compensated for with an ability to unite versus an external enemy – generally Catholic nationalism and at times the British state. However, the Protestant community has always been deeply internally divided. Different denominations have set against one another, single denominations have been bitterly split and subgroups broken away. Anglicanism was originally the established religion in Ireland whilst Presbyterianism was imported into Ulster later by settlers. Presbyterians resented the privileges enjoyed by Anglicans; these privileges were denied to them in the Penal legislation of the seventeenth and early eighteenth century (until this was later reversed to stem Presbyterian support for Catholic demands for rights). Some high-church versus low-church tensions still exist amongst these denominations.

Intra-denominationally, Presbyterianism has historically shown the most extreme tendency to schism, and is characterized by constant debate and dialogue at best, and bitter power struggles at worst, between liberals, conservatives and fundamentalists (McBride, 1998). Anglicanism too has comprised a broad coalition of pro-British, Anglo-Catholic high churchmen, moderate theological liberals and an evangelical wing (Brown, 1981). There are various offshoots of Methodism, such as Independent Methodism and Free Methodism. Other denominations, such as the Brethren, the Baptists and the Free Presbyterians have not had such pronounced internal divisions; however, they are smaller groupings that do not necessarily have much in common with one another. Whilst evangelicalism has provided an umbrella for the most devout Protestants to unite under, it too experiences internal divisions between liberals, conservatives, charismatics and others. Ecumenism in recent times has divided some Protestants as much as it has united others. Indeed, the depth and nature of religious commitment continues to deeply divide contemporary Protestants, just as it did their predecessors.

Religious diversity stems very much from the Protestant emphasis on individualism and personal conscience (see Chapter 6). However, class issues have always played a large part in Protestants' fragmentation. Elliott (1985) also argues that class antagonism has always suffused Presbyterianism and still divides Ulster unionism. Class issues in Protestant history, in terms similar to theological divisions, have often been subdued because the Protestant community, despite being a broad coalition of competing interests, has consistently displayed a crucial ability to transcend internal differences when faced with an external challenge. The United Irish movement is one of the few examples where Presbyterians made common cause with Catholics; however, the failure of the 1798 rebellion led to re-establishment of the old formula of a veneer of Protestant communal unity combined with opposition to the Catholic other. Religious communal membership then has historically been the domain of communal identifications and power struggles, rather than class.

This tenuous unity in the face of opposition has important implications for Northern Irish politics. Because communal, rather than class, politics have been dominant, Catholics have been consistently cast as the 'other' by Protestants. Catholics have responded to this by trying to present a united front. Although internal divisions have always belied 'real' Catholic unity, due to their particular history, institutional as well as imagined togetherness have been prioritized in the Catholic community. For Protestants, perceived Catholic togetherness has been a source of insecurity as they contrast it with their own perceived fragmentation. The sense amongst Protestants that the Catholic community is more united than their own is pervasive (Boal et al., 1997). This produces unease amongst Protestants, many of whom feel that their failure to act as a united body is ultimately detrimental to their political goals and leaves them open to attack.

In fact, whilst discussion of religious community occurred naturally with Catholic interviewees, this was not the case for Protestant interviewees. Instead, presentations of the Protestant churches were always, where mentioned, about weakness and disunity. Protestants believe that they are much more inclined to argue and split than the Catholic community. Whilst there is seldom a purely theological explanation given for this, many interviewees attempted to make connections between Protestantism and unionist politics:

> I think I said earlier about factions in churches, I think it's the same within unionism as a whole. (Jonathan, Co. Down)

> Our churches are a bit like our politicians, we don't have one, they separate over their differences ... whereas if you're a Catholic you just go to the chapel ... I feel that Gerry Adams and all them ones, you know the Catholic ones, are doing a lot more for their community, and they all stick together and cooperate, whilst we are falling apart at the seams, we are falling apart at the seams. (Jane, Belfast)

> The Roman Catholic culture as I perceive it is essentially one unit, the Catholic culture, the nationalist culture – whatever you want to call it – is a bloc, whereby you've got your credit unions where Roman Catholics put in money and Roman Catholics take out money – it's one unit. Whereas the Protestant community is so fragmented – you've got your Church of Ireland, Presbyterians, Methodists, and then other peripheral groups – so we're not a unit. (Donald, Co. Down)

> I think that the Catholic religion, their way of life is more bound up with their Church, and the Protestant religion less – and people don't go to church in the same way that Catholics do, I mean it's a very social thing I think for Catholics – it's more bound into their way of life and their culture. I think that Protestantism has kind of come away from that. The Protestant community is much more fragmented – we don't have the same unity. (Victoria, Belfast)

This is a range of churchgoers and nonchurchgoers explicitly making connections between the lack of community in Protestantism and unionism, as opposed to what they perceive as the strong community of Catholicism and nationalism.

A lack of communalism is often perceived ambiguously by Protestants. Another interviewee, Jim, a nonchurchgoer from Belfast, says 'I think that the problem is that there's so much diversity I suppose – which is a good thing – I mean our weakness is our strength as well.' The strength is often seen to be the freedom to follow one's own conscience; an anti-authoritarianism that is often contrasted with Catholicism (see Chapter 6). The contrast with the Catholic Church is important. Here Victoria says that the Catholic Church is at the heart of the social life of that community, and Donald argues that the Catholic community is 'essentially one unit'. This is in opposition to the plethora of Protestant churches, which seldom if ever present a united front, and which play much less of a role in the organization of Protestant social and economic life. This is a classic case of social stereotyping that glosses over the actual complexity of the other community. As Gallagher (1989; 1989) notes, in Northern Ireland members of the Protestant community struggle amongst themselves to define the meaning of British and unionist identity, whilst over-simplifying, ignoring or denying the same complexity to Catholic identity – and vice versa. A dominant self-image of Protestants would appear to be one of disunity.

However, it would be unwise to ignore the roles that religious practices *do* play in the construction of Protestant community. Evangelicalism, which represents a significant percentage of the Protestant population (25–33 per cent, Bruce, 1986; Mitchell and Tilley, 2004), is a particularly active faith that requires frequent practice on behalf of the individual: it is rarely a nominal religious identification. Although evangelicalism is a diverse movement containing liberals and conservatives, it has a core commitment to a 'triad of beliefs and practices' (Johnston, 2000, p. 219). These are a belief in authority of Scripture, the need for personal conversion and the necessity of evangelism or at least the active practice of their beliefs (see also Thomson, 1998; Jordan, 2001). Evangelicals are found in a broad range of denominations, from the smaller Baptist, Brethren, Elim and Free Presbyterian to mainstream Anglican, Presbyterian and Methodist churches (Johnston, 2000; Boal et al., 1997). However, despite this internal diversity, it is probably evangelical practices that provide the most recognizable mechanism for the active construction of Protestant community in Northern Ireland. Although forms of worship and messages from the pulpit may differ, the common commitment to being born again provides a shared understanding of who is inside and who is outside the community of believers. This is reinforced through private and public rituals of prayer, Bible study, religious meetings and communion.

Although most evangelical practices take place within single congregations or denominations, there are also pan-evangelical organizations and events that help construct a Northern Ireland-wide sense of religious community. Extended conferences such as New Horizons, or festivals such as Summer Madness for teenagers, foster links between a wide variety of people from different denominations. These large annual events are supplemented by smaller and more regular meetings during the year where people may come to hear a visiting speaker or discuss a specific theme. In addition to these pan-evangelical events, many individual congregations run evangelistic missions, generally in the summertime. Sometimes these are indoor, and other times they are outdoor meetings, often in marquees hired especially for the occasion. 'Tent missions' focus on preaching the Gospel and gaining conversions, and those who attend are encouraged to bring along their 'unsaved' friends. Recent interviews with evangelicals indicate that these are important rituals in establishing networks of relationships. They are also highly ritualistic, and a familiar message of sin, repentance and forgiveness is repeated in sermons and testimonies and acted out through 'altar calls' and conversions (see also Buckley and Kenny, 1995). Often there are conversions but this is not always reflected by significant growth of congregations. In other words, the fallout rate is high. This might indicate that these rituals can be euphoric events where there is a heightened awareness of evangelical norms and expectations. These expectations may later be difficult to live up to. However, the salient point is that evangelical religious practices provide a forum where individuals from all over Northern Ireland can come together and reaffirm their identity and belonging. These rituals are often respected, if not practised, by many non-believers as well.

Certainly not all Protestants are evangelicals and not all engage in these practices. Moreover, a small minority of Catholics are evangelicals, and their commitment to being born again usually supersedes their Catholicism in gaining access to the community. Some Protestants are disapproving of evangelical culture and feel that 'fire and brimstone preachers' give Protestants a bad reputation. Of course, an insider's critique of evangelicalism is different from an attack from the outside, for example, from a Catholic, and some anti-religious Protestants may be reluctant to completely condemn such an integral part of Protestant culture. However, since the central opposition within evangelicalism is salvation versus damnation, non-born-again Protestants are cast outside from the evangelical imagined community in a way that anticlerical Catholics are not excluded from the wider Catholic community. Therefore, whilst evangelicalism is central in providing the practices that bring many Northern Ireland Protestants together, the requirement of being born again is non-negotiable and therefore excludes many other Protestants.

Religious practices can also provide identity resources for non-devout Protestants in times of uncertainty. Des Bell's (1990) work is instructive here. In his study of working-class Protestant adolescents in Derry, Bell identifies various factors that bind religiously non-practising Protestant youths to Protestant identity, for example, images of violence and masculinity offered by militant loyalist politics. He notes that many of his interviewees attended churches to hear militant political sermons, but argues (1990, p. 164) that for some, their motivation seemed secular rather than sacred, 'involving some sort of a search for political answers rather than for spiritual uplift'. This was also the case for several evangelicals I interviewed recently who attended Revd Ian Paisley's sermons in the 1970s to hear political, rather spiritual, messages (see also Taylor, 1999). Subsequently, these interviewees became saved. Bell concludes that whilst Protestant identity is not reducible to religious commitment, it still depends on religious representations and practices to construct belonging. Bell's work indicates the role of conservative evangelical religion for a group wider than committed believers. Although he chooses to call religion a 'marker', he actually highlights how religion can be constitutive of communal identity, as churches and meetings, if not spirituality, can help in the search for political answers. Once individuals go to meetings for social or political reasons, they come into contact with religious messages that may later become meaningful in and of themselves.

Arguably, similar processes are at work in the most controversial of Protestant rituals, Orange Order marches. Bruce points out (1986, p. 138) that 'parades are the very stuff of Protestant politics.' The religious ethos of the Orange Order, and related institutions such as the Royal Black Preceptory, has already been outlined in Chapter 3. Jarman's study (1997) of parades and visual displays in Northern Ireland reveals considerable biblical content. More than a third of banners Jarman surveyed were explicitly religious, showing the Crown and the Bible, Jesus, biblical stories, sayings such as 'My faith looks up to thee', local churches, portraits of Luther and others. The majority of the rest portrayed scenes from Protestant history. Some of these images, for example, the open Bible and Crown, create the impression of interdependence between Britishness and Protestantism that is not real but looks to a more coherent identity. Others, such as images of local churches, link Protestantism to a sense of place and belonging. Buckley (1985) sees parallels between these themes and the responses of many Protestants to their own situation: many of the stories deal with the Israelites being led to the Promised Land, prophets who emphasize the relationship between God and the individual, and characters who have done whatever God has demanded of them. Indeed, parades are an important ritual through which the substantive content of Protestant identity and community is constructed.

Of course not all Protestants approve of the increasingly divisive parades. Moreover, those who watch parades, or even carry these banners, will not necessarily interpret their meanings in the same way. However, these religious images cater exclusively for the Protestant community. They alienate Catholics and provide moral evaluations of the boundary. Significantly, in the years following 1995 and the beginning of the controversial Drumcree disputes, there has been growing tension within the Orange Order between religious and rowdy elements (Bryan, 2000). Protests against the rerouting of marches at Drumcree and elsewhere have often spilled over into violence and a loyalist drinking culture has grown. One interviewee who owns an evangelical Christian bookshop told me that he opens the shop on the 12th of July and lamented that he has no customers whilst there are queues for the off-licence next door. He says that people like himself are leaving the Orange Order because it is losing its religious underpinnings (see Bryan, 2000, for more on Orange Order decline). None the less, it is premature to describe Orange Order marches as wholly secular occasions. Sermons often follow the parading, much of the symbolism remains religious and some clerics continue to be involved in proceedings. In a community that lacks overarching collective practices, the emphasis during the marching season on symbolism, rituals and parades reinforces many Protestants' sense of communal identity. As Bryan et al., stress (1995, p. 60) marches 'are symbolic of the identity of the Protestant community, play a specific political role within that community and [are] a resource within the politics of unionism'.

Whilst not a weekly practice such as churchgoing, other occasional unionist protests and rallies can provide practical rituals through which the Protestant community is constructed. For example, at Belfast City Hall at a mass protest, and at province-wide rallies against the Anglo-Irish Agreement in 1985, hymns such as 'O God our Help in Ages Past' were sung by the crowd (Porter, 1996). Even if superficially and temporarily, this creates an image of collective solidarity that resonates with believers and non-believers alike. Indeed, there appears to be an affinity with Protestant rituals and practices amongst some non-attenders and non-believers. Wright (1973) reported that parents who were not church attenders themselves often sent their children to Sunday School. As pointed out above, recent interviews conducted with Protestants by this author indicate that this still happens. So in assessing the significance of religious practices in the construction of Protestant community, we need to examine religious rituals in secular spaces rather than limit the analysis to churchgoing.

Finally, it is important to highlight the role of Protestant churches in the social and economic construction of community. This issue has been discussed in Chapter 3, which concluded that although Protestant churches have helped organize social life to a lesser extent than the Catholic Church, they have none the less played a significant role in running a variety of social and recreational activities. Many Protestants have links with churches through a mother's group or crèche, for example, rather than attending Sunday services.

The role of religious practices in the construction of Protestant community is a complex issue. On one level, religious practices within individual congregations, and within specific evangelical religious networks, are highly significant in fostering identity and belonging. On another level, because there are so many fragmented Protestant denominations, no religious rituals are able to unite the bulk of the community, imaginatively or in practice. Many other Protestants have distaste for evangelicalism and its accompanying rituals. On another level, there are important religious elements in more secular practices, such as marching or rallying and the churches are involved in a variety of social activities. However, despite these nuances, when one asks a variety of Protestants about their 'community', one is likely to hear stories of division, disunity and schism. The tendency to juxtapose Catholicism with Protestantism – to understand Protestant weakness in the light of Catholic strength – is a standard discourse.

Conclusion

Whilst religious practices play an important role in constituting community for some Protestants, the general trend is for Protestants to be more aware of their religious and political fragmentation. On the other hand, religious practices play a highly significant role for Catholics. In the context of partition and conflict, Catholic community in Northern Ireland has been reinforced by high levels of religious practice and the continuing centrality of the Church within social life.

There is, however, a danger that in making these kinds of arguments we would over-emphasize the impact that these perhaps rather limited types of 'religious' activity can have. Just because people are attending churches for social reasons does not mean that their sense of belonging in Northern Ireland is primarily religious. Similarly, just because a sense of group belonging is created through religious attendance, the constructed community may be local and relational rather than religious. People may engage in religious practices, or activities related to the churches, because of pressure from family, social expectations, cultural or political reasons, or simply lack of choice about types of provision, for example, of childcare facilities. Even when engaging in rituals, different people will have different levels of commitment and will have different interpretations of what it is they are participating in. Moreover, whilst practices like churchgoing or parading may provide shared experiences for many, other members of the community will be completely uninterested and even hostile to them. There is also the consideration of falling church attendance, noted in Chapter 2, which has serious implications for the role of religious rituals in community construction.

Moreover, in addition to religion, there are other areas of social life with important ritual elements. Ethnonationalism has accompanying rituals such as commemoration of historical events and national anthems. There are also significant ethnonational dimensions to Orange Order parades. Irish, British and Ulster-Scots culture also sustain popular practices such as dancing and singing. Sporting events, in particular soccer and Gaelic sports, are opportunities to come together and express belonging. There are less ritual activities associated with class identities. However, none of these rituals are as regular or pervasive as religious practices. No institutions, organizations or political parties can claim to have such regular contact with such a breadth of community members as the churches. Since all social groups engage in practices that mark out identity and belonging at one level or another, it is reasonable therefore to suggest that these widespread religious practices are at least partially constitutive of Protestant and Catholic communities in Northern Ireland.

Of course this does not mean that anyone who brushes up against religious practices, or even fully engages in them, has a primarily religious identification. It does not mean that communities can be classed simply as religious communities. However, in modern societies where individuals are pushed, pulled and entangled in various competing commitments and convictions, there is still an important role for the churches in community life. Communities, whilst cognitive constructions, are practically constituted by a range of practices. Certainly not all of these practices are religious. However, religion in Northern Ireland is one of the most important practical mechanisms through which shared understandings, expectations and behaviour are created. Even community members who critique the religious norms of their community do so from the inside. As family and community members it is highly likely that nonchurchgoers will still come into contact with their respective churches for weddings, funerals and other occasional activities. Moreover, the social and civic activities of the churches cross over into civil society in many ways, often reaching those with no formal beliefs or practices.

Even when the churches are used self-consciously for social reasons, for example, to transmit communal identity to children or to hear political sermons, people come into contact with religious ideas, norms and behaviour. Even if they do not subscribe to traditional tenets of faith, they instinctively recognize their surroundings and know what to do. In contrast, if they entered a church of the 'other' religion, there would be less familiarity and less confirmation of identity. One Catholic friend in the Republic of Ireland related to me her total disorientation when she moved to a new area and accidentally walked into the local Anglican church thinking it was a Catholic chapel. When the first unfamiliar bar of music was played, she turned around to examine her physical surroundings, and realizing they were unfamiliar she panicked, got up and ran out the door. This conveys well how religious activities can confirm or disconfirm belonging, regardless of any supernatural or theological considerations.

Where groups or individuals deliberately instrumentalize religion and attend church to bolster ethnic identity, familiarity with religious ideas and teachings is increased. This may provide the foundations from which religion itself may be rehabilitated at a later date. Chong (1998, pp. 266–8), for example, found that although her research respondents initially began to attend Korean-American evangelical churches for social and cultural reasons (such as to maintain social networks and 'keep up' the culture and language), their newfound participation led to genuine religious conversions and religious renewals. Although this is not always the case, the religious content of identity can be reactivated in a time of personal or political struggles. After this, religious identity takes on a logic of its own and Chong's respondents actions were simultaneously informed by their evangelicalism as well as their Korean cultural identity. The following chapter examines this process in more detail. Suffice to say with regard to religious practices that continuing participation in religious rituals, regardless of motivation, engenders familiarity with religious terrain. It is not unlikely that somebody who uses a church as a community centre will be familiar with some of its religious messages and may later want to turn to this institution in a time of personal crisis. Whilst people retain some connection with recognizably religious practices and religious institutions, religion is still socially important and may have the capacity to rehabilitate itself.

Overall, despite falling church attendance, levels of religious practice remain extremely high in Northern Ireland. Whilst people participate in religious practices for a variety of reasons, they continue to be important in constituting Protestant and Catholic communities. This is particularly the case for the Catholic community, where there is higher church attendance and more involvement of the Catholic Church in areas of social life. If church attendance were to fall significantly over the next twenty years, it is likely that arguments surrounding religious rituals and community construction would need to be re-evaluated. Obviously the less regularly practised, the less socially significant rituals become. However, at least for the foreseeable future, religious *practices* are likely to remain integral to the construction of communities and the maintenance of separate identities. It is to the role of religious *ideas* in identity formation processes that we now turn in the next chapter.

6
Religious ideology and politics

Key points

- *Religious ideology is a system of concepts about self and others, informed by religious doctrines.*

- *Religious ideology is unconcerned with answering spiritual questions.*

- *Religious ideology is significant for those without strong religious beliefs or practices as well as religious people.*

- *Religious ideology requires some familiarity with religious teachings, usually acquired in childhood.*

- *Religious ideology is particularly pronounced amongst Protestants.*

This chapter is concerned with the persistence of religious ideas amongst ordinary Protestants and Catholics who do not necessarily see themselves as religious. It maps the ways in which religious ideas are used to understand politics, and the ways in which politics influences religious ideas. The term 'religious ideology' is used. This simply refers to concepts that are informed by religious doctrines but that are not concerned with answering spiritual questions. In this way religion can be socially significant for those who have had a religious socialization but do not have strong religious beliefs or do not practise regularly in the present. This chapter argues that this trend is particularly pronounced amongst Protestants.

A couple of bodies of work are useful in elaborating on this process. First, there have been many attempts in recent years to theorize non-traditional forms of religious persistence. As numbers attending church have declined throughout Europe, a variety of sociologists of religion have tried to show that this does not necessarily mean that Europe has secularized its religious ideas accordingly. Most famously, Davie (1994) has argued that the dominant trend in Britain is 'believing without belonging', that is, whilst less people go to church most still believe in God or are interested in some form of spirituality. Therefore, measuring the social significance of religion through survey data on churchgoing and rituals gives an incomplete picture. It is vital to also examine how individuals use religious ideas and beliefs to give meaning to social life.

More recently, Davie (2000) has introduced the idea of 'vicarious religion'. By this she means that the seemingly small amount of active religiosity that can be observed in many modern societies is merely the tip of the iceberg. Most people, she contends, continue to have respect for and affinity with their religious heritage. Beneath the surface of the water, a wealth of religious ideas and concepts simmer, ready to erupt in times of crisis or hardship. Davie points to events such as death of Diana, Princess of Wales or the tragic massacre of schoolchildren in Dunblane in Scotland as times of heightened religious awareness when churches brought mourners together in solidarity. Similarly, the death of Pope John Paul II in 2005 catalysed a tide of emotion that created the impression of a religious community united in mourning, if only for a time. In notoriously secular Sweden, after the Estonia ferry disaster where 800 drowned, large numbers of people attended religious places (Pettersson, 1996). Walter (1991) and Davie (1992) highlight the spontaneous outpouring of religious sentiment after the Hillsborough disaster where the Catholic Church was as much a site of pilgrimage as Anfield football stadium. These moments of disaster can shed light on the dynamics of modern religion. For Davie, religion persists in an understated, non-traditional way. It is highly responsive to social and political developments, which can cause it to resurface in more dramatic ways.

Hervieu-Léger is another sociologist of religion who is keen to understand the ways in which contemporary Europeans are both religious and modern. In the context of France, she argues (2000) that religion operates as a 'chain of memory'. She contends (1994, p. 125) 'religion as a memory passes from generation to generation in interpreting the formation of religious identities of young French Catholics'; feelings of belonging and the process of religious identification 'depend on the group or individual being conscious of sharing with others a stock of references to the past and remembered experience to hand down to future generation'. Hervieu-Léger's (2000) argument is that memories are carried through institutions, and in the French context, her prognosis is one of declining significance. However, given the continuing salience of religious institutions in Northern Ireland, one can readily see the importance of religion as a chain of memory through which shared understandings of social life are passed down through generations.

With the imperative to analyse the social significance of religious ideas in mind, the question becomes one of how we might go about this. One of the most useful concepts to have been integrated into the study of religion in recent years is that of habitus. Formulated by Pierre Bourdieu (1990), it has been used by Inglis (1998) to analyse Irish Catholicism. Most recently Ruane and Todd (forthcoming, 2005) have utilized it as a mechanism for analysing national, ethnic, colonial as well as religious dimensions of communal identity in Northern Ireland. Habitus refers to a culturally specific way of doing, speaking, seeing, thinking and categorizing. We are all predisposed to sort social life into categories and make comparisons between people and groups (Hogg and Abrams, 1988). Habitus describes how we assimilate cultural categories and meanings into our sense of self, and then think and act in ways that actually reproduce the categories. These become unconscious, taken for granted, shared understandings. They are embedded in how we perceive things, how we react and respond to situations.

In such a way, religion can become part of common-sense knowledge about social life. Its meanings and interpretations are taken for granted. As Hervieu-Léger (2000) argues, categories are also embodied in the institutions we have set up to organize society, which in turn pass these meanings back down to us. Therefore, religious ideology must be analysed in conjunction with an assessment of religious institutional power, described in Chapter 3. Berger argues (1967, p. 46) that 'the reality of the Christian world depends upon the presence of social structures within which this reality is taken for granted and within which successive generations of individuals are socialized in such a way that this world will be real to *them.*' Whilst individuals create the social world through their words and actions, they also internalize what they have created (Berger and Luckmann, 1967). Historically, religion has been one of the most effective forms of social legitimation, providing answers to questions about way things are the way they are. Thus these explanations of social life become embodied in individuals as well as institutions. Moreover, they do not necessarily depend on continued active religious practice for their maintenance.

It is possible to qualitatively analyse the religious dimensions of Protestant and Catholic habitus in Northern Ireland. This chapter draws on interview material to explore how religious ideas might live on in Northern Ireland outside those groups of people who are religiously devout. It asks how far ordinary 'nonchurchgoing' Protestants and Catholics carry religious ideas and use these ideas to understand their personal and political situations. It understands that religion does not have to be defined simply by the search for ultimate truth or belief in the supernatural. Moreover, following Davie (1994, 2000), it suggests that religious ideas can be important outside of regular religious practice. Instead, religiously derived ideas can be structured into a system of concepts from which identities are formed and social action produced. They can become part of common-sense knowledge of 'what they are like' as opposed to 'what we are like'. This knowledge is passed on in groups and individuals through generations like Hervieu-Léger's (2000) chain of memory. These ideas can be called religious because whilst they are not concerned with answering spiritual questions, they are informed by specifically religious teachings and concepts. In this way, it is not simply the case that religion acts as an empty boundary marker, providing labels of us and them. Rather, the content of religion is actively harnessed to construct the meanings of identity and group belonging.

This chapter elaborates on the political importance of specific religious ideas. It very briefly outlines the theological roots of these ideas. In certain instances the theological content is discussed in more length in the following chapter, and this is indicated, where relevant, in the text. This chapter can therefore be read in a stand-alone manner, or, if the reader wishes to understand the doctrinal lineage of various concepts, it can be read in conjunction with the following chapter on theology.

Religion as a cultural reservoir

Before commencing discussion of specific religious ideas and politics, it is pertinent to establish the nature of the relationship as well as to note the context in which it takes place. First, as we have seen in Chapter 2, Northern Ireland is an incredibly religious society. Ninety-six per cent of the population have grown up as a Protestant or a Catholic. Churchgoing rates remain very high. But even most of those who do not go to church are familiar with religious codes and symbols. In this section, we argue that childhood socialization is full of religious ideas that 'stick' to a certain extent in later life in so far as these ideas continue to make sense of people's social and political relationships.

Religious codes, symbols and categorizations are part of the habitus of Protestants and Catholics in Northern Ireland. They are embodied and unconsciously reproduced in everyday life. As Ruane and Todd point out (forthcoming, 2005, Chapter 3, p. 3 of draft manuscript) each religious tradition

> ... has its own core beliefs, rituals and symbols, its own form of organization, architectural style, religious paraphernalia, accepted forms of piety and dress, style of clergy and clerical authority, characteristic relations between clergy and laity'. [They argue that] 'for those brought up within a particular faith ... the beliefs, symbols and rituals of their own denomination have the quality of the familiar, the natural and the normative, and it is in their terms that others appear different, strange, unsettling, threatening.

The landscape of Northern Ireland is littered with religious imagery. A short drive through the countryside immediately brings one into contact with signs hammered to trees stating that one must 'repent for one's sins for the end of the world is nigh' and other religious messages. In cities, it is not unusual to see religious slogans on colourful banners outside churches and religious images integrated into loyalist and republican murals. Street-preaching and evangelism are regular occurrences, as likely to be found in well-to-do Hillsborough's high street on a sunny afternoon as outside a rural nightclub in the small hours of Sunday morning. Religious tracts are often pressed into the hands of shoppers throughout the towns and cities of Northern Ireland. Catholic, as well as Protestant, imagery looms large in the landscape, whether this is shrines to saints on country roads or pictures of the Sacred Heart of Jesus behind shop counters. These messages and paraphernalia are both privately and publicly embedded. They adorn mantelpieces, greetings cards and self-help books in households throughout the region. The point is that irrespective of active religious belief or practice, religious ideas and symbols form a kind of cultural reservoir in Northern Ireland. They are symbols that are familiar to most people, even if their exact doctrinal significance is not known. Moreover, nearly everybody will recognize the religious messages that relate to their community and those that appear unfamiliar and strange.

It is in this context that Martin Smyth described Shankill Protestants as 'Bible lovers if not Bible readers'. Whilst this is probably a hopeful overstatement, it taps into the tendency amongst people in Northern Ireland to have at least some familiarity with religious traditions, regardless of active participation. Bruce (2001), for example, describes the trend for loyalists to become 'saved' inside prison and describes how becoming 'born again' is seen as a legitimate reason for leaving a paramilitary organization. This is because salvation is a familiar discourse that can be activated in times of stress (of course, becoming saved in prison may also be for more strategic reasons). Similarly, in terms of party politics, the DUP carries most of the associations of Ulster's evangelical past and whilst many of its supporters reject its religious overtones, there seems to be an affinity with their message beyond evangelical elements in the Protestant community. Bruce (1986, 1994), suggests that this is because evangelicalism provides the core beliefs, values and symbols of what it means to be a Protestant, and that even the unchurched can identify with its terms, emphases and language. Especially in times of challenge, there can be an increased attraction to a unionism or loyalism that makes its moral foundations clear (Todd, 1998). So religious ideas may still reverberate with those who are not actively religious.

As outlined above, many Protestant children are still sent to Sunday School, even in cases where parents are not themselves regular churchgoers. In the Catholic Church, many children make their confirmation and First Communion despite the fact that their parents do not usually frequent mass. The persistence of parental desires to educate children about religious teachings despite their own lack of participation demonstrates a residual attachment to religious ideas. It is also an effective method of transmission of information and identity. A variety of recent interviewees who had newly become born again cited their early attendance at Sunday School as instilling knowledge in them about right and wrong. Many youth clubs are run through the Catholic Church, with priests and lay people at the helm. Reinforced by religious imagery in schools, at an early age children become familiar with religious symbols. Religious ideas are also relationally transmitted as many friends and relations of religiously active people are persuaded to go to church, at least on special occasions (see Morrow et al., 1991 for further examples).

It is perhaps unsurprising that growing up in such a religious climate can impact on individuals in later life. Kelley and de Graaf (1997, p. 654) argue that religious socialization is very significant and that 'the religious environment of a nation has a major impact on the beliefs of its citizens.' Furthermore, they find that in religious nations, even those born into secular families are likely to acquire religious beliefs. In this way, it is possible to argue that the religious character of a society is important at the level of ideas even for those who are not themselves dedicated believers.

Morrow et al.'s findings show how ideas gained through religious childhood socialization play out in adult life. They found (1991, p. 22), that even where church attendance falls, communal boundaries reflect ecclesiastical boundaries; and where religious doctrines are no longer accepted, churches are still 'likely to carry the memories of community experience'. Even amongst those who do not go to church, 'the language of religious identity is not very distant' (1991, p. 3). An example of this is their discussion of Belfast Protestant drinking clubs, where they point out that religiously informed ideas and values, given weight by conflict, are pervasive. In recent times, Alpha courses, providing an introduction to evangelical Christianity, have been held in some of these pubs. Furthermore, Morrow et al. found many forms of participation by clergy in civic activities such as local festivals and events organized by the Orange Order. In such a way, churches help shape not just communal life, but the nature of memory, for example, intertwining Protestantism with ideas of Britishness in Remembrance Day services. This is not so much about theology, they argue, but about how difference is experienced.

Where religious ideas help explain difference, they may also inject a moral dimension into identification, providing reassurance that one's cause is right. This often takes the form of myths and 'stories of the people'. As Fentress and Wickham (1992) argue, social identity can be considered cognitively as a group of ideas, sustained through representations of social memories. In relation to Protestants, Morrow (1997) suggests that religious myths and interpretations of history, sustained through rituals and symbolism, unite the community. Religious ideas allow people to 'read back' events in Ulster into a mythical interpretation of the Bible, assuring themselves that despite persecution, their cause is good. Morrow (1997, p. 56) maintains that

> The explanatory power of fundamentalist religion resonates with the experience of persecution and violence. In the face of violence and chaos, people are driven back to the comfort of a knowledge of righteousness and order … Neither theological liberalism nor secular modernity offers such solace in this context, while traditional religion offers both immediate comfort and the hope of triumph.

This does not mean that most people subscribe literally to a theological interpretation of history. Certainly a small number do. But more important is the capacity of biblical discourse to evaluate political conflict as good versus evil for many moderately religious, and even non-religious, unionists. It helps construct morality.

So religious ideas delineate difference and provide moral evaluations of social relationships. One way they do this is by conveying codes of belonging through language and imagery. This transmits an identity narrative that does not just tell a 'story of the people', but in so doing also influences people's actions in the present (Samuel and Thompson, 1990). It is not that Protestants have a unanimous or clearly defined doctrinal position that they use to understand politics. Rather, religious ideas help people know commonsensically the differences between right and wrong, good and bad. Brewer (1998) argues that although people's experiences are individual, their expression through language translates them into categories that suggest that experiences are shared. Language helps structure people's experiences and beliefs, allowing them to see their common-sense knowledge as part of a broader social world. As language reproduces rather than merely represents society, it can help transmit shared social beliefs. Culture is not only mirrored by, but also shapes and conditions, language. Culture assists in speaking – defining the appropriate ways of articulating ideas; it assists in listening – helping 'inferencing', or the way to 'hear' ambiguous words, and it assists understanding words used as 'codes'. So language helps construct identity. In Brewer's words (1998, p. 183):

> Language provides the categories, units, typifications and stereotypes by which one 'knows' common-sensically, one's own identity and those of others. For example, moral boundaries are drawn by means of language, and notions of social distance and the identities of 'the stranger' and 'the outsider' are expressed in linguistic form.

To use familiar slogans such as 'No Surrender', 'not an inch', 'for God and Ulster', 'fuck the Pope', 'ye must be born again', confirms the user as an insider, excludes the outsider, and helps construct a Protestant identity (Brewer, 1998). This blurs the boundaries between religion and politics in Protestant culture. An interesting example is liberal unionist Ken Maginnis' view, given in a television interview, that the Protestant community considered itself 'more sinned against than sinning' (cited in Morrow 1997, p. 55). His use of language resonates with the key themes of Ulster Protestantism – the persecution of the righteous and the identification of others as sinners. McKay (2000) found people comparing former British Secretary of State for Northern Ireland, the late Mo Mowlam to the biblical temptress Jezebel. Finlayson (1997) describes the post-Agreement loyalist narrative of David Trimble as Judas Iscariot, the traitor. These create oppositions between good and evil, and as Morrow points out (1997) they are 'description[s] of the moral universe to which both doctrine and reason speak'.

In his seminal article on 'Protestant Ideology', Wright (1973) provides sharp analysis of the relationship between religious ideas and political identity. Speaking about 'extreme' Protestantism, he argues that ideologies provide a source of values which give legitimacy to the 'Protestant' cause in conflict, and that they may at times be an ostensible expression of conflicts of a more material character. In fact religious ideologies can structure their adherents' notions of the actual condition of Catholics. Wright is saying that Protestant ideology can be woven into common-sense understandings of social life. He argues that in a deeply divided society, 'knowledge' of the other is 'comprised very largely of indirect experience and socialized teachings rather than by first hand experience' (1973, p. 213). While the presence of the other is a constant preoccupation, what is unknown is enormous, and this gap is bridged by a 'vast body of ideas, theories and mythologies' (1973, p. 218).

Wright also argues that religious elements of Protestant identity can be shelved in times of cooperation and understanding, but lie ready to be asserted when times are tough. Indeed, in a situation where political and institutional change was (and still is) perceived by many Protestants to be in favour of the Catholic community, Wright's (1973, p. 273) analysis is still extremely salient: 'Ideological pre-disposition coupled with occupation of a situation apparently threatened by the Catholic demands, synthesised the twin components of the sense of being threatened. It combines the general assumption of Catholic hostility with the awareness that oneself is the particular target of that hostility.'

So, religious ideology and perceptions of one's political position become intertwined. Wright points out some key constituencies of those most likely to adhere to a strong kind of unionism. These are those most exposed to socializing processes of evangelical preaching; those whose personal experiences of the other community provided evidence of the 'truth' of extreme perspectives; those whose geographical location is in a situation where hypothetical conflict would be most damaging to their security (Protestants in a border area, for example); and those who are in a socio-economic position where they feel that Catholics pose a threat.

In such a way, religious ideology and socio-economics reinforce each other. The point is that religious ideas can be used to make sense of political situations. In turn, political situations can influence the importance, or otherwise, of religious ideas. In times of political calm, religious ideology may not be needed to interpret the situation. In times of crisis, it may take on extra explanatory power. Developing this point, Wright focuses on the theme of Protestant liberty, arguing that this comes from a combination of religious and political ideas, that is, a fusion of evangelicalism and a concern for the maintenance of Protestant power. So 'Protestant' beliefs and position can be deeply intertwined in ideology. In such a way, religion may not simply mask deeper political desires, but may fuse with them, each giving the other meaning.

Below, we explore some of the specific components of religious ideology that have influenced social relationships and interpretations of politics in Northern Ireland. These form a kind of cultural reservoir, or a pool of religiously-informed concepts, which acts as an identity resource. Most of these concepts relate to Protestants. This is because, as is also argued in the next chapter on theology, Protestants have more familiarity with religious teachings and doctrines.

Protestant liberty

When asked by a woman at an open meeting whether someone from the Shankill Road who had no affiliation to any church could still be defined as a Protestant, Revd Ian Paisley (in *Beyond the Fife and Drum*, 1994, p. 6) made a good point:

> There are those who are Protestants nominally and who do not have a religious experience but have embraced the principles of Protestantism in regard to their own life … if you suggested to such a Protestant that he go to the Roman Catholic church, he would say, 'I'll do nothing of the kind, I'll make my own choice'. So when he says that, he is actually spelling out a principle of personal liberty. Because Protestantism is a religion of choice – that every man before God in his conscience makes a choice.

It is significant that Paisley tries to point out that Protestantism is a way of thinking and being, rather than just attending church or being born again. Here he is reproducing common-sense knowledge for his audience about the way Protestants are, as opposed to Catholics.

Liberty has always been a key concept in Protestant identity. It is based on Protestant ideas of freedom of thought versus the perceived authoritarianism of the Catholic Church. It can be present in stronger theological, or weaker ideological, forms. The weaker formulation comprises arguments about why Catholics seem to have less social freedoms and why they seem less able to think for themselves, as opposed to individualistic Protestants who have much more autonomy of choice. The stronger form focuses on theological ideas of religious control versus religious free will.

Protestant ideas of freedom have a long historical lineage. Hamilton Rowan, County Down landowner turned United Irishman, outlined some Protestants' ideas of Catholic politics in the late eighteenth century, saying that 'one part of the nation seems content to remain in a sort of willing servitude, merely to lord it over another part' (cited in Elliott 1985, p. 26). Ian Paisley (in *Beyond the Fife and Drum*, 1994, p. 4) outlined early twentieth-century radical churchman Dean Inge's definition of Protestantism as the 'inward conviction in the place of unquestioning obedience, docile acceptance and the surrender of the right of private judgement. Protestantism … emphasises the absolute worth of the individual and so rejects extreme forms of institutional loyalty.' Indeed, according to Miller (1978a, p. 85), liberty is the defining characteristic of Protestantism. This is more than the right of private judgement, but a 'freedom of the soul deriving from the saving truth of the Bible' – an opportunity perceived to be long rejected by Catholics. Miller goes on to suggest that Catholic attacks on street-preaching and resistance to Bible reading in schools have been interpreted as an attempt to use the power of their numbers to destroy the liberty that has mattered so much to Protestants. Here we can see the underlying structures of ideas, 'othering' communities and translating a general fear of the power of the Catholic Church into specific fears about the intentions and failings of individual Catholics.

Indeed, these ideas remain popular today amongst a variety of Protestants. One conservative evangelical Protestant interviewee describes his faith thus:

> What role Protestantism would play in my life? Well, it means I am a free born and free person and Catholicism believes in something that curtails people, you can't do this, and you can't do that, or don't look there at somebody … Catholicism? I believe Catholicism isn't right because the Pope is all-powerful, they say that he is allowed to direct the people.

This interviewee's ideas of Catholics are very much based on traditional Protestant assumptions of enlightenment versus superstition, liberty versus enslavement, and freedom of thought versus blind obedience. The impact of the idea of freedom is clear: banned Orange marches are presented starkly as a matter of freedom: 'free born … free [men]' should not be prevented from walking where they want. Similarly, individual Catholics are presented as unfree – forbidden from various activities by their Church. However, we might expect conservative evangelical Protestants to use this discourse. What is striking though, is where ideas of liberty are used in a weaker ideological form by otherwise nonreligious individuals.

Victoria is a young nonchurchgoer from Belfast, who rejects a lot of her traditional Presbyterian upbringing, has no time for 'fire and brimstone preachers' and was once married to a Catholic from Germany. She describes herself as a moral person, but not religious. She still describes herself as a Protestant, and identifies with the Protestant community. Whilst secular and radical in her political views (she may vote for the Worker's Party or the Women's Coalition), Victoria still has rather fixed ideas about the consequences of religion for people's lives. She feels that she has more social freedom as a result, especially as a woman. Constant in her self-presentation, is her independence, her right to choose and to think for herself. She talks about her Protestantism in this manner:

> Interviewer: What does Protestantism mean for you?
>
> Victoria: Well I've always been like, it's a way of life – but that's just a personal choice, it's what suits me.

In contrast, Victoria talks about the power of the Catholic Church and sees her Catholic friends as having a lot more pressure and guilt about their religion. She speaks of their 'strictness' and the brutality and indoctrination of Catholic schools. So Victoria, although she sees herself as nonreligious, categorizes her Protestant culture as a source of freedom, as opposed to her Catholic contemporaries, who she feels are still 'driven' in some way by the Catholic Church. This forms part of a common-sense understanding of 'what Catholics are like'. It also has social consequences, for example, when Victoria describes her knee-jerk reaction not to let her son be baptized into the Catholic Church.

A similar theme ran through other interviews. One man in his twenties from a suburban Protestant town says that whilst he had a very religious upbringing, he no longer attends church and now has no religion. However, he also says that Catholics 'seem to have such fear about things' and attributes this to the role of priests. This is juxtaposed with his self-presentation of independent reasoning. When asked 'what do you associate with being a Protestant?', another nonchurchgoer says, 'well, I think you are much freer.' These categories of liberty versus repression have clear religious roots in Protestant teachings about freedom of thought and beliefs about the authoritarianism of the Catholic Church. Yet people with no active religious commitment use these categories to understand social relationships. This is not a position argued theologically, but from Protestants' observations of the ways in which Catholics seem different to them. In their strong form, there is a clear relationship between religious ideology and politics, where Catholics are seen as unfree and politically duped. In their weaker form, such as with Victoria, they are more compartmentalized, affecting some social relationships but not an overall political analysis.

It has been argued that ideas of liberty directly inform unionist politics. There is a strand in modern unionism that, although not hostile to Catholicism on religious grounds, conceives of political rights through a frame of Protestant freedom. Aughey, for example (1989, 1995), argues that in an individualist and pluralist British state, diversity and liberty can flourish. His notion of liberty is freedom of individual opportunity and choice. However, this version of freedom does not reflect what liberty means for Catholics in Northern Ireland. As Finlayson points out (2001, p. 91), such a unionist claim to freedom is particular, not universal. For Northern Ireland nationalists, the British state is not 'difference-blind', as it embodies the will of one part of a polity and tends itself to be exclusive. Although there are no religious overtones in Aughey's argument, its individualist premises are actually quite close to those of stronger Protestantism. At their heart is an idea of individual liberty rather than communal recognition, which cannot understand or deal with the communal claims of nationalism.

In such ways the Protestant idea of liberty has been a central identity narrative for this community. It often influences the self-understanding of many Protestants as free and independent individuals. It constructs an opposition with Catholics, who are often thought to enjoy less freedom. Thus, liberty is a religiously derived concept that has created important stereotypes of Northern Ireland Protestants and Catholics. Whilst ideas of liberty are seldom motivated by ideas of the supernatural, in terms of content they none the less have clear religious overtones. In contemporary Northern Ireland, there is a perception amongst many Protestants that the grip of the Catholic Church has weakened in recent times, but they are not sure how much. Thus, although many modern Protestants feel that Catholics are freer than in previous decades, without the information or experience to support this, as Wright (1973) suggested, there is also a tendency to rely on older assumptions about Catholic strength and control.

The 'Honest Ulsterman'

Honesty is another important aspect of Protestant religious ideology. The idea of the 'honest Ulsterman' has some foundations in doctrine and theology and represents an additional discourse that excludes Catholics from the Protestant imagined community. A faith in which individual conscience and personal responsibility are paramount may predispose its adherents to believe that they have a better ability to access the truth as they have not been manipulated or spoon-fed by their church. As a result, Catholics have sometimes been stereotyped as lazy, slovenly and deceitful (Harris, 1972). Moreover, with the uncertainty of settlement, many Protestants needed to believe that they were on the right side, and that there were good reasons why the natives could not be trusted. Many needed psychological justification that they could do a better job, in work and in politics, than the natives. For whichever combination of motivations, this self-image of honesty has persisted into the twenty-first century. That this self-image of trustworthiness is imagined is not as important as the fact that it has been accepted as common-sense knowledge in some quarters. It is the gut feeling amongst some Protestants that they have higher standards than Catholics, that makes the 'honest Ulsterman' such a formidable stereotype.

The use of honesty in religious ideology has a long historical lineage in Northern Ireland. Miller argues (1978a, p. 115) that 'the "honest Ulsterman" was a central motif in the loyalist myth structure which emerged from about 1885', popularized during the Land League years when Catholic tenants were stigmatized as greedier and more dishonest. In the early 1900s, one commentator, James Logan, rated the characteristics of 'the Belfast Man' (that is, the Protestant man) as: determination, 98 per cent; business capacity, 94 per cent; courage, 91 per cent; trustworthiness, 90 per cent; mental vigour, 78 per cent; hospitality, 70 per cent; general culture, 55 per cent; artistic tastes, 48 per cent; and social graces, 44 per cent (cited in Miller 1978a, pp. 114–15). Orange Order leader S. E. Long (n.d., p. 8) also highlights his perception of how Protestants are different when he states as fact, 'There is the "Protestant ethic" with a strong emphasis on honesty, sobriety, industry and morality.' How far this reflects the actual character of Protestants is not as important as its default definition of what a Catholic is not.

These assumptions have been easily adapted to recent conflict in Northern Ireland. In a pamphlet discussing propaganda, Clifford Smyth (n.d.), an ex-DUP member, uses truth to distinguish between republicans and loyalists. He argues that republicans have succeeded in building an effective propaganda machine that is built on deceit, lies and violence. In contrast to this, he says loyalists have lacked the same propaganda skills. For Smyth, this represents not their hopelessness at publicity seeking (after all, he was a colleague of Paisley) but loyalists' commitment to humility and truth in their refusal to resort to propaganda. He states (p. 20) 'far from acknowledging the sanctity or centrality of truth, propaganda manipulates truth and subordinates truth in the quest for political domination.' This idea is not uncommon in contemporary Northern Ireland. A variety of Protestant interviewees spoke of nationalists' expertise in propaganda, as opposed to unionists' failure to present their cause in a positive light. 'Propaganda' implies deceit: it implies, in one woman's words about the Catholic Church, 'twisting' the truth.

John Dunlop and Godfrey Brown, two leading and reasonably liberal Presbyterian figures in Northern Ireland, agree that Protestant ideas of honesty have influenced unionist approaches to politics. They argue that Protestants have little time for ambiguity, do not want to read between the lines, and instead are very literal in their approach to politics (cited in Opsahl et al. (eds), 1993, p. 37). Indeed, there has been a perception amongst some commentators on Northern Ireland that this self-image of the 'honest Ulsterman' has resulted in a communication problem between the two communities. Griffin (cited in Opsahl, 1993, p. 37) suggests:

> Protestants are really puzzled by what they feel is the ambiguous attitude of Catholics and their failure to define ordinary concepts in a clean, straightforward way. There is much more of what I would call sophistry, casuistry in the Roman Catholic approach to honesty. Protestants generally find that Catholic concepts of right and wrong and truth and honesty are more complicated ... Protestants sometimes find it very difficult to understand the sophistry, the playing with words which [we] sometimes get from Catholics.

Similarly, Revd Sidney Callaghan argues that Protestants believe that Catholics do not say what they mean, and are 'masters of the art of the fine point, the innuendo and the half truth' (cited in Opsahl et al. (eds), 1993, p. 37).

Another contributor to the Opsahl Commission, Peter McLachlan, suggests (1993, pp. 37–8) that thinking processes in Northern Ireland have been influenced by the theology that operates in each culture – the pre-Reformation theology of Aquinas which was deductive in nature, and the post-Reformation theology of Calvin and Luther which was inductive. Throughout political negotiations, McLachlan argues that the SDLP puts down a deductive principle – a general framework – and does not budge from it, whereas unionists put down a number of propositions or demands. Unionists then struggle to clarify what nationalists' aims are, whilst they in turn appear intransigent to nationalists. This can be understood as paralleling religious notions of interpretation versus legalism. In turn, this has led many Protestants, who do not relate to this kind of thinking, to believe that Catholics are not being honest and that they have a 'hidden agenda'. Indeed, these ideas are not just referenced by theological experts. Donald from Co. Down, for example, spoke of the Drumcree issue in terms of a nationalist 'agenda' compared to the single 'focus' of Orangemen. Unionists he says, see 'a series of issues, to be dealt with one at a time', whereas nationalists have a 'far-seeing strategy'. He concludes that he is not hopeful of getting agreement 'whenever you are talking in completely different terminology, and the parameters of your thinking are totally different'. Indeed, this logic is often applied to conflicting nationalist and unionist interpretations of the Good Friday Agreement.

For social groups in conflict, the perception that the other is dishonest and deceitful is common, and does not need to be justified by religion.[1] However, in the context of a divided society, where people tend to seek refuge in the familiar and fear the strange, the vocabulary of honesty has fed back into misinterpretations and conflict. Apart from misunderstandings in communication, for some Protestants the idea persists that Catholics simply do not tell the truth. As one woman, nonchurchgoing Betty from Belfast, says 'It's all one-sided stories – they never tell the truth about the times they were tried to be helped.' Another man, churchgoing

Sam from Co. Down, tells a story about republicans infiltrating a police station, and concludes 'It goes to show, you just can't trust them.' This theme also arises in Harris's work, for example, her respondent who felt that all Catholics were telling lies and 'milking' the British welfare state: 'There's not one Roman Catholic in the country that hasn't got two pairs of spectacles and false teeth' (1972, p. 174). These ideas of course cannot be reduced to theology. However, if we look at the role of religion in helping create values and assumptions about the values of other groups, it may be suggested that there is a relationship between religious values of truth and some Protestants' analyses of politics. The changing emphasis of many unionists towards engagement with the pragmatic political game of politics as opposed to restating fixed principles has caused some disillusion. One woman says:

> At least I feel that the DUP are there, at least I know that when they come out and say this is what's going on in there, this is what's going to happen, that this is going to happen. At least I know. I feel that when the unionist party [UUP] talks they speak with a foreign tongue, with their fingers crossed behind their backs at the same time. I would rather someone would tell me, give it to me straight between the eyes than telling me all these little things that they think I want to hear, but it's not really the reality. I like honesty and I don't think we've got it.

Truth versus deceit, honesty versus hypocrisy, clarity versus hidden agendas: these ideas form part of the cultural vocabulary of many Protestants in Northern Ireland today. They are pronounced amongst Protestants with strong theological beliefs, but they also exist amongst many nonchurchgoing Protestants, especially those who have been raised in religious families. These constructions of the differences between Protestants and Catholics generalize and simplify; however, they are effective in reproducing classic stereotypes of straightforwardness versus sneakiness. They also provide moral evaluations of the communal boundary. Many Protestants have thought these ideas to be common-sense. These concepts provide a means of evaluation of groups as well as a means of explaining current political issues, such as Drumcree or decommissioning. It could be argued that these evaluations of truth and deceit would happen regardless of religious input, particularly in a social situation where trust is lacking. However, at the very least, the way that language has evolved in Northern Ireland has caused theological ideas to become entangled with political ideas over time. When people use these concepts to understand politics, even if they do not recognize their theological roots, it none the less reproduces religiously informed social stereotypes and alienates many Catholics.

Anti-Catholic ideology

The following chapter discusses in more depth how theological anti-Catholicism is a dominant narrative in Protestant culture. But ideological anti-Catholicism can also have explanatory power for Protestants who do not regularly go to church and who are not strong believers. Again, this depends on an individual's socialization. Those who gained familiarity with notions of the evils of Catholicism as children can find this idea difficult to shake off. This is particularly the case in the context of the perceived strength of the Catholic Church within the Catholic community. Generally, the strength of the Catholic Church is juxtaposed with criticism of the weakness and fragmentation of the Protestant churches (see Chapter 5). In fact, there is a sense of jealousy of, and threat from, the perceived unity of the Catholic community, which is thought to be driven by the Church.

Jim is a young nonchurchgoer from Belfast. He says:

> Jim: The Roman Catholic Church to me – in some strange way, I still feel a threat from it.

> Interviewer: Can you explain that?

> Jim: It's strange, I feel threatened by it in the sense that I feel it has done so much for their community, em, and it's done so much, and maybe, I think, I'm annoyed, because our church has done so little for this community, but then when you wonder why they are doing this for the community – what is their desire, what is their motivation – is it a more political thing you know?

Although a nonchurchgoer, Jim has a religious father and is familiar with conservative Protestant theology. It is perhaps unsurprising that he calls upon the religio-political discourse of the threat of the Catholic Church to make sense of the lack of strength he currently perceives within his own community. In contrast to the weakness of the Protestant churches, the Catholic Church is presented as suspiciously omnipresent. What we see here is Jim's ideas forming in relation to powerful agencies, interpreting his current political situation through the religious ideas learned in his formative years. Although Jim says his political views have moderated in recent times, he is very aware of the influences of his upbringing:

> I have all these influences and I have a very sort of evangelical, anti-Rome influence … in the later stages of my life I have become much more moderate to that whole concept of Roman Catholicism [but] I have these sort of triggers … still these influences are there, that there's either right or wrong and there's no in-between … I mean for example, you have all this sort of 'the Roman Catholic Church' as a system, in terms of the customs and some of their philosophies and practices that I totally disagree with, but it's really difficult – who am I to judge them if I'm myself not a practising Christian?

This is an example of religious ideology, concepts rooted in negative gut feelings about the Catholic Church and its theology. And for Jim, these ideas are not just abstract, but affect his daily life. For example, he says that he has always had problems with Jesuits, suspecting that they had political motivations, but now works with Jesuit priests and considers some as friends. However, negative perceptions of the political situation for Protestants in Northern Ireland draw him back into ambiguity. Jim describes his continuing struggle in building personal relationships with Catholics, not least his Jesuit colleagues, and his confusion about their intentions.

In short, Jim is actively renegotiating his religious identification, struggling to separate positive individual relationships from a wider negative analysis of his place within political structures and his group's lack of power. However, the seemingly zero-sum structure of communal politics in Northern Ireland makes Jim backtrack on some of his openness. The ideological formulation of anti-Catholicism is triggered when it seems to make sense of structural conditions. As he points out himself, it is ironic that he seems to care so much about the churches and religious ideas, when he takes no part in religious life. But whilst it may be ironic, these religious explanations sometimes help to make sense of what was, at the time of interview, a very tumultuous political situation. As Todd (1998) has argued, religious explanations can provide certainty of position in a way that secular loyalism and unionism cannot. This does not necessarily mean that personal religious revivals are provoked; however, the explanatory power and gut reactions of religious ideology, in this case anti-Catholicism, seem difficult to shake off.

Whilst religious ideology is more likely to be politically significant for Protestants, it is worth at this point asking how it may operate amongst Catholics. For a historically disadvantaged community, Catholicism also provided an idiom of identity. In Millar's (1999, pp. 202–204) work, for example, republican interviewees question whether Protestants have a conscience, and speak of their 'ingrained wickedness'. This is in contrast to Catholics, whom they say have been brought up with a moral theology and know what sin is. However, for Catholics, religious ideology does not generally stem from theology as it does for Protestants. Instead, liturgy and practice are the bases from which politically significant Catholic ideology has been constructed. Some of the most important of these religio-political ideologies for Catholics are outlined below.

Catholic victimhood and sacrifice

Ideas of victimhood are deeply embedded in the history of Irish Catholicism and the post-1922 Catholic community in Northern Ireland. The religious overtones of victimhood are important. Rafferty argues (1994, p. 2):

> Northern Ireland catholics do not regard the religion of their political opponents as essentially evil, or its practices as blasphemous. Nonetheless, catholics in Ulster have, in the absence of political or economic prosperity, historically placed their hope in a sort of 'eschatological vindication', believing that their reward for suffering endured at the hands of protestants would be a blissful union with God in heaven. The community saw itself, too often perhaps, as an island of catholic piety in a harsh sea of protestant heresy. To some extent their clergy encouraged Ulster catholics in this attitude.

Catholic theology is infused with notions of spiritual reward for earthly suffering, and a sense of righteousness in persecution. Whilst the extent to which ordinary Catholics were or are influenced by this is impossible to quantify, it is however significant that the victim is a familiar theme, and is one that provides hope, at least in terms of the next world.[2] The idea of the victim in the Christian tradition is powerful, with Christ the central illustration. The proper Christian attitude to persecution, as exemplified by Christ, is to turn the other cheek, accept what has happened and look to heaven for later vindication. Irish Catholic liturgy contains many references to heavenly rewards for the passive victim, and images of the sacrificial lamb being led to the slaughter. It is possible to argue that eschatologically, Irish Catholicism has often encouraged passivity when faced with suffering, and in extreme circumstances hope for redemption through sacrifice or martyrdom; these ideas have impacted upon political, as well as religious attitudes.

Take the hunger strikes,[3] for example, when Catholicism played heightened ideological and symbolic roles. Alongside the input of the institutional church (trying to convince the prisoners to end the strike, yet visiting and praying with prisoners), religious imagery was used to gather support in the community. The hunger strikers were portrayed in murals and literature as Christ-like figures, claiming 'blessed are they who hunger for justice.' Marian themes were drawn upon, and saying the rosary was a common feature of political meetings at that time (Ruane and Todd, 1996). Whilst Bobby Sands saw himself solely as a political, not a religious, prisoner, he frequently used the language and imagery of martyrdom. Consider his poetry: 'To walk the lonely road/ Like that of Calvary/ And take up the cross of Irishmen/ who've carried liberty' (cited in O'Malley 1990, pp. 51–2).

By identifying with Christ in this explicit way, Sands portrayed his actions as having a transcendent purpose. Although he could, of course, have been using religious ideas instrumentally for popular appeal, this in itself is significant as it indicates that he thought this discourse would have been well received amongst ordinary Catholics. Whilst the demands of the hunger strikers were exclusively political, they were coming from a prevalent, if not shared, cultural understanding of the story of Irish martyrdom, where the oppression of the community could only be broken by the sacrifice of individuals, as in the Easter Rising of 1916. Although republicans are often harsh critics of the Church, they are also capable of drawing on Catholic ideas and institutions as symbolic resources. Even Catholics for whom this myth did not match their understanding of real life – the fact that the prisoners were dying and being buried in such a constant stream – could not but affect the community far beyond the parameters of those with a mystical reading of Irish history.

Victimhood and sacrifice are not necessarily theological concepts, although they do have religious parallels. They are narratives of morality, helping define Catholic innocence and British and Protestant guilt. O'Connor has argued (1993, p. 99) that at least until the 1990s, republicans have used a 'pure, distilled Catholic victimhood' to block out their guilt for violence and to justify the IRA. O'Malley (1990, p. 157), perhaps overstating the case, argues that Sands came to symbolize the accumulated wrongs done to Catholics and that the hunger strikers' funerals 'awakened a deeper Catholic awareness of their own inner sense of victimization'. For many nationalists at the time, this could be seen as the latest instalment of an historical precedent. It fitted in with an historical narrative of persecution and was utilized to make sense of the present. The strikes may have been seen as unnecessary by some, but they still could be understood and often sympathized with. The British state could be perceived as heartless, uncaring, guilty of persecution, and the prisoners as selfless, sincere and 'innocent' victims. So religion played a significant symbolic role in fostering a sense of common grievance and shared purpose. In the context of the early 1980s, religious and moral meanings became fused with political diagnoses of a terrible situation for the Catholic community. To quote O'Malley (1990, p. 284) the hunger strikes 'brought into sharp focus the religious dimension of the conflict – differences in the definition and meaning of moral concepts, underwriting our notions of right and wrong that make reconciliation difficult, differences that transcend the politics of conflict'.

Indeed, victimhood has been a persistent frame through which to relate past and present. Fox describes northern nationalists after partition as 'the sacrificial victims of intransigence and intolerance' (1997, p. 88). This imagery creates continuity between past and present, and reproduces ideas of a communal boundary defined by Catholic powerlessness. Politicians too have been apt to tap into this narrative. As Gerry Adams reflected (in an interview with O'Connor, 1993, p. 293):

> To be a Catholic in Northern Ireland is still a political thing: it identifies you as a Fenian, a Taig. People are killed for being Catholic, or they can't go to certain places without that danger. And they have an affinity with the Church which has to do with its history, echoes of the penal days, punishment by death for being a priest or a bishop – the Church was part of the people's struggle.

This demonstrates the tendency to construct narratives of the present with reference to the past; it recreates the idea of historic community and implies something about the constancy of the moral failings of Protestants.

Victimhood hinges around a variety of key themes such as violence, socio-economics and politics. Fay et al.'s (1999, p. 164) research shows that in absolute terms more Catholics than Protestants died during conflict (although republican paramilitaries were also the most significant perpetrators). In response to this loss, a vibrant culture of victims' support groups amongst the Catholic community has emerged. Indeed the Agreement has focused attention on victims of conflict: setting up the Bloomfield Commission that culminated in a sympathetic report, 'We will remember them', and has since spawned a Victims Commissioner and Victims Unit. In addition to violence, many Catholics feel they have also been victims of political oppression and socio-economic discrimination. Denial of democratic rights has been a core issue since the inception of the state, and one that dominated politics particularly since the late 1960s. Socio-economic inequalities have also been on the top of the political agenda.

The scope of these has been mapped extensively by Smith and Chambers (1987, 1991), who attribute the recent phase of conflict to the presence of these inequalities (for more recent analysis, see Osborne and Shuttleworth, 2004). However, reflecting on how much discrimination there was during the Stormont years, Whyte's (1983, p. 31) observation remains pertinent: that the most serious charge against the government was not that it was directly responsible for widespread discrimination, but that it often allowed it to happen. Suffice to say there continues to be much contention about the degree, if not the existence, of Catholic disadvantage. None the less, an important cultural narrative has arisen out of these real experiences and grievances. Liam Kennedy (1996, pp. 217–18) has famously coined the phrase 'MOPE' – the story of the 'most oppressed people ever'. He argues that there is a 'cultural processing' of history, where a 'palpable sense of victimhood' in the presentation of the Irish national past is used for present political purposes. But as Kennedy suggests, it is not necessary to establish the 'facts' of Catholic disadvantage to understand how these grievances have been layered on top of one another to construct an historically orthodox, and often politically charged, narrative of victimhood. This is significant because, as Somers argues (1994), social actors use narratives, or stories, to make sense of, and act in, their lives. These narratives define who we *are* and help us know what to *do*.

How far these ideas are used by Catholics after the Good Friday Agreement to make sense of their political situation is debatable. There is a strong sense in which victimhood and sacrifice are narratives of the past. As we saw in Chapter 2, Catholics have been overwhelmingly in favour of the Agreement and have felt that they benefited from change. Although the Agreement does not deliver everything that nationalists and republicans might have hoped, it has none the less been welcomed as a positive direction of change. Moreover, many Protestants are presenting themselves as the new victims of change (McKay, 2000). In this context, an ideology of victimhood has less explanatory power (Mitchell, 2003b). When asked what is the first political event he can recall in Northern Ireland, Fred, a young churchgoing Catholic interviewee from Co. Armagh replied, 'I certainly don't remember the hunger strikes.' This response perhaps implies that this is an expected traditional reference point, but one which he does not really identify with. He goes on to say that he is aware of Catholics' suffering during the civil rights era and the hunger strikes, but that he prefers to focus on the future and opportunities provided by the Agreement. He disassociates himself with a traditional narrative of Catholic victimhood. This shift is exemplified by another republican interviewee, Sean from Belfast, who says that he has 'sacrificed' his hope for a united Ireland. However, he also says that things are improving for the Catholic community and that he will not sacrifice his demand for equality. Moreover, he is confident that this demand will be met. This is an interesting inversion of the concept of sacrifice, which is unrelated here to political powerlessness or helplessness. In this way, we see how religious ideology is contextual. As political circumstances change, the dynamics of religious ideology can change accordingly and may even recede from view.

However, it is perhaps premature to write off the political implications of victimhood. Northern Ireland remains a deeply divided society, and conditions are by no means improving for everyone, particularly for those in the most deprived areas. Moreover, interface conflicts persist at community level, and those affected often feel that their troubles are not being addressed by those in power. This feeling is heightened as the political process stalls and lurches from crisis to crisis. Events such as the Holy Cross School protests in 2000–01 serve as dramatic reminders of Protestant persecution and continue to provide the logic of victimhood, innocent children contrasting starkly with protesting loyalists. In the case of Holy Cross, one parent went on hunger strike to highlight the issue, creating a symbolic continuity with Catholics' plight in the past. The parish priest, Father Aiden Troy, walked the schoolgirls past the jeering crowds each morning. This not only creates symbolic unity between the Church and the Catholic community, it also reminds us how politics and religious ideology often become bundled together because of the necessities of dealing with conflict. So just as aspects of religious ideology may fall in relation to political circumstances, so too may they rise again when the situation demands. Thus, whilst victimhood and sacrifice are less politically salient than they were during the height of conflict, they have not yet gone away.

Anti-Protestantism

It is often argued that conflict for nationalists and republicans lacks the religious overtones of unionism, and is solely based on ethnonational politics. Catholics, it is held, are not sectarian and do not have a problem with Protestants *per se*, only their politics (White, 1997; O'Duffy, 1995). Republicans frequently make assertions that theirs is an anticolonial struggle that has nothing to do with religion (Juergensmeyer, 2000, p. 37). However, the assumption that politics is disconnected from negative ideas of the 'other' is problematic (Bruce, 1997). This section challenges the assumption that Catholics do not have negative feelings about Protestants, and begins to unpick how religion might play a part in constructing the content of these ascriptions. It fleshes out what Sinn Féin's Tom Hartley explained to Juergensmeyer (2000, p. 38) were the different 'thought processes' of Catholic and Protestant religions and cultures. It argues that religious ideas have provided a resource for identification through narratives of anti-Protestantism. Anti-Protestantism is a much more subtle phenomena than anti-Catholicism, lacking the latter's stark religio-political language and imagery. This, however, is exactly the point. Catholic identity has been constructed as a negation of Protestant religious fervour. It is framed in opposition to strong religious ideas. The religio-political dimension of Protestantism acts as a key concept against which to define Catholic identity and 'normality'.

History has bequeathed to Irish Catholicism on the one hand, a sense of being the powerless underdog, and on the other, a sense of strength in one's own community and values. The Protestant community are identified as the aggressor, whose religious convictions have often been perceived as the motivation for their discriminating tendencies. As such, Catholic identity has been constructed as open and tolerant, as a negation of ideas of Protestant fervour. This construction is dramatized and reproduced in the present, as Catholics look to events at Drumcree and Harryville, where Our Lady's Catholic Church in Ballymena was picketed throughout 1996–98 by conservative evangelical Protestants. This leads many Catholics to conclude that there is something about the nature of Protestantism that allows this to happen. Often Catholics argue that they are not like Protestants; they do not take their religious beliefs to these extremes. But this itself is othering – casting the Protestant community as wayward, and religious Protestants as sinister. It is the assumption that Protestants have got it wrong, and must become more like Catholics, that can sometimes lie at the heart of strained social and political relationships.

Although it is rarely articulated on theological premises by Catholics in contemporary Northern Ireland, anti-Protestantism may partially stem from religious ideas. Conservative Catholic theology holds that Protestant beliefs in 'Sola Scriptura' (the Bible alone), private judgement and justification by faith alone are illogical and dangerous. This is because of the perceived sin of pride implicit in the concept of private intellect. Faith in Catholicism is about submission and the combined wisdom of interpretation. It is argued that private judgement may be dangerous in that people may have particular prejudices and can twist the Bible to suit themselves. Whereas 'faith consists in submitting; private interpretation consists in judging' (Herbermann et al. 1911, p. 497). Thus there is a focus on the 'unhappy divisions' within Protestantism that are 'destructive of unity' (Herbermann et al. 1911, p. 593).

Many of these ideas about Protestants' inflexibility are echoed today at the level of common-sense knowledge amongst a wide range of Catholics. First consider some general responses to the question 'what do you associate with Protestantism?':

> Very austere, law abiding, I'll try to be fair about it. Law abiding, austere, em … uptight, uncompromising people. (Fred, Co. Armagh)

> Church and formality and hats and suits and I associate obeyance, there's very little dissidence – they listen to what the minister, vicar, director – whatever the terminology – rector, pastor – has to say, obedience. The laying down of the law. There's little room for questions or liberalism. (Michael, Co. Armagh)

> Their dress sense is immaculate … where we would go in, well I wouldn't go in in runners – but they are seen as much more reverential than ours to a certain extent. You know you get the Bible thumpers in ours, going on about the Holy Rosary and all this here, but theirs is something different. (Vinny, Co. Armagh)

This constructs a picture of Protestantism as very formal and inflexible – Protestants as well dressed, serious and unbending. Ironically, many Catholics perceive the authoritarianism within Protestantism that Protestants perceive within Catholicism. Whilst it is generally conceded that not all Protestants are inflexible, the stereotype is deeply rooted. This is in contrast with Catholicism. When Fred was asked what he associates with Catholicism, he says:

> Being a Catholic, being born a Catholic. More a minority, we are fun, is fun the right word? Laid back probably, much more than our Protestant counterparts, laid back to the extent of being lazy, can be quite defensive also … A lot of mysticism about Catholics, Catholicism has a lot of mysticism about it, Protestantism is more scientific. Does that make sense?

Indeed the idea of Catholics being more relaxed than Protestants was pervasive. Fred goes on to say that the Catholics he knows take their religion less seriously. Ironically, even though he feels Protestants are more 'uptight', and says he has 'a lot of ill-feeling' towards them, he reveals that he envies some of them for their commitment to their beliefs:

> Em, well I have a perception that Protestants won't do things if they don't see it in the Bible, or if it's not written down or it … it's em, well you know I have to go back to this to make sure I can go forward this way. Obviously that is a complete generalization. Catholics, well, church comes in somewhere, I'm sure it's in somewhere. You know, mass, yeah it's great you know, we'll get up for mass on Sunday. Well sure, what's the point of going in anyway? We can sit outside – I've got a hangover anyway, it doesn't really matter, you know? I can sit outside. The whole point about Catholic mass is to go and receive communion and one of the things that I would blame on Catholics is the ones that actually leave the mass before the communion, what the hell are you talking about in the first place? You've just missed the whole bloody point. That really annoys me about Catholics, really. I suppose that Protestants' devotion to religion is something that I would have to … em, I would quite envy some I would say.

So, it was not always an unequivocal criticism to say Protestants are more serious about religion. In fact it sometimes even resembled a half-compliment from Catholics who wished they felt the same kind of devotion. But Fred's is not a full compliment; his 'envy' is conceded reluctantly: 'I suppose, I would have to …'. Fred is struggling to make sense of his own desire to take religion more seriously, but also with his association of Protestantism with 'serious religion'.

Others inadvertently make the same association between Protestantism and serious religion as they talk about themselves. Indeed there seemed to be something of a self-abnegation amongst many Catholics, for whom being 'holy' was routinely denied. Amongst those I spoke to this was particularly evident amongst those most dedicated to their faith. Michael, a churchgoer from Co. Armagh, says that even though he is a eucharistic minister and feels proud of his faith and role in the Church, that, 'even now I wouldn't see myself as holy. I wouldn't see that as being, myself as being holy or judging myself to be holier than thou.' Catherine, a churchgoer from Co. Armagh, says, 'Well, going to mass, I would get some peace. I would feel peaceful and I always hope for my children – it's not that you're very holy or that you would join your hands, kissing the ground or the altar, but I enjoy going to mass and I like other people's religion too.' Brendan, also a churchgoer from Co. Armagh, presents himself in a similar way when he says, 'Although we practise our faith, we don't class ourselves as saints, and we don't kiss the altar rails and say we are totally proponents of our religion, because I know there are a lot more things we could do.' Barry says 'I wouldn't be going round with the Rosary beads or anything'; Eamon, 'I mean I wouldn't be a raving religious fanatic or anything.'

There seems to be a trend towards Catholics who take their faith seriously, to make it clear that they are not religious fanatics. It seems that expressive religious enthusiasm is not an acceptable self-image for many Catholics. There could of course be elements of self-censorship amongst interviewees on account of the interviewer's perceived Protestantism; however, the frequency with which these ideas arose is striking. Religious identities in Northern Ireland are constructed in a context of regular conservative evangelical Protestant disputes and claims. Whilst this may only represent a minority of Protestants, it is often noisy and disruptive, demanding a response. Numerous Protestants seek to distance themselves from strong religion, so it should not be surprising when Catholics do so too. However, it seems that a Catholic religious identity is not just distant from strong religion in general, but is constructed in opposition to an 'uptight' Protestantism. As such, it is not just an interesting cultural stereotype that Catholics are 'laid back' – it also constructs morality around different religious identities. As we see above, Vinny says that although there are some 'extreme' Catholics, this is 'something different' from Protestantism. In short, an opposition between humility and arrogance is being constructed here. This contrasts strong, formal and inflexible Protestantism, with a quieter, humbler Catholicism.

This point is even clearer when we explore the common claim that Protestants use their religion against Catholics, but that Catholics do not reciprocate. There is a tendency to present Catholic faith as less aggressive than Protestant faith. This is of course understandable in the context of a very vocal and often threatening anti-Catholicism – from being handed anti-Catholic literature in the street, to larger arenas of conflict such as Harryville. Indeed, this is a good example of reflexive identification, where what others think and feel about one, feeds back into one's sense of self. In this case, there is a rebellion against the proscriptions of others, inclining Catholics to define their identity defensively against the attackers. Again, because the focal point of anti-Catholicism is often religious, ideas about the different nature of Catholic faith and Catholics have been constructed.

Niamh's narrative provides a good example of a defensive response to the proscriptions of others. She is very aware of Protestant ideas of Catholics, and turns their moral evaluations upside down. Niamh says, 'It is not normal to stand in the street and scream and shout about God and the Bible and the Devil and quote from the Old Testament.' Her comments on having Sinn Féin's Martin McGuinness as Minister for Education are revealing. She says that whilst this must be difficult for some people,

> [Unionist] political leaders have given the false belief that you know, people like Gerry Adams and Martin McGuinness are the devil incarnate and they're bad and they're evil, you know, we're represented by the RUC and a group of defenders and supporters and all this kind of stuff, we're clean from any badness and these people are evil and we're good. It's not as simple as that and I think it's very hypocritical.

In Niamh's narrative, there is a strong awareness of the rhetoric and concepts of religious Protestants. Perhaps this is informed by her working in a mostly Protestant company, where some people have tried to give her evangelical literature to read, which would contain similar messages about cleanliness and badness. She presents Protestants in a very oppositional way, using their own discourse – 'God, Bible, devil, evil, clean' – to evaluate them, concluding that this is abnormal and hypocritical. By extension, Niamh's rejection of these constructs a self-image of Catholics being more down to earth and normal.

This often leads to a stereotype of the Protestant community being formed in a way that does not distinguish between members. This has important implications for social and political relationships, as it casts a cloud of suspicion over the intentions of a wide range of Protestants. Drumcree and Harryville were the main focus for highlighting the impact of anti-Catholicism in the present. Vinny says 'at the end of the day, if that is what their religion is about – that's not what Catholicism means to us. There's no way I would march down a road in defence of a particular religion.' Mark says:

> I think that Protestants would use religion more against, now I'm not being bigoted, I don't want to put my foot in it, but they would tend to say things about Catholics – especially Paisleyites – he doesn't like the Catholic Church, Paisley, he's got a big problem with Catholicism as such – I don't think that Catholics have the same problem with Protestantism.

Similarly, Brendan makes associations with the 'staunchness' of Protestants at Drumcree and Harryville, and highlights the religious dimension,

> We're not saying that all the atrocities are starting from the Protestant side – certainly not – Protestant places of worship have been burned and I would condemn those things. But I can't understand how people could stand outside a place of worship and heckle people that were in praying to God … I couldn't understand why, I don't think, correct me if I'm wrong, but I have never seen a Catholic demonstration outside a Presbyterian Church or a Church of Ireland Church or any other type of Protestant religion. And I found that, actually I found it disgusting … it makes you feel … resentment would be the first thing that comes into my mind, not that I would, actually, what I'd say, is it

would make you feel very strong sort of hatred against these people. I'm being honest, and I'm not saying this out of badness or anything, but it would certainly, em, I would feel, would stir up an anti-Protestant feeling, if that's the right term to use, in the very ordinary, middle-of-the-road Catholic, not even staunch, but a middle-of-the-road Catholic would turn round and say that's disgraceful.

Brendan is saying a lot of things here. First, he emphasizes the centrality of religion and of churches as symbolic sites of conflict in Northern Ireland. Secondly, his presentation of Catholicism is in opposition to this type of religiously motivated conflict. He locates himself within this tolerance – 'I'm not saying this out of badness', and presenting himself as 'ordinary' and not staunch. Thirdly, there is a strong negative evaluation of Protestants – 'disgusting, resentment, hatred, disgraceful' are used in relation to the actions of the protesters – but interestingly Brendan formulates this as anti-Protestantism. 'These people' are the other against which he articulates his own Catholic identity.

These narratives often lack distinction between Protestantism and unionism. Whilst many Catholics think that there are also 'good' Protestants, in general, people presented Protestants as the bigots in Northern Ireland, not Catholics. Indeed, it was expressed to me with surprise by some, that I actually seemed normal – for a Protestant. This indicates that religion is of crucial importance – not that anti-Protestantism is articulated theologically, but rather that the religio-political dimension of Protestantism acts as a key concept against which Catholic identity and 'normality' can be defined. In turn, Protestants are often expected to be religiously inflexible and humourless. This leads to ideas of Catholics and Protestants having certain characteristics. Even if people realize these are generalizations, they can still list typically Protestant or Catholic traits. The result of this is to make communities seem more fixed and more polarized than they really are; these ideas help prop up the structural perpetuation of communal division in Northern Ireland.

Anti-Protestantism is not a clearly worked-out ideology. This is precisely because it is articulated as a negation of being 'anti'-anything. It lacks the theological references of anti-Catholicism; so too does it lack the latter's vociferousness. It does not relate to a comprehensive theological exegesis on what is wrong with the Protestant faith, although it does have doctrinal parallels. However, it is a mechanism of othering. That is, it is concerned with similarity and difference, evaluating the former positively and the latter with fear and negativity. In many respects, Catholic identity seems to be constructed as a negation of perceived Protestant arrogance and inflexibility. Anti-Protestantism is reproduced around fears of the intensity of the other's religious beliefs: Catholic identity is constructed in opposition to this perceived threat. As such, oppositions emerge around humility and arrogance, laid-backness and seriousness, normality and abnormality. Moreover, these formulations are deeply informed by religion, in the sense that Protestantism, rather than unionism, is frequently seen as what drives the other. It is the seriousness of Protestant principles which are cast as incomprehensible by many Catholics, because these principles are seen as hostile to them, as zero-sum and uneasily accommodated in a 'normal' society. These ideas appear to help make sense of political relationships for many Catholics. Whilst this dimension of Catholic identification might not appear *religious*, it has historically been constructed in negation of Northern Ireland

Protestantism and Protestants. Although none of these ideas are articulated as a critique of Protestant theology, it is none the less significant that there exist such parallels between traditional theological teachings about, and contemporary political ideas of, Protestant inflexibility and arrogance.

Conclusion

But what is the political significance of these concepts and how far can they even be described as religious?

This chapter has argued that religion can manifest itself as ideology in Northern Ireland. This is where religious concepts are used to imagine what Protestants and Catholics are like, inform identity and mediate social and political action. Unsurprisingly this trend is most pronounced amongst those familiar with religious concepts. Familiarity can be gained from childhood socialization and can persist at the level of common-sense knowledge, independent of religious practice or belief in the present. Over time, however, ideology that is unsupported by religious structure and participation will become less coherent. However, as Northern Ireland is still a rather religious society, as indicated by its high levels of affiliation, practice and belief, it is unlikely that this dimension of division will disappear any time soon. Furthermore, the religious dimensions of ideology ebb and flow in relation to socio-economic and political conditions. In times of communal difficulty or crisis, ideology can become more intense; in times of calm, it can recede into the background.

Protestantism has provided the language and ideas for moral evaluations of the boundary. Although Protestantism puts much more emphasis than Catholicism on the Bible and doctrine, Protestants have never been a theologically coherent group. However, Protestantism has provided a system of ideas and values that have been used as a resource for identification. It has provided a discourse, much of which originally stems from reformed Protestant theology, which has evolved in relation to the political circumstances of the community. These ideas construct something like an identity narrative in the present – which is not universally accepted or always coherent, but which is a resource for identification. Religious ideological narratives have created political culture, just as they have been informed by it. Ideas such as the inherent liberty and honesty of Protestants helped to justify their dominant historical position as well as explain why Catholics were so antagonistic. For many Protestants, subsequent political events confirmed these ideas. In such a way, common-sense understandings based on religiously derived structures of ideas, of the political climate and of an historic power struggle, have become widespread in Northern Ireland. This has had implications, not only for devout believers, but a wide range of cultural Protestants, as conflict encouraged communities into oppositional patterns of thought. Thus, religion has been much more than a mere marker of communal difference. Religious ideology is both a cause and product of conflict. Protestants have sought to understand their situation through the lens of traditional religious concepts, and have in turn reproduced the social and political importance of these concepts. This is how Protestant political culture has become infused with religious ideology.

For Catholics, this relationship has been less pronounced. As we argue in the next chapter, theology is less socially salient in the first instance for Catholics. So it should not be surprising that religious ideology, its offshoot, is also less politically relevant. That said, Catholic ideas of victimhood and sacrifice have at times had explanatory power for a community bruised by conflict. Anti-Protestantism, or a tendency to cast religious fervour as the downfall of the Protestant community, also has a significant place within Catholic identity. These ideas are to some degree rooted in theology, but are also informed by liturgy and practice. Most of all, religious ideology is relational. It evolves from a combination of the cultural 'stuff' within a given community as well as their experience of social relationships, politics and power. This is why ideas of victimhood are declining in the present period. As political circumstances change so too do the dynamics of religious ideology.

Religious ideology is politically significant. It can affect social and personal relationships as well as political attitudes. People often draw upon religiously informed stereotypes of each community to understand what is happening in Northern Irish politics. By using these concepts as an interpretive framework, people reproduce these religiously informed categories of thought. This reifies ideas of what we are like as opposed to what they are like. These feed back into political culture. They can create suspicion between individuals, between communities and between political parties. Thus, religious ideology often sets the boundaries within which politics operates. But is religious ideology then just a boundary marker? The tendency to draw social boundaries and to stereotype others is universal. Does it matter that some of the cultural resources used to construct these stereotypes in Northern Ireland are religious in origin?

In fact it does matter. This is because of the two-way relationship between religion and politics. We have seen throughout this chapter that religious ideas do not just *cause* political attitudes, but that politics affects people's religious ideas. When people feel politically threatened, certain religious ideas may become more salient and cause people to question their beliefs. When Jim feels that Protestants are losing out after the Agreement, his feelings of anti-Catholicism resurface. When Sinn Féin are seen to fudge yet another call for decommissioning, this reinforces ideas of Catholics' dishonesty. Conversely, when political conditions improve for nationalists, traditional Catholic discourses of victimhood recede. Indeed, times when political difficulty has led to an outpouring of religious sentiment are well documented in Northern Ireland (Bruce, 1986). This is not to say that all political crises will bring religious revivals. Society is changing in other ways as well, and post-industrialization, increased travel and communications also influence the relationship between religion and politics in various directions. However, it does mean that in times of political difficulty, religious ideas are still 'out there'; people still understand them and can use them to identify insiders and outsiders. They remain an important cultural resource and reference point. And as Davie points out (2000), this means that religious ideas may simmer, ready to resurface in less favourable social or political climates. This is why the issue of religious ideology is a live one.

However, as we have seen, the persistence of religious ideology depends to a large extent on the religious character of the society and on religious socialization.

Increasingly unsupported by religious institutions and religious practices, even optimists, such as Davie (1994), have argued that beliefs will become more fragmented, individualized and less socially important. Brown (2000) maintains that this is what has happened in Britain. He argues that whilst people may still be interested in spirituality, Christianity is no longer a discourse that is used to make sense of the world, particularly by the young. This is a possible scenario when looking into the future of Northern Ireland. But, in the long term, anything is possible. On the other hand, for the foreseeable future it seems likely that the salience of religious ideology in political culture will persist. Northern Ireland still has extremely high rates of religiosity, and some religious subcultures such as evangelicalism may even be growing. Although attendance is declining amongst the under-35s, nearly half still attend regularly (see Chapter 2). It seems that there will be no immediate change in the provision of religious education so children will continue to gain a degree of familiarity with religious concepts. Moreover, it is also apparent that there will be no immediate resolution of social conflict even if political structures were to begin to work more effectively. Low-level conflict seems set to persist. In this context it would seem that the two-way interaction between religious and political ideas is likely to continue, at least for the next generation. Moreover, the importance of religious ideology must be seen in so far as it overlaps with other dimensions of religious significance in Northern Irish society. The next chapter turns to religious theology and politics, a pairing that is closely related to, and also props up, the religious ideology described in this chapter.

7
Theology and politics

Key points

- *Theology is the least socially significant dimension of religion.*

- *Theological beliefs are politically important mainly for evangelical Protestants.*

- *The theological element of Catholicism is less significant than ritual and liturgy.*

- *Theology can compel believers towards peace and reconciliation as well as political opposition.*

- *People's theological beliefs can change in response to political effects.*

Generally, theology is thought to be politically salient only for a minority of evangelical Protestants. Whilst this is the indeed the case, the relationship is not as straightforward as might be assumed. In this chapter we examine the connections between theological beliefs and political attitudes in Northern Ireland. The central concern is the ways in which religion provides meaning in what sometimes seems to be a meaningless world, and in turn, how this can affect people's political attitudes and actions. This dimension of religious significance has been left until last because although it is the most dramatic manifestation of religion in politics in Northern Ireland, it is actually the least prevalent. Of course, it is intricately connected with the other dimensions of religious power, ritual and ideology, and this reinforces the theological components of politics. This chapter concentrates mainly on Protestants, and in particular evangelicals. The reason is because evangelicals are the largest social group in Northern Ireland for whom theological teachings and doctrines have political significance. This of course does not mean that Catholics lack devotion or commitment to their faith. It simply indicates that the doctrinal element of religion has less social significance than ritual or liturgy.

The approach taken by many theologians, and some sociologists, is that religious beliefs inform social action because people are grasped and motivated by a spiritual quest. Glock and Stark (1965), for example, see religion as a means of answering 'ultimate' questions and problems. Christian theologian Tillich (1963) argues that religion is a state of being grasped by an ultimate concern about the meaning of life.

Wilson (1979) regards religion as pertaining only to those activities that make some explicit reference to a supernatural source of values. This is the frame of reference within which this chapter operates: spirituality, theology, doctrine and the supernatural.

Before commencing this exploration, a word of caution is needed about relationship between the social sciences and theology, which is often rather fraught. Tension generally arises because many social scientists see religion as an irrational force and as something that masks other material or political interests. Flanagan (1996) argues that sociologists have little understanding of theology and tend to ignore signs of the sacred in their own lives as well as their work. He maintains that this lack of reflexivity on behalf of most sociologists has led to the dominant association of modernity with secularization and instead calls for 'the enchantment of sociology'. Martin (1997b), addressing the same question, feels that social scientists have difficulty with theology because their analyses must deal with socially grounded empirical generalizations that often challenge theological claims. Sociology's remit of course is to analyse the social patterns surrounding religious belief rather than judge the veracity of these beliefs. For our purposes these issues need not be resolved, merely handled sensitively. There is no need to have an opinion as to whether theology is meaningful in and of itself, or that humanity is somehow connected to the supernatural, in order to analyse how these beliefs affect individuals and communities. The impetus is upon the responsible researcher to accept the claims of believers at face value. If people perceive that religious ideas and teachings provide guidance in their lives, it is inappropriate to write this off as false consciousness or mere boundary maintenance. This would fail to grasp the nature of their self-understanding, which is the key to understanding social action. We may of course tease out how beliefs are related to processes of boundary maintenance, without concluding that they can be reduced to this.

Weber (1958) is extremely helpful on this point. He argued that religious beliefs are centrally important in guiding social action and was concerned with the connections between certain types of beliefs and certain types of social behaviour, in particular, economic activity. Weber builds a theory of religion that could be described as psychological – taking into account the intellectual as well as emotional bases of religion, and then linking it up to social factors. He rejects theories of religion that claim that it is simply a product of social conditions, and also those, such as Marx, who say that religion is merely a response to powerlessness and deprivation, such as Marx. Instead, for Weber, life is inherently uncertain and people seek to find meaning, especially to explain good and bad fortune. As different groups occupy different social positions, they use different sorts of religious ideas to explain and understand their place. It is not so much that religious ideas are used instrumentally to justify political dominance, for example, rather that they are useful as people seek reassurance and try to make sense of their place in the world.

However, for Weber, ideal and material interests, rather than religious ideas *per se*, are what motivate human behaviour. By this he means that we are driven by a need to explain our social, cultural, economic and political position in the world as well as look out for our own material well-being. It is in the context of these needs that charismatic leaders, thinkers and prophets inject religious ideas. Once these ideas of the sacred are 'out there' they can begin to shape our views of the world, the questions that we ask and the types of reassurance that we seek. So there is a two-way relationship between religious ideas and social action. Our social and economic position determines the kinds of questions that we ask about life's meaning; we find answers to these questions in appropriate religious ideas and explanations; these ideas and explanations in turn create a world image that helps us reformulate our ideal and material interests and we think and act accordingly. This is of course a simplified version of Weber's model. In reality, nobody starts with a blank canvas. Religious ideas are already 'out there' culturally, not least in Northern Ireland, helping to shape people's interests. However, it is useful to bear in mind the reciprocal way in which religious beliefs and social action influence one another. The relationship between theology and politics is not a one-way street where the former simply influences the latter. Politics sometimes influences religion, not just the other way round.

This chapter draws out some of the main themes in which theology has been related to politics in Northern Ireland. It shows the theological roots of certain beliefs, their political application and how they have been appropriated by people in an attempt to provide meaning to life and to the political situation in Northern Ireland. It also explores how politics affects theology. As indicated, most of the sections in this chapter concern Protestants, although there is some discussion of Catholicism provided and reasons for this disparity are suggested.

Anti-Catholicism

Morrow argues (1997, p. 58) that 'theological Protestantism and anti-Catholicism can lay claim to a longer unbroken historical pedigree in Ulster than any other still-existent ideological rival.' Traditionally, Ulster Protestants have objected to Catholicism on many grounds: that popery enslaves its followers, that it is superstitious, conformist and antithetical to individual freedom. This opposition to perceived authoritarianism helps explain the intensity of anti-Catholic feeling enshrined in the Westminster Confession of Faith (the statement of beliefs of the Presbyterian Church), which identifies the Pope as the anti-Christ. The decision of the Presbyterian Church in 1993 not to remove this reference shows that it is by no means a marginal idea. This statement emphasizes the role of Catholic priests in confession, mediating between man and God, and argues that this prevents Catholics from thinking for themselves. Instead, Catholics are thought to be controlled by their Church. Furthermore, in Protestantism, salvation is achieved through faith alone. That is, there is a relationship between the individual and God in which the individual repents for their sins and is forgiven through God's grace. Subsequent contact must take place between the individual and the divine. Thus, traditional Protestant theology holds that 'superstitions', such as prayers to Mary and the saints, insignia and medals are not only a waste of time, but are idolatry. Ideas that Catholicism is fundamentally wrong, even evil, and that individual Catholics are deluded at best or damned at worst has informed Ulster Protestantism and loyalism for centuries, from the Covenanters and Seceders in the eighteenth century through to Revd Ian Paisley and his followers today.

Brewer (1998) outlines three active modes of anti-Catholicism that he sees as prevalent in contemporary Northern Ireland: covenantal, Pharisaic and secular. The first two are based in theological teachings and articulate and act upon their beliefs about Catholics in different ways. The covenantal mode of anti-Catholicism is based in prophetic Old Testament ideas of God, land and a 'chosen people' (see below). Conflict is interpreted as a battle between good and evil, truth and error. As such, covenantal Protestants or 'Bible Protestants' have no relationship or dealings with Catholics. This mode of anti-Catholicism has strong political implications. Akenson (1992) shows how Ulster-Scots Calvinism helped many Protestants justify their settlement in Ireland. By distinguishing the saved 'elect' settlers, from the damned natives, Protestants were able to draw political lessons from biblical parallels with the Israelites. If the natives did not accept their religious beliefs they were wrong, and moreover, if they were hostile to the settlers, refusing to give up the 'promised land', they were also deemed to be evil. For Akenson, this explains Protestants' traditional willingness to discriminate, their rejection of religious pluralism and their distinctive political language. Brewer (1998) too feels that covenantal Protestants' total revilement of Catholicism makes them almost impossible to work with politically. Seeing the hand of Rome behind all forms of nationalist and republican politics, they tend to shun contact altogether. This helps explain the DUP's traditional reluctance to negotiate with Sinn Féin (although there are signs that some DUP members are moderating this stance).

In the Pharisaic mode of anti-Catholicism, Brewer (1998) points out that theology emphasizes New Testament biblical truth and Catholic doctrinal error, rather than ideas of a chosen people. Pharisaic Protestants tend to believe that Catholics are Christians, but that they are in error, and need enlightenment and conversion to bring them truth. In other words, Catholics can be taught to realize the freedom that Protestantism offers as well as the benefits of the union. McBride (1998), Elliott (1985) and Miller (1978b) point to this tendency, amongst the New Light and Reformed Presbyterians in the eighteenth and nineteenth centuries, and amongst Church of Ireland clergy in the early twentieth century. It is found amongst a wide variety of evangelical Protestants today.

Religion can be associated with withdrawal from this-worldly concerns and a subsequent lack of attention to politics (Bruce, 2003, pp. 83–7). For a group of Pharisaic Protestants, politics is often ignored and Catholics are reached out to in order to 'save' them. Brewer argues (1998) that Pharisaic anti-Catholicism is not used to legitimize political superiority or social segregation. It allows for a degree of ecumenism and social contact with Catholics in nonreligious settings. Pharisaic Protestants may even be pro-Catholic to a degree in their politics, as is evidenced by the extent of cross-denominational cooperation in United Irish Movement in the 1790s. However, at this time, contempt for Catholics' intellect was still the most common objection to their immediate political emancipation and the predominant feeling amongst the Presbyterian New Lighters was that freedom should be introduced to Catholics gradually as a learning process (Elliott, 1985). Thus, Brewer is correct when he argues that Pharisaic anti-Catholicism breeds its own form of exclusivity. It still involves negative stereotypes of Catholics that can have negative social effects. As one evangelical interviewee from Co. Down, John, describes:

> I was explaining to a girl in work one day, who was a Catholic, that, about my belief, that you have to be saved. And I could see it in her face that she was taking great offence at this, because she thought I was attacking, she thought I was just being nasty because she was a Catholic, and I says to her – no, I believe that you have to be saved, and I believe I've to be saved, and if not you're going to hell. And I says to her, it's not just about persecuting Catholicism, I says it's about anyone who is not saved, Protestant or Catholic.

The impact of salvation beliefs on social relationships can be alienating and this interviewee is aware of the sensitivities of this Catholic workmate, using words like attacking, offending, persecuting to describe her feelings. He has an acute sense that his views are unpopular and that he may be seen as intolerant. He is also correct that many other Protestants, not just Catholics, can be offended by his beliefs. However, the imperative to spread one's religious convictions is a key feature of this strand of Protestantism. This can complicate social relationships with people outside the evangelical subgroup. If combined with unionist political attitudes, strong Protestant religious beliefs may be seen as even more antagonistic to Catholics.

It is important, however, not to over-simplify the social and political consequences of theological anti-Catholicism. It is inaccurate to say that people's theological problems with Catholicism and a desire to convert inevitably lead to bad social relationships. Rather, it depends on the relationship of those involved, and their willingness to accept other people, if not their views. Fundamental religious beliefs do not make social intolerance inevitable. Kerry, a young, unemployed born-again Christian with very strong religious beliefs, is convinced that people need to be born again, and gives examples of times when she has explained her views to others, including Catholics. She admits that sometimes her ideas are not well received, but with close Catholic friends there is more of a mutual exchange of thoughts. A story she tells about a Catholic man who has married into, and is shunned by, her loyalist family is revealing:

> My cousin got married to a Catholic and he got snubbed something shocking by our family. They were really cruel to her. There was me and a few others who didn't mind. At my grandfather's funeral, he was really creaming it, and I went down in a Rangers top,[1] and he sort of looked at me, and I changed it because I didn't want him to feel ... I mean he was really nervous and I went over to talk to him and I says, don't worry, I've nothing against you. I was raging at my family. I talked to him for an hour and a half about the Celtic/Rangers game that weekend. He said you didn't have to take that top off, and I said but I didn't want to make you feel uncomfortable.

Kerry's strong views about her faith have not in this case caused her to be negative towards Catholic individuals. In fact, she plays for a Catholic football team. She constantly repeats that she accepts other people's beliefs, that her friends accept hers, and that if it were not for her parents she would have no problem dating a Catholic (and has done so in the past). So, although Kerry's views on faith are strong, her narrative is one of religious privatization on a personal level. She shares her faith with like-minded people around her, but says she studiously avoids getting into conversation about issues that may cause social conflict. Although she has a fear of Catholicism in a united Ireland, and she describes mass as having 'freaked [her] out' with 'candles, the priest and scary music', in the main her religious beliefs are not overly oppositional. Church for Kerry has been a sanctuary from a life of drink and drugs and paramilitarism, and she uses words like 'home, welcome, happy, security, safety, trust' to describe it. Although unemployed, Kerry feels more secure than she did before – where there is danger, it comes from feuding loyalist paramilitaries in her neighbourhood rather than Catholics. Her self-presentation of strong, personal Protestant faith is one of something that has positively changed her life and has not hindered her relationships with her Catholic friends.

Both strong and weak forms of anti-Catholicism translate into fears or concerns about a united Ireland, albeit in different ways. Although theologically rooted, anti-Catholicism is also a Protestant response to the nature of politics in the Republic of Ireland after partition. The special place of the Roman Catholic Church in the Irish constitution (until 1973), the degree of political implementation of Catholic social teaching and actual clerical involvement in politics in the Republic of Ireland have added to the perception that the Catholic Church is still a tyrant to be feared (Fulton, 1991, 2002). Although the Irish Republic never was a theocracy, and the Catholic Church was never totally dominant (Whyte, 1980), the image of the all-powerful, superstitious Church is no less potent for many Northern Protestants (and indeed for many Catholics). For covenantal Protestants, fears of a 'priest-ridden' Irish state in which they would be persecuted loom large and they attempt to avoid all contact with it.

On the other hand, Pharisaic Protestants have more appreciation of the consequences of rapid economic growth and value change in Ireland. Although they may see the Republic of Ireland as culturally different, it is not considered likely to be as oppressive as covenantal Protestants think it to be. In fact, recent interviews with a range of evangelical Protestants suggest a growing tendency to view the Republic of Ireland as godless as a result of the Celtic Tiger, and thus, see Irish citizens as potentially ripe for conversion (Mitchell, 2004b).

Anti-Catholic theology has a long lineage in Northern Ireland. That said, it should not be assumed that theology is something fixed which functions as the basis for action. Theology does not provide a total world-view outside of individuals' experiences. In fact, the strength and type of anti-Catholicism amongst Protestants has gone up and down in waves in relation to wider political conditions. McBride (1998) argues that in times where no serious Catholic 'threat' was perceived by Protestants, there was much more optimism that Catholics were actually capable of enlightenment and deserving of freedom. In interviews after the Good Friday Agreement, where Protestants perceive the Catholic community as strong and their own community as weak, the role of the Catholic Church in promoting this strength was often highlighted with suspicion. In such ways, anti-Catholic theology is rather malleable and religious ideas often respond to different political contexts. When Protestants were secure in their dominance, there was more flexibility in how Catholics were perceived and treated. When structural conditions seem to be worse for Protestants, some fall back on a harder anti-Catholic position (see also Chapter 6). In contrast, other Protestants' personal experiences with Catholics and of politics can defuse anti-Catholic beliefs. In these ways, politics can affect theology and the ways in which theology is used to interpret the world, just as theology can affect politics.

The chosen people: covenant and contract

The idea of a covenant between God and man was at the heart of early Protestantism. This is the notion that God made a deal with the children of Israel that he would lead them to the 'promised land' and that in return they would devote themselves to him. If God did not deliver on his promise, then the children of Israel no longer owed him their loyalty. The group of, in Brewer's (1998) terms, contemporary covenantal Protestants see parallels with Israeli Jews (and Afrikaaners in South Africa) and feel that they have been led to Ulster by God (Akenson, 1992). They are a 'chosen people' and Ulster is their own promised land. Their enemies are the forces of Satan led by the Antichrist, the Pope, whilst the Protestant people wait in hope of salvation in the promised second coming (Todd, 1998). Thomson (1995) points out that a variety of Protestants believe that Ulster is the last defender of the faith. This theological interpretation of the modern world and of Ulster Protestants' role within it has important political parallels.

There has been a long-standing association, especially in Ulster Presbyterianism, between loyalty to the Protestant Crown and the Bible. The Scottish universities where Ulster Presbyterian clergy were trained were intellectual centres for the most advanced contractarian ideas in the age of the Enlightenment (Elliott, 1985). Religious notions of covenant have translated into political notions of contract and mutual obligations between citizens and the state. Many Protestants interpreted their obedience to government as conditional on the latter's avoidance of corruption and the protection of Protestants' individual liberties.

This helps explain why Ulster Protestants have had a difficult relationship with Britain. Indeed, one of the ironies of Protestants' identification with Britain is that there has never been any surplus of affection for England and that their loyalty has always been conditional. When Protestants have felt ignored or betrayed by the British Parliament, many have focused their loyalty on the Protestant Crown instead. A further irony is the increasing de-traditionalization and de-Protestantization of the modern British monarchy. The royal family can hardly be described as upholding long-established Protestant principles. However, a degree of cognitive dissonance can persist about this so long as the monarchy is formally a Protestant institution. What is more striking, however, is Protestants' willingness to stand up to central authority when they perceive their rights as being trampled on. This has been reflected in various periods, evidenced in the Volunteering of the 1780s–90s, the Ulster Unionist Convention of 1886, Ulster's resistance in 1912–14 and the 'Solemn League and Covenant', to the Ulster Worker's Council of 1974 (Elliott, 1985; Stewart, 1986).

Religious ideas of covenant take on a heightened political resonance in periods wrought with Protestants' insecurity about Britain's commitment to them, and Catholic threats from within. McBride (1998, p. 109) argues that the British connection was always problematic for Presbyterian settlers. Britain at once represented their only source of protection on an island where there was an increasing Catholic majority, but was also a source of exclusion and often hostility. Even when full political rights were extended to Presbyterians in the eighteenth century, their ethos of conditional loyalty did not die out. Miller (1978a) maintains that the result of this frustrated loyalty has often been a trend towards self-reliance and the prioritization of Ulster over Britain. Wright argues (1973, p. 236) that although the Protestant monarchy is a central idea, it is in fact loyalty to Stormont over Westminster that has been emphasized by Protestants. Although Anglicanism lacked the same historical tension with Britain, circumstances in the nineteenth and twentieth centuries changed this, as no particular section of the Protestant community enjoyed special treatment from Britain, or exemption from the threat of nationalism.

As Miller points out (1978a), modern Ulster Protestants have not strictly regulated their lives according to the contractual tenets in Locke's Second Treatise or the Solemn League and Covenant of 1912; however, he argues they have continued to think in terms reminiscent of these. He cites Ian Paisley's warning to the British Secretary of State that 'government is not a one-way street. It is a civil contract in which each party has a duty' (1978a, pp. 5–6). Fulton (1991, p. 107) argues that those still hanging on to a theological covenantal history are especially antagonistic to nationalism, and may increase in number as people become disillusioned with British identity and see Paisley's words about the treacherous nature of the British government become reality. So for many evangelical Protestants, there are distinct theological dimensions to the political conflict in terms of the religious concept of covenant.

Coulter (1994) has argued, however, that ideas of contract are anachronistic and do not square with ideas of citizenship in modern liberal democracies. Aughey (1989) agrees and argues that unionism's confusion over loyalty is the result of British government failures to provide basic rights of participation and statehood, rather than religious ideas of contract. However, strong parallels may still be found. Cochrane (1997, p. 69) quotes David Trimble, who acknowledges the possibility that the UK might at some point want unilaterally to end the union. Trimble says:

> Yes, there is a sort of contract relationship … I don't agree with all of Miller's book but I think it is quite interesting. But the idea of a covenant – I use that word instead of contract – is of course very central to Presbyterian theological thinking, and a lot of people's political thought – it is true here, it has been true elsewhere as well – it is closely related to their theology.

Sometimes ideas of covenant and contract are explicit in evangelical discourse. Bruce (2001) reports that the Loyalist Volunteer Force's (LVF) code word for its murderous acts was 'Covenant'. Tara, another small loyalist paramilitary organization, ends a pamphlet calling Protestant men to arms citing the Bible, 'your enemies shall fall before you by the sword … for I will establish my covenant with you … and I will cut off the names of idols out of the land and they shall no more be remembered … for the mouth of the Lord hath spoken it' (Tara Proclamation, n.d.). Another movement that has explicitly stressed ideas of covenant has been the British Israelites, who have exercised some influence in Northern Ireland, for example, Revd Robert Bradford, former Westminster MP for South Belfast, who believed that the British race is descended from the lost tribes of Israel. Indeed, this is one of the strongest ways in which religious legitimation is given to paramilitary violence. However, Bruce (2001) argues that only a handful of evangelical unionists have actually been influenced by some form of British Israelism and undue influence should not be attributed to it. In its strong form, this is undoubtedly the case; however, field notes taken by this author after a variety of interviews show that it is not unusual for conservative evangelicals to own books on Jewish history and other memorabilia. This may indicate that there is at the very least a continued awareness of British Israelism and covenantal ideas.

Overall, whilst ideas of covenant are often implicit in Protestant discourse on Britain's disloyalty, they may be less influential in contemporary Northern Ireland than ever before. This is because a growing number of Protestants believe that Britain can change its relationship with Ulster without unionist endorsement. Indeed, covenant and contract have little explanatory power in the light of British government policies that have shown willingness to let Northern Ireland leave the United Kingdom. In fact, since the Sunningdale Agreement in 1973, both British and Irish governments' acceptance of the consent principle has meant that the constitutional status of Northern Ireland can change in a referendum. In this sense, there is realistically no contract with Britain. However, for most Ulster loyalists and some unionists, particularly in times of low-level conflict, an acknowledgement of this fact seems to coexist easily with the notion of basic loyalty to the Crown. But given how theological ideas can simmer and surface in response to structural conditions, should there be a prospect of an imminent united Ireland or other form of British disengagement it is possible that ideas of broken contract and covenant may resurface. For the meantime, though, covenant appears to be a secondary dimension of politically relevant Protestant theology.

The end times

The second coming of Christ, or the end times, is a recurring theme in conservative evangelical Protestant theology, although there are differing interpretations of the logistics of this. The biblical book of Revelation outlines a process by which the end of the world will draw near. Those Protestants who interpret Scripture literally have constructed a narrative of the end times that has been politically influential. Higgins and Brewer (2003, pp. 116–20) outline the main features of Antichrist beliefs in Northern Ireland. It is believed that soon there will be a 'rapture' where true Christians will be taken into heaven. After this, a world leader shall emerge, known as the Antichrist, and shall unite the world religiously and politically. There will then be a time of tribulation where anyone who has subsequently come to Christ shall be persecuted. Ultimately there shall be a final battle, Armageddon, which will end with the second coming of Christ who will rule the earth for a time and triumph over Satan.

The narrative of the end times has been very influential in a subsection of unionist and loyalist political culture in a variety of ways. First, as indicated above, the Antichrist is often thought to be the Pope (or at least the Pope is thought to be an agent of the Antichrist), and the Roman Catholic Church to be his means of spreading domination. The influence of the Pope is thought to reach right into the heart of Europe, and the European Union in particular. Alan, a conservative evangelical from Co. Down, talks about the instrumentality of Catholicism in bringing about the end of the world. He says that nationalists want to uphold Roman Catholicism as a religion in a united Ireland. However, nationalists are not as big a threat as the EU. This is because the EU is alleged to be part of a Roman Catholic plan for world hegemony as is foretold in the book of Revelation. European monetary funds, political unity and moves to create a European army are seen as signs of a new world order. Alan believes that the heads of Europe are going to be canonized by the Pope – proof that the EU is in the grip of Rome. He says that he expects that soon we will have identity cards and numbers that will bear the 'mark of the beast'. This represents a Northern Ireland Protestant identity constructed and developing in response to the perceived changing balance of power in the world, and given meaning through religious belief. Nationalism and Catholicism are perceived to be aligned with the dark side of world politics. In contemporary conservative evangelical publications such as the *Protestant Bulwark* and *The Battle Standard*, these themes continue to be promulgated.

In Northern Ireland, some Protestants read the political situation through the lens of Revelation, associating each new Protestant 'defeat' with the trials and tribulations outlined in the Bible. Those who subscribe to this theology are constantly on alert to distinguish signs of the end times. As evidenced by international organizations like 'Rapture-watch', in all generations it has been expected that the second coming will happen sooner rather than later. A handful of conservative evangelicals also pointed out that political events in Israel will signal the beginning of the end times. Indeed, premillenial theology indicates that the end times will see a decay of society, and that the situation for evangelical Christians will get worse before Christ can return.

For those who subscribe to this theology there may be various courses of action. Either one can sit back, do nothing politically and wait for the prophecy to be fulfilled. Or one can try to engage with society and politics in order to dampen the negative impact of change upon evangelicals, for example, by arguing that Christian morality should be upheld in the public sphere. Contemporary conservative evangelicals in Northern Ireland adopt both strategies. The Caleb Foundation, for example, engages with media and government in an attempt to put across evangelical positions on homosexuality, abortion and religious education. Similarly, Paisley's European Institute for Protestant Studies (EIPS) encourages political activism. However, other evangelicals reading Biblical prophecy into political events can be prone to political apathy. For example, Bruce (2001) points out that the political rhetoric of Paisleyites is often apocalyptic: murders, bombings and political betrayal are read as proof that the world will become even more violent as the Day of Judgement approaches. Sometimes this stunts political will to compromise – after all why back down on politically unpopular theological points when the Bible says that the righteous shall inevitably be persecuted? Bruce (2003, p. 12) argues that at times Ian Paisley's uncompromising politics is underpinned by an expectation of imminent revival. In this sense, end-times theological convictions can lead to political inflexibility.

Juergensmeyer (2000) points to two trends in relation to theological positions on the end times and violence. Some Christian groups believe that violence is an acceptable means of achieving a godly society on earth, based on the Ten

Commandments. On the other hand, dispensational premillennialists, believing that the end of the world is drawing near, may instead prepare themselves for the final battle and stockpile arms and other supplies. Juergensmeyer (2000) views loyalist paramilitary violence in Northern Ireland in the light of both of these types of theologies. As argued in the previous section, Bruce's work (2001, 2003) indicates that these types of religious doctrines are certainly not at the forefront of loyalist paramilitarism. However, these ideas do appear to be salient for a handful of convinced religious believers within loyalism. They are also influential amongst some of their sympathizers.

The main influence of end-times theology, however, is not in directly informing loyalist violence, but in fostering everyday interpretations of the political situation in Northern Ireland for ordinary believers. For some conservative evangelicals, the Good Friday Agreement of 1998 is seen as the latest instalment of the end-times process. One anti-Agreement Protestant, Helen from Co. Down, for example, talked about how she felt that there was an 'attempted eradication' of Protestants in Northern Ireland and says that there is 'religious apartheid' afoot. This echoes long-standing historical narratives of siege within Ulster Protestantism (Stewart, 1986) where the righteous are persecuted by hostile external forces. It is perhaps no coincidence that this interviewee has become a born-again Christian in recent years, as well as switching her political preference from the UUP to the DUP. As she tries to understand what is happening in Northern Ireland, a religio-political interpretation is used to explain, to justify and to give hope of deliverance: 'The thing that always sticks in my mind is what the Lord says, 'the truth is mine, and I will repay', and I really do hold on to that because I do believe that ultimately he will stop it this time. Not just the Agreement, but generally [immoral, corrupt] society.'

Whilst the book of Revelation speaks of the final days of the world, it ends with judgement and salvation, which this interviewee believes will soon be underway. Indeed, a variety of conservative evangelical Protestants agreed with this interviewee that the Agreement may be another sign of the times. One said of Drumcree, 'It's like the final battle, if we don't go in here we are finished' – the final battle with overtones of Revelation. Another says the only thing that can salvage the political situation after the Agreement is 'divine intervention'. In more recent interviews with evangelicals in 2002, nearly a third (out of 20) of DUP supporting conservative evangelicals spontaneously brought up the idea that the Agreement was a sign of the end times (Mitchell, 2004b).

There are two processes at work here. First, believers are using their theological convictions about the end times to impose meaning on their political situation. At the same time, their response to what they see as threatening political developments feeds back into their religious ideas, in many cases strengthening their sense of impending apocalypse. Again, this is not simply theological conviction being used to justify opposition to political change. Rather, religious and political beliefs help shape one another. In some cases, politics reinforces theology rather than simply the other way around.

Protestant theology and reconciliation

Generally, it is the oppositional dimensions of religion in Northern Ireland that get the lion's share of attention. However, religion can also act as an impetus for inclusion and reconciliation. Both Protestant and Catholic theology can be interpreted in ways that promote good ecumenical relations and even political integration. Martin (1997a) goes so far as to argue that although religion is often entangled with political conflicts, where individuals correctly interpret Christianity's relationship to society, it tends to contribute to peace rather than war. With regard to Protestant evangelical religion, Jordan (2001) calls the conciliatory strand 'inclusive evangelicalism'. This subgroup also contains liberal evangelicals and some Catholic evangelicals, and is not seen as authentically evangelical by conservative Protestants.

A key example of an evangelical Protestant group committed to reconciliation is Evangelical Contribution on Northern Ireland (ECONI), which applies Biblical concepts to conflict and its resolution (Mitchel, 2003). Ganiel (2002) points out that ECONI has a very different perspective on constitutional questions than other conservative evangelical groups. Whilst the latter argue that Ulster is the promised land, ECONI evangelicals are not concerned with geographical territory. Instead, they emphasize the Kingdom of God both in this world and in the world to come, and characterize citizenship as heavenly rather than to do with nationality (Mitchel, 2003). This sentiment is reflected by one of Ganiel's interviewees, 19 year-old UUP-supporting Grace from Co. Antrim. She says, 'I think a lot of Christians believe that [Northern Ireland] should be part of the United Kingdom whereas I don't really see that as the big issue. For me citizenship is in God's kingdom, not in a country down here, so to me it wouldn't make any difference' (Ganiel, 2002, p. 14).

Forgiveness is at the heart of a theology of reconciliation. Hurley (1994) argues that this entails giving up any desire for retaliation, a willingness to view situations from all sides, accepting responsibility may well be shared, and making amends. As McCullough (1994) points out, in the Bible restoring the vertical relationship between God and the individual is always accompanied by the restoration of good horizontal relationships between individuals. ECONI stresses the biblical message of forgiveness with regard to peace-building in Northern Ireland. They challenge conservative evangelical assumptions that Irish nationalism is a tool for spreading Roman Catholicism and have engaged in ecumenical dialogue with Catholics as well as other Protestants (Thomson, 1995). Through their newsletter *Lion and Lamb*, organization of conferences, publicity by information officers and activism within a variety of congregations, ECONI have diffused their message throughout wider evangelical circles. They successfully tap into, as well as pioneer, a wider discourse of religious reconciliation.

Indeed, there are a variety of religious organizations involved in peacemaking at grassroots level in Northern Ireland (Brewer, 2003). Corrymeela, a religiously run reconciliation organization providing a retreat for cross-community groups, also promotes a dialogue of reconciliation. Similarly, individuals such as Revd Ken Newell, a Presbyterian minister at Fitzroy Church in Belfast and current Moderator of the Presbyterian Church, actively promote ecumenism and political reconciliation. They regularly run events in conjunction with Clonard monastery. However, despite high levels of social and political activism, this strain of 'inclusive evangelicalism' does not have significant party political representation in Northern Ireland. Although its influence appears to have grown in recent years, as yet it does not characterize the predominant political attitudes within wider Northern Irish evangelicalism.

In light of this, it is inaccurate to assume that strong theological commitment to evangelical Protestantism leads to political oppositionalism. Even non-negotiable belief in the Protestant faith does not necessarily produce anti-Catholicism in social relationships. Tim, a Church of Ireland minister from Co. Down, makes clear distinctions between personal faith and 'Protestantism' in its Northern Ireland context. Tim has been influenced by his time spent in theological college in the south of Ireland, and he contrasts Protestant/Catholic relationships there very starkly with those in the north. In the south he says there is trust, no sense of threat and a spirit of accommodation; in the north he says there is no trust, a need to defend one's own, a fear of 'giving in' and a sense of hurt. As he says, 'Having lived in Dublin for three years, I relate to Catholics differently, because the Catholics in the south relate to Protestants differently than Catholics relate to Protestants in the north.' This captures well a sense of reflexive self-identity – how one's ideas are socially constructed in negotiation with others. Other people's ideas about what I am like and how they treat me feeds back into my sense of who I am. Tim's self-presentation is one of a 'moderate', a 'bridge-builder' who is opposed to 'hardliners' on all sides. Furthermore, he presents his experience of Catholicism outside of Northern Ireland as the impetus for his openness. His narrative on Catholicism is couched in terms of liberalization after Vatican Two, 'progressive Catholics' and his experiences of cooperation.

Whilst Tim says that his Church 'has its truth which we believe is the truth', he says he does not judge other people for believing differently. He says he will try to pass on what he thinks is the truth, but at the end of the day does not condemn anyone for believing otherwise. What we see in Tim's narrative is strong faith, but which is held in such a way that it does not preclude relationships with people whose beliefs differ. He focuses on God's love, lack of judgement, equality, support, welcoming and sharing experiences. He has concluded from his time in the south that there is nothing inherently persecuting about Catholicism, and he tries to find a wide centre ground where he can meet with Catholic moderates in the north, despite the context of mistrust. Politically too, themes of moving beyond the past, giving and taking on all sides predominates.

It is unclear why these different articulations of evangelical faith, and their political applications, differ. Does a theological emphasis on God's love come before more inclusive social relationships, or do positive social experiences and feelings of political security allow one space to focus on God's love rather than on God's judgement? Similarly, does a religious preoccupation with the attempted corruption of purity of faith come before and inform political fears, or do negative social and political experiences (real or perceived) incline one to give these a theological interpretation? Whilst causality is unclear, however, it can be argued that there is a two-way relationship between theological emphases within Protestantism, and social and political analyses, and that both spheres inform one other. Strong religious beliefs need not lead to damaged social and political relationships with Catholics.

Rather, it depends on how theological differences are framed, and on a person's experiences and interpretations of the social world.

Catholic theology and politics

In contrast to Protestantism, there is very little relationship between Catholic theology and political attitudes in Northern Ireland. Indeed, as Weber (1958), champion of the causality of religious ideas, pointed out, Catholicism cannot be measured by the same kind of religious ethic as Calvinist Protestantism. The role of priests as intermediaries and the logic of confession release the existential pressure on the individual to justify their own beliefs and actions. Thus, Catholicism may be better assessed in terms of ritual and institutional dimensions, and by the relationship between its communal ethos and ethics. Similarly, Inglis (1998) argues that salvation can be achieved in Catholicism by adhering to the rules and regulations of the Church, through good works and through the miracle of grace. The role of the Church in interpreting what constitutes good and bad conduct is of central importance. Inglis (1998, p. 23) believes that this removes the 'necessity of developing an individual pattern of life based on ethical principles'. In recent times Inglis argues that Irish Catholics are putting more emphasis on individually principled ethics than ever before and are moving to a more 'Protestantized' faith. However, he maintains that adherence to the rules and regulations of the Catholic Church, alongside some willingness to break these rules, remains the dominant form of religious behaviour.

This historical orientation of Irish Catholicism away from individual interpretation of doctrine has important implications for the relationship between religion and politics in Northern Ireland. It has meant that theological intricacies are not something that most Catholics spend a lot of time agonizing about. This of course is not to say that theology is irrelevant to Catholics; doctrine matters deeply to a wide variety of Catholic individuals. But doctrine does not play a role in the explanation of personal and social relationships for Catholics to anywhere near the same degree it does for many evangelical Protestants. In the course of this research, no Catholic interviewees ever mentioned theology or alluded to specific religious teachings when discussing what their faith meant to them. Only once did an interviewee refer to Protestants as 'heathens' and this was entirely devoid of theological content. This was in direct contrast to the dominant narrative of religious community that was continually brought up by Catholic individuals.

There is discussion of victimhood and sacrifice in the previous chapter, and these concepts have theological underpinnings. However, these reflect more closely the imagery, liturgy and practices of Catholicism than they do doctrinal debates. Anti-Protestantism, also discussed in the previous chapter, is the antithesis of theological interpretations of society and politics. In short, whilst every religion is underpinned by a certain belief system, it does not necessarily follow that these specific beliefs inform social and political attitudes. In Northern Ireland, application of theology to politics is simply not a primary way in which Catholics understand their place in the world. This is due to the specificities of Catholicism as a ritualistic religion as well as the way it has developed in the context of the Northern Ireland conflict.

Conclusion

There is a long-standing historical relationship between theology and politics in Northern Ireland. This is particularly pronounced amongst Protestants who for a long time occupied a position of uneasy dominance in society. Theological reassurance was sought by many Protestants to help explain and understand their uncertain settler status. A Protestant world image developed which soon began to shape their political desires and interests. It is important to remember that theology and doctrine are not simply used instrumentally by individuals because they want to retain power and a superior identity. Theology is not just a thin veneer masking underlying Protestant desires to oppress nationalists. An instrumentalist conceptualization does not capture the ways in which religion is used from the bottom up by people trying to make sense of their place in the world. As Flanagan (2000, p. 234) points out, sociology must 'seek a theology to resolve the limits of understanding faced in dealing with issues of identity, and the self in a culture of postmodernity'. Flanagan is saying that people grappling with existential questions, constructing their identities and searching for meaning in the social world often find answers in religious beliefs. This is very different from arguing that Northern Ireland Protestants are stuck in the past, following battle lines drawn in the Reformation, where backward theological views render them unable to adapt to a new political context.

Neither is theology simply a divinely inspired total world-view that governs all action. Theologies must always be seen as constructed in particular times, places and historical contexts. They reflect as well as help create political ideas and behaviours. So there is not linear causality from strong religious beliefs to specific political attitudes as is often assumed. Individuals mediate theological beliefs through their own experiences. In Northern Ireland some evangelicals remain committed to strong religious beliefs but have peacemaking social and political attitudes with regard to relationships with Catholics and ideas about union with Britain (Ganiel, 2002). Just as the religious dimensions of identity, community building and ideology respond to individuals' experiences in life and of politics, so too, interpretations of theology are works in progress. Evangelicals in Northern Ireland use theology to understand politics, and politics to understand theology, in order to help them make sense of their position in the world.

For Catholics, the theological dimensions of politics are much weaker. This is because of the ritual, liturgical and sacramental emphases within Catholicism, as opposed to Protestantism, which concentrates on individual interpretation of Scripture. There is much more familiarity with theology amongst the Protestant laity than amongst the Catholic laity. For these reasons it is unsurprising that doctrine matters little to political attitudes for Catholics in Northern Ireland.

In sum, theology is sometimes politically salient in Northern Ireland, mainly for evangelical Protestants. Conservative evangelicalism is often associated with anti-Catholicism, and religious beliefs about the end times can help form interpretations of the political situation for Protestants in particular and society in general. Occasionally, but probably not very frequently, these theological beliefs have spilled over into physical violence. More often, they complicate social contact between evangelical Protestant and Catholic individuals who are each aware how ideas about salvation and damnation may impact upon the relationships between them – with evangelical Protestants feeling they must speak the truth about their beliefs in order to offer salvation, and Catholics feeling aggrieved that they are considered to be sinners. In other cases, evangelical Protestantism is framed in such a way that it implies forgiveness and reconciliation in society. In both situations, theology and politics are mutually conditioning. Each informs the other in a complex two-way relationship.

8
Conclusions

Religion, identity and community

This book has explored the ways in which religion gives substantive meaning and content to the communal boundary in Northern Ireland. The argument here challenges previous approaches to religion and politics in Northern Ireland, where an academic consensus had begun to hang around the idea that religion is an ethnic marker that is relatively insignificant in and of itself. However, this research has shown that religion is, in part, constitutive of ethnicity. Far from being an empty marker, it gives meaning to Protestant and Catholic labels. Religion is part of what is signified, rather than just the signifier. Whilst conflict in Northern Ireland has not been about religion *per se*, religion has given meaning to the overall system of community relationships and to politics. Of course, it is inaccurate to say that these meanings are theological – although sometimes they are – but rather that religious ideas, structures, social practices, powerful agencies and morality, fuse with other dimensions of difference in constructing the meaning of communal identity and membership. Moreover, religious ideas and practices overlap and interact with other differences such as ethnicity, nationalism and inequality. In a context of conflict, together these dimensions have come to constitute communal identities. In this way, religion gives meaning to identity and community just as much as, if not more so than, other dimensions of social difference.

In any case, it is problematic to talk of 'empty' markers. It is rare that something that provides such a dominant communal label would not also have some substantive content to accompany it. Imagine, for example, that the primary ethnic marker in Northern Ireland was relatively superficial, for example, having ginger hair or not. If this were the case, we would all associate various meanings with ginger hair, perhaps as more powerful or ruthless. However, just because ginger hair might demarcate a wealthy and powerful social group, this does not necessarily mean that their hair colour lies behind their ideas or informs their behaviour. On the other hand, if having ginger hair were accompanied by ritual practices, symbols and beliefs, even if not all people with ginger hair subscribed fully to these, gingerness would begin to be more meaningful. Even if ginger hair was an arbitrary distinction in the first place, it is likely that certain beliefs and rituals would emerge over time to support it. It is very clear that religion does entail these kinds of institutions, practices, symbols, moral evaluations and beliefs in Northern Ireland. The question then, is not one of *whether* religion has meaning, but rather one of *what meanings* and *for whom*.

However, previous studies of religion in Northern Ireland that asked what meanings and for whom had a rather narrow focus in that they honed in on just one dimension of religion, such as theology or the churches as powerful actors. This leads to the common misconception that religion is only politically important for 'ultra' Protestants and the Catholic Church. Whilst it may be true that religion is more important for these groups, this focus ignores everybody else. Using a multi-layered characterization of religion is necessary in order to reframe the debate. In order to understand the relationship between religion and politics, it is necessary to refrain from stamping any essential definition upon it from the outset. Rather, religion must be seen as important to people in a range of different ways, and as playing a variety of roles in social and political relationships. However, for the purposes of the current research, religion in Northern Ireland is also characterized as related to institutions, practices and ideas that are recognizably Christian rather than just anything that gives meaning to life. This approach enables us to capture a much wider spectrum of ways in which religion has given meaning to conflict. Moreover, by not reducing religion to theology, or power, or boundary marking (and indeed acknowledging the relationships between these), differences in Catholicism and Protestantism as religions can be tackled better analytically. It also allows for better theorization of differences within each community.

Placing this conception of religion in the specific context of communal relationships in Northern Ireland is vital. In such a way we see that the salience of religion cannot be assessed simply in terms of church attendance, beliefs in the afterlife or Christian doctrines in the constitution. Protestantism and Catholicism have communal meanings that do not depend simply on levels of individual religiosity. These meanings are often as concerned with ideas of community, power and the other, as they are concerned with ideas of God. Frequently, these ideas are so entangled with one another, that it is difficult to tell where the social stops and the spiritual starts.

Of course, different people relate to religion, and use it to understand politics, in different ways. Similarly, they respond to the relationships between religious and political organizations differently. Previous chapters outlined five different ways in which religion and communal identities interact: through powerful agencies, through boundary marking, through ritual practices, through ideology and through theology. Although religion constitutes a relatively empty identity marker for some, as discussed in Chapter 4, this is not the dominant trend. More usually, religion provides substantive content to identity and community amongst many who do not go to church and even for some who do not regard themselves as religious.

For the still large number of churchgoing Catholics, ritual and religious practice reinforce a sense of communal belonging and enhance physical as well as cognitive separation between groups. Many nonchurchgoing Catholics understand that Church structures are still needed to be a full member of the community and thus retain a degree of contact with the Church. Whilst they may be 'cafeteria Catholics', picking and choosing which aspects of Church teaching are most meaningful for them, none the less, masses, priests and sacraments continue to be involved in the transmission of communal identity. This relationship is partly organic, as Catholics have looked to the Church for alternative forms of social organization and representation in an otherwise hostile political situation. It is also attributable to dynamics of power relationships in the region, as the British government has historically tried to promote the Catholic Church to maintain stability in Northern Ireland, and as the

Church has sought to promote its own strength through control of education and provision of structures to social life (Fulton, 1991). In this context it is hardly surprising that religion occupies such an important place in the habitus of Catholics in Northern Ireland.

For many Protestants, it is more likely to be religiously informed concepts and ideas, rather than separate religious practices, which help construct categorizations of self and other. This holds even for many Protestants who are no longer religiously active nor have a strong faith. Whilst many of these Protestants are invisible in conventional measures of religiosity, the concepts they use to understand social life are not just morally, but also pseudo-theologically, charged. Again, it is unsurprising that religion has become entangled with wider communal identifications in these ways when we consider the historical context of a dominant yet embattled Protestant group in a small state that most Catholics deemed illegitimate. Religious difference became intrinsically connected to other inequalities in political, economic and cultural power. Religious interpretations of siege and justifications of defiance by some Protestant clergy and organizations like the Orange Order are pervasive and are transmitted to a constituency much broader than the religiously devout (Bruce, 1994). This is because these interpretations have often made sense of structural conditions. Indeed, it is difficult to transcend these religious ideas when they continue to make sense of many Protestants' situation in Northern Ireland. For others again, theological conviction and doctrine provide a further layer of cultural information, this time with a sacred stamp of authority, that can be used to establish and evaluate one's place *vis-à-vis* other social groups. In these ways, religion is an essential part of the identification process in Northern Ireland and it is at least as much about the social, as it is about the spiritual.

The scope of religion in everyday life

A central question must be whether there is anything in particular about religion that makes it more important than other cultural differences. If the answer is negative, then we might postulate that religion is merely one of a number of differences that divide communities in Northern Ireland. The reason it is an important dimension of difference in the present may simply be down to historical experience and cultural context. It could be substituted with any other difference, such as nationalism or ethnic identity, and communities would be just as divided. If this was the case, then conflict could persist centuries into the future without necessarily having any religious basis.

However, this is not the case. Of course there is nothing intrinsic about religious differences that *cause* conflict. People of different religions coexist quite peacefully in many countries around the world. However, because conflict *has* developed in Northern Ireland, and because religion *has* historically played a role in that conflict, it has now taken on a special social and political significance. Religion is different from other cultural differences because it contains supernatural, moral and ritual elements that lift it above the rest. Whilst nationalism and ethnicity matter deeply to people in Northern Ireland, and they have some accompanying rituals, moral evaluations and creeds, they do not make such a wide appeal to the sacred nor offer extensive otherworldly answers to people's psychological needs. Nor do nationalism and ethnicity provide a regular meeting place or forum for community building like religion does. Thus, nationalism or ethnicity alone might be seen as somewhat weaker dimensions of difference in everyday life than religion.

A good, if necessarily simplistic, way of thinking about the causes of conflict in Northern Ireland, is hypothetically to eliminate the factor at hand and then reimagine the situation asking if conflict would still be likely. Thus if one feels that the root of conflict is economic deprivation and poverty, then imagine that everybody in Northern Ireland was given employment and a decent wage. Given that deep cultural, national and political inequalities would still exist, it is unlikely that conflict would disappear. Although the amelioration of poverty would make a huge contribution in easing the situation and reducing incentives to participate in paramilitary activities, it is likely that social divisions would persist. Based on this, we may conclude that whilst deprivation certainly contributes to conflict, it is not the essence of what conflict is about. The same exercise can be performed with the border question solved: British and Irish passports replaced by an undifferentiated European citizenship, mathematical equality implemented in all aspects of employment and so on. The fact is that removing any of these divisive elements entirely would reduce, but not eradicate, communal conflict. Whilst each may play an integral role in propping up the communal division, none of these factors may be seen as the essential underlying cause of discord. This is not a question of what caused conflict 400 years ago or 35 years ago. We could certainly say that if x, y or z had never happened, then Northern Ireland would not have had the type of conflict that it did have. However, the question is one of what conflict is about now, what it has become over many years of divisions and what causes it to be reproduced every day.

So, what would happen if we pulled the religious rug out from under the feet of social relationships? It would entail many changes. Neither community would have the church as a weekly meeting place. It is difficult to think what other organization could provide a forum to facilitate regular contact for such a wide spectrum of the population. Schooling would also not be segregated along religious lines and would have no clerical input. This would make an enormous difference, as it is harder to imagine how children could be divided up by other criteria. Would children whose parents have British passports go to one school, and those whose parents have Irish passports go to another? Could parallel education systems be run by different states? What would have happened in the 1960s where only two out of five Protestants identified as British? In addition to these practicalities, we would need to remove the psychological and emotional supports that religion gives to a community in conflict. Any hints of divine justification or sacred legitimization of the political situation would have to go. Thus, people would need to explain their actions, rationalize their feelings and comfort themselves by some other means. Some have suggested that nationalism can provide such legitimations. However, would a more entrenched ethnic identity, or stronger cultural traditions, be able to perform these roles as well as religion?

At the very least, we must conclude that if religion in Northern Ireland disappeared tomorrow the situation would be very different indeed. Each community would be stripped of a major regular meeting place, of religion's capacity to explain and justify their situation in otherworldly terms and, especially in the case of Catholics, of the institutional anchor of their education system and key agency for the transmission of communal identity. Protestants would be left with an ambiguous sense of Britishness that could not be fortified by religious ideas or symbolism. Of course, social and political conflict in Northern Ireland would continue to exist if these factors were removed. Questions of territory and inequality would remain in place. But would divisions be sustained so easily in the future without the input of religion?

The fact is that there is something about religion that makes it different from other cultural differences. This is its penetration of everyday life. As argued in Chapter 1, human beings are naturally predisposed to sort social life into categories, to make comparisons between us and them, and to operate on a principle of difference from others. However, some of these differences are more salient than others. The most significant differences are the ones that affect our daily lives. They are the differences that are most deeply entrenched in social and political structures as well as in people's everyday practices.

A good example of a very obvious difference that deeply penetrates everyday life is language. In Canada or Belgium, for example, people carry out their daily activities and are most familiar with cultural resources in their own language. For those who cannot speak the language of their co-nationals, this difference is extremely pressing because they cannot actually communicate with others. Although human constructions, language differences are socially very real. Another socially constructed difference is race. Whilst there is nothing intrinsic about skin colour that means people are actually *different*, skin colour has acted as an important code of one's social position and relationship to power. It is a visible difference that has made it easy to identify in-groups and out-groups in certain contexts. Of course neither language nor race *cause* social conflict in and of themselves; however, where there are disjointed power relations, language and race are audible and visible bases on which to make social distinctions.

People in Northern Ireland, however, lack any physically obvious divisors. And it is in the absence of deeply entrenched linguistic or racial differences that religion has become so socially significant. This is because unlike economic position or national identity, religion reaches into more areas of life. It encompasses a wider spectrum of the population than any other difference; it comes with powerful institutions such as churches and other religious organizations that attempt to spread their influence; and it provides a forum for regular social practices and also helps organize other social activities around the churches. Religion provides a rich source of symbolism, ideology and moral evaluations, and it offers a variety of supernatural explanations and theological reassurances about social and political events. No other dimension of difference in Northern Ireland has such a wide scope. For the most devout, religion may be important in all of these ways. How important these various aspects of religion are for everybody else depends largely on whether they are a Protestant or a Catholic, churchgoer or nonchurchgoer, believer or nonbeliever. But even if one does not attend church or believe in God, it is likely that religion still reaches into many areas of everyday life. Very often, where it appears on the surface that religion simply marks out a deeper ethnic difference, it is in fact playing some of these extra roles.

Religion, politics and conflict

The discussion thus far has concentrated on the relationship between religion, community and identity. This can be categorized as politics with a small 'p'. In other words, religion is highly influential at the level of stereotypes and relationships that reproduce conflict in everyday life. What then of the relationship between religion and politics with a capital 'p'? We can answer this question at the level of political culture and also of political parties and institutions.

First, on political parties at an organizational level. Whilst in Northern Ireland most political parties do not have an overtly religious ethos or membership (with the notable exception of the DUP – although this too is changing), no major political party operates without a certain degree of cooperation from the churches. It is not that churches dictate party policy, but rather that they work together with political parties in fostering a sense of mainstream Catholic or Protestant opinion. As we saw in Chapter 3, both political parties and churches benefit from this mutual relationship. Parties gain legitimization and churches gain influence. Only rarely do churches and parties break ranks with one another.

Churches are involved in politics in a wide variety of other ways. They are often included in processes of political consultation and negotiation and sometimes act as intermediaries between states, politicians and paramilitaries. Their influence is not usually one of critical policy input, but it is important in so far as they are perceived as respectable representatives of their community. The churches' participation in political life gives them a significant degree of social influence and is thus self-perpetuating. Not only do they have the ear of the powerful, but they are interpreters and mediators of community experience. This influence is further reinforced by the large number of roles that the churches play in the organization of social life. Their reach extends from education in the case of the Catholic Church, through to a range of economic initiatives, social provision and cultural activities.

In these ways, religion is politically important from the top down in Northern Ireland as well as from the bottom up. Of course, this does not mean that the churches are successfully spreading ideological monopolies across Northern Ireland. There is much popular dissent from both traditional Catholic and Protestant religious teachings. The official separation between churches and the state is well established. Moreover, many figures within political parties are anxious to distance themselves from religious ideas and institutions. Churches have tended not to support radical republican or loyalist political movements. Added to this is the fact that some of the churches are undergoing their own crises and internal challenges to their authority and cannot claim to have as a far a reach as they did in the past. But despite all these caveats, it is none the less clear that there is a two-way, and mutually beneficial, relationship between the churches and politics.

It is therefore unsurprising that religion plays such an important role in political culture as well as in political structure. Again, what is politically important is not theology or practice *per se*, but how these have been used to construct and give meaning to political culture. This has heavily influenced the language and concepts used by political elites as well as community members. One important set of concepts is the opposition between communalism versus individualism. We have outlined the ways in which Protestant ideas of liberty and individualism, and Catholic ideas of community, have been politically significant. Moreover, we have demonstrated the ways in which Protestant individualism and Catholic communalism have been constructed *vis-à-vis* each other. These concepts have influenced Protestants' and Catholics' different understandings and expectations of certain political policies and processes.

That is not to say that these concepts represent Catholic and Protestant experiences accurately, but that in a specific context of conflict, they have formed part of people's self-understandings and ideas of the other. Each community trades in stereotypes and often has an apprehension of the other. Sometimes, people have a begrudging respect for difference. In fact, many Protestants look across the boundary and almost envy the way in which they perceive the Catholic community to be more united than them. This often leads to an over-estimation of Catholic unity, alongside fears of what this strong, highly organized 'unit' can achieve, and fears about the role of the Catholic Church within this. However, many Protestants perceive authoritarianism behind this 'unity', and believe that Catholics are unduly controlled by their Church, afraid of their religious leaders and unquestioning of rules. So too, many Catholics are both repelled and sometimes a little attracted by Protestantism. What some admire is that Protestants seem to take their faith more seriously – where it is practised, they perceive this to be not out of habit, but out of conviction. Many compare this to Catholicism, which they portray as less demanding. However, the line between sincerity and austerity is fuzzy, and a great number of Catholics associate Protestantism with being uptight, unbending, unwilling to compromise. These ideas are embedded in political culture in Northern Ireland.

This is because religiously informed ideas have been used to make sense of, and cope with, political and structural conditions. The content of Protestant and Catholic religious traditions have been applied, in varying degrees, to a context of conflict. In such a way, the insecurity of Protestant settlement was imbued with religious notions of siege and contractual loyalty. Many Catholics gave meaning to social and economic consequences of invasion through religious ideas of suffering and victimhood. The role of the Catholic Church was enhanced by experiences of struggle as a faith community, as it built alternative social structures to British and Protestant power, and provided resources for identification. This helps explain why the Irish state after independence took on a very Catholic ethos. In this context, Protestant fears of going under politically as a community were infused with religious ideas of freedom and individualism versus a seemingly authoritarian Catholicism. So, we see a two-way relationship between religious content and political culture and structure.

However, conflict in Northern Ireland has undergone periods of low and high intensity. A striking feature of communal identities is that they are not essential and they are not static. They can change in emphasis and can reconstruct in relation to structural conditions, in turn influencing possibilities for structural change. In this way, the role of religion in communal identity and political culture can simmer, surface and sometimes recede from view. In times of high-intensity conflict or political insecurity, the religious dimensions of identification may be strengthened. At crisis points, they may be thrust to the forefront of communal understandings, such as some Catholics' ideas of sacrifice during the hunger strikes, or some Protestants' ideas of religious siege after the 1998 Agreement. On the other hand, in periods of low-intensity conflict, or when a community perceives it is doing well politically, the religious components of communal identity may become more secondary, such as many Catholics' narratives of victimhood in the early 2000s. Moreover, it is not just structural relationships within Northern Ireland that impact on the religious dimensions of communal identity, but also wider processes of social change and regional and international politics. An example is the toning-down of religious language and imagery of contemporary Protestant politics in order to appear more socially acceptable on the international stage and in the media. Religion then does not simply *cause* social and political attitudes; it is both responsive to, and constitutive of, politics.

Future prospects

Religion continues to play a variety of roles in civil society and politics in Northern Ireland. However, we must ask in a period of accelerated social change, what roles might religion play in the future in Northern Ireland. It might be that religion becomes less important, as a result of slow processes of secularization and individualization. In the present, many people are 'believing without belonging' (Davie, 1994) and belonging without believing, but one might ask how long this might continue with declining institutional support on one hand, and changing ideological reference points on the other. Secularization has not yet made a huge impact on current communal relationships in Northern Ireland because most people have been socialized into some form of religious belief and activity. However, future generations who have been raised in a society that is more publicly secular than before may use religious ideas and practices less often to give meaning to social and political relationships. It may also be that the prognosis for the continuing social significance of Catholicism and Protestantism is somewhat different.

First, the institutional power and moral authority of the Catholic Church is waning. This is due to an increased questioning in Irish and Northern Irish society in general as well as to the specific problems that the Church encountered in relation to their handling of cases of child abuse since the 1990s. This has of course impacted upon Catholics in Northern Ireland, amongst whom distrust of religious institutions has grown in recent years. The Church now must compete more convincingly with other agencies that seek to speak up for and represent the community. It also faces internal restructuring. An acute manpower crisis (Inglis, 1998) means that it must respond to internal calls for greater democratization of religious life from the laity. As Casanova suggests (1994), the role of modern churches is often to fill the gaps left by secular society by articulating a message of alternative morality in order to maintain their public significance. Whilst this may be the case with the Catholic

Church in Northern Ireland, it is more difficult to see how this role would prop up the politics of conflict as was the case in the past. The Church may agitate in a less partisan fashion for the 'good of society' rather than simply the Catholic grouping within it. Moreover, as nationalism becomes more integrated in the structure of Northern Ireland, the Church is beginning to cater less for a community in conflict. It no longer needs to play the political roles it was called upon for during civil rights or the hunger strikes. Although, of course, events like the Holy Cross School protests contradict this trend, overall the Church's brief is changing.

As well as facing institutional change, Catholics in Northern Ireland are also in the process of substantial behavioural change. Rates of religious practice, whilst extremely high overall, are declining amongst the young. This may mean that religion will play less of a community-building role in the future amongst Catholics. Churches may be less likely to form the basis of shared experience. It might also mean that there would be a decline not just in the religious dimensions of community but also, as indicated by Putnam (2000), less experience of community full stop. At the present time there are no institutions or practices comparable with the Church in terms of organizing shared rituals or practices. Cultural and voluntary associations, and rituals surrounding sporting activities, come nowhere near the Church in their ability to unite in practice the entire spectrum of the community. As less people enact the same religious rituals every week, community membership may become more imagined than practised.

Religiously derived ideas have traditionally provided an idiom of identity through which many Catholics have come to see themselves and relate to Protestants in Northern Ireland. These ideas have been politically salient because they have made sense of social and structural conditions for many Catholics, at least up until the present. Ideas of victimhood helped identify and evaluate the Protestant victimizer whilst providing some form of consolation for suffering. So too, religiously informed ideas of sacrifice helped some put the hunger strikes into perspective. However, these explanations are clearly not required of religion by social groups in more fortunate positions in society. As Weber suggests, when we occupy different social positions we have different types of ideal interests and existential questions, and consequently, we call upon religion to play quite different roles. Inglis (1998) suggests that this is what is happening amongst Catholics in the Republic of Ireland. As the laity move from rural farming to urban professional-class backgrounds, their religious interests move from demand for compensation to demand for symbolic legitimation. So too Catholics in Northern Ireland have entered the middle classes *en masse*; they are becoming ever more integrated into social and economic structures, and, although many republican political goals are still far from being achieved, there is a sense in which Catholics are beginning to see themselves as equals in society, not as victims (Mitchell, 2003b). As such, religious ideas of rewards for suffering are less likely to have explanatory power for Catholics in contemporary Northern Ireland. Other, more secular, narratives may be used to imagine symbolically the community, and community relationships, as time goes on.

This, however, represents the pessimistic version of the future of Catholicism in Northern Ireland (or the optimistic version if one wishes religion to disappear). It is deeply misleading to leave it at that. It is in fact highly likely that Catholicism will continue to play important public as well as private roles for the foreseeable future. First, at an institutional level the Catholic Church, despite all its problems, remains the most significant communal organizer. Nearly four out of five Catholics still state that they have some degree of confidence in the Church, and overall rates of religious practice remain very high comparatively speaking (Fahey et al., 2004). The Church continues to monopolize the Catholic market in the education system. Although there is a majority of lay teachers in the Catholic Maintained Schools, clerics continue to be influential at management level and Catholic symbolism and ritual continue to form an integral part of school life. Similarly, the Church remains involved in a wide variety of other areas of social and cultural life – its personnel and resources are pumped into community welfare and development schemes throughout Northern Ireland. Priests continue in some ways to be gatekeepers of the community. This is evidenced whenever political crises erupt. In times of stress, clergy often assume the mantle of the people's representative and protector and they often try to provide guidance. Once again, Holy Cross provides a striking example. As low-level conflict persists in Northern Ireland and community relationships continue to be strained, there is still a role for the Church in these types of political mediations – albeit now a part-time job.

Furthermore, Catholicism maintains public significance where it intersects with ethnicity. Concepts such as the habitus help us appreciate the ways in which religion can give meaning to ethnicity. This can be done in both practical and imagined ways. Group formation and boundary maintenance are a universal part of social relationships. These are integrally human processes and are at work in peacefully pluralist, never mind deeply divided, societies. It is highly unlikely that the Catholic/Protestant boundary in Northern Ireland will be replaced by something more secular in the near future, despite attempts to cast the conflict as a purely political one. Often through marking out boundaries, religion actively helps constitute what it means to belong to a particular community. It gives meanings and values to the boundary. In this sense the religious, and indeed moral, dimensions of group belonging would seem set to continue. They are deeply embedded in the habitus of Northern Ireland Catholics.

The situation is rather different for Protestants in Northern Ireland. Protestant church attendance has not decreased very much over time. In the present there may even be a growing conservatism within Protestantism and, strikingly, within young Protestantism. Evangelicals are not shrinking as a social group and do not appear to be liberalizing morally or politically (Mitchell and Tilley, 2004). The DUP are currently growing rather than declining in strength. Although they have dropped some religious issues such as Sabbatarianism from the political agenda, they remain resolutely committed to other conservative moral principles such as opposition to homosexuality and abortion. In such ways a sizeable minority of Protestants in Northern Ireland remains religiously committed.

On the other hand, Protestants are more likely than Catholics to move over time to a position of having no religion. Whilst attendance at evangelical Protestant denominations may be growing slightly, attendance at mainstream Protestant denominations is decreasing, which means that there is no overall growth in rates of Protestant church attendance. Overall, the Protestant churches remain as disunited as ever. In this sense, there is no prospect of overarching religious unity ever fusing a wider Protestant community together. Moreover, the declining membership of the Orange Order, alongside the growing ambiguity over its actual religiosity, means that Protestant identity in a religious sense is less practised than ever before.

Despite the lack of significance of religious rituals amongst the wider Protestant community, this was never the primary way in which religion has been socially or politically important for this group. Instead, religious beliefs and ideas have been more socially and politically salient. For some Protestants, religion itself continues to be prioritized as a political issue. In some cases, there is a strengthening of specifically religious purity, righteousness and salvation – in part at least in response to a pessimistic political diagnosis. This can be accompanied by apocalyptic predictions of the end times, which the Good Friday Agreement is sometimes thought to signify. In such instances, religious beliefs may be strengthened by political developments, as each subsequent turn of events is seen to fulfil religious prophecy. It should be noted of course that other groups of Protestants have reached positive, or benign, conclusions about political change and religious beliefs inform desires for political reconciliation.

Because religious beliefs amongst many Protestants continue to be strong and politically relevant, it is unsurprising that religious ideas and symbols continue to be important in the imagination of Protestant identity. Concepts of Protestant freedom, honesty, religious siege and anti-Catholicism still permeate the language and values of many Protestants, even amongst those who do not go to church or see themselves as religious. Whilst not specifically referring to theology or doctrine, Protestant ideology continues to help people make sense of social relationships in Northern Ireland. Protestant ideology retains strong explanatory power, particularly when it overlaps with other cultural, political and economic issues. This is especially the case when viewed in the context of the Good Friday Agreement and subsequent political changes that have been received negatively by many Protestants. For many people, oppositional religious ideas compose a discourse of morality, rather than being concerned with theology.

Of course, Protestant ideology unsupported by at least some religious familiarity may become increasingly diluted. Without religious reference points it might become thin to the point of no longer constituting a religious ideology. Familiarity is gained through going to church, Sunday School and receiving religious education in state schools. It is also gained by hearing religious concepts discussed in the media and in the home. Religious ideas are strewn through unionist, and particularly loyalist, discourse. They are found on gable walls, marching banners and signs pinned to trees. These images and discourses are often translated for ordinary Protestants through religious spokespeople who explain the political significance of various religious concepts. But whilst familiarity was very pronounced in the past, it might be less so in the future. Certainly evangelicalism remains strong and persistently uses these religious concepts, but other Protestants may not be as influenced by evangelicalism as their predecessors. If the gap widens between evangelicals on one hand, and mainline Protestants on the other, religious ideology may well become a less influential dimension of religious significance in Northern Ireland. For the meantime, though, this disengagement has not happened.

Evangelicalism continues to be an influential subgroup within the Protestant community and still provides a rich repository of ideas and symbols of Protestant identity.

It is much too hasty to predict that religion will lose its relevance as a dimension of difference in Northern Ireland. The religious dimensions of identity and community are of course contextual. Certainly, we get a sense of its capacity to change and evolve, to simmer and sometimes recede from view. But we also see its tendency to burst forth into communal and political consciousness in times when politics is not working. Extra structural and symbolic roles are demanded of religion in times of crisis and uncertainty. The current social and political significance of Protestant ideas of freedom and Catholic authoritarianism may be strongly related to the fast-changing and uncertain political climate. As so many Protestants perceive the Good Friday Agreement as entailing loss for their community, we might expect that more oppositional formulations of identity, along with moral and religious explanations of change, to emerge. Should Protestants' interpretation of the political situation become more positive, then we might expect identifications to reconstruct accordingly.

Similarly, should the conflict wane considerably, it may well be that Catholicism recedes into a more private sphere, concerned with spirituality and the inner lives of its members. Whilst, as Casanova suggests (1994), the Church may continue to articulate alternative conceptions of morality in the public sphere, its current widespread institutional and ideological contributions to political life may fade away. On the other hand, should conflict persist even at this lower level (which seems most likely), Catholicism and indeed Protestantism will probably continue to play many of the social and political roles outlined above. In such a way, we are able to conceive of religion, not just as something that causes political attitudes, but also as something that responds to politics. What roles Catholicism and Protestantism will play in the future in Northern Ireland then depends as much on politicians and community relationships as it does on the laity and their religious leaders.

The point is that although religions often claim the unchanging nature of their traditions, beliefs and spiritual vision, we must look beyond this and recognize also their capacity for movement. We must recognize that individuals and communities often go through religious journeys, where beliefs and practices can deepen, loosen and change. Generally, we can find at least partial explanations for these changes in the context of people's experiences of the here and now. Social and political context plays an important role in the ongoing construction of religious identity. Moreover, political changes can make room for religious changes, as well as vice versa. Whether this will lead to an increase or decrease in oppositional religious identities in Northern Ireland depends on the nature of political change.

Glossary of terms

Born-again   This describes the evangelical belief that an individual must have a personal relationship with Jesus Christ. This happens where an individual confesses that they are a sinner and receives forgiveness from Christ. Evangelicals believe that this is the only route to heaven. Also known as being 'saved'.

Civil religion   Where societies attach sacred qualities to their own rituals and institutions without making reference to the supernatural. Popular examples might include Americanism, or royalism in Britain.

Communal conflict   Characterization of the conflict in Northern Ireland as multi-levelled, encompassing a variety of overlapping differences such as nationalism and religion.

Community   Feelings of belonging to a certain social group that may be based on region, class or religion amongst other things. Communities can be local and small-scale where individuals have face-to-face contact with one another, or they may be regional large-scale groups where belonging is more imagined. Individuals can belong to more than one community.

Constructionism (or constructivism)   Refers to theories that stress the socially created nature of social life. It emphasizes how individuals actively create meaning and invent the world, rather than taking social organization as something that is already 'out there'. It also pays close attention to the limitations of human agency by recognizing how social structures shape people's thoughts and actions.

Cultural religion   Demerath's (2000, 2001) argument that people often have a sense of belonging to a religious group but do not make reference to theology (similar to civil religion).

DUP   Democratic Unionist Party, currently the largest political party in Northern Ireland and led by Revd Dr Ian Paisley. Strong on the maintenance of the union with Britain and moral conservatism. High level of evangelical personnel and has links with the Free Presbyterian Church.

Ethnic marker   This is where something is said to act as a badge or label of ethnicity, without actually being very important in and of itself. An example is that whilst football tops mark out identity in Northern Ireland, the conflict is not about football.

Ethnonationalism   It is the dominant view that the conflict in Northern Ireland is ethnonational, that is, that two separate nations (British and Irish) want their territory to be governed by their own state.

Evangelicalism   A global, mainly Protestant, pan-denominational religious movement. Evangelicals subscribe to the core ideas that the Bible is the word of God and that individuals must have a personal relationship with God, although they may differ on other theological points.

Fundamentalism   A sub-category of evangelicalism, characterized by an opposition to liberal theology, which not all evangelicals share. In common usage, the term fundamentalism is increasingly perceived to be backward and dangerous. Whilst it is sometimes used as a proxy for evangelicalism, fundamentalism has become a broader term to describe extreme versions of any world religion (Berger 1999; Bruce, 2001).

Good Friday Agreement   Settlement reached by all the major Northern Ireland parties, including Sinn Féin and excepting the DUP, in 1998. Reinforced the right of Northern Ireland to remain in the union with Britain until voted otherwise in a referendum. Set up institutional linkages between Northern Ireland and the Republic of Ireland, and between all parts of the British Isles. Also set police and equality reform in motion. Positively received by most nationalists at the time, whilst unionists were, and remain, bitterly divided. Also known as the Belfast Agreement.

Identity   How people understand themselves. Self-understanding relates to how we compare ourselves with other people and how we think we fit into wider society. We all have many different identities, but not all are equally important in all situations.

In-group/out-group   Where individuals distinguish between them and us, often preferring those who they deem as similar to themselves.

Loyalism   A stronger form of unionism, associated with historical public banding traditions where groups of men loyal to the Queen would join together to defend their community. Has been associated with Protestant paramilitary violence; however, politically, loyalists are now broadly in favour of the Good Friday Agreement. Its adherents are more working-class than their unionist counterparts.

Nationalist   In the context of Northern Ireland, a nationalist is someone who identifies with the Republic of Ireland and would like to see Irish unity. It is sometimes used in a more generic way, as an alternative 'catch-all' term for Catholic.

The 'other'   Social groups who are viewed as different from, and perhaps threatening to, other social groups.

Religious ideology   A system of concepts about self and others, informed by religious doctrines but not concerned with the supernatural.

Republicanism   A stronger form of nationalism that aspires to setting up a socially and politically radical united Ireland. Associated politically with Sinn Féin, and militarily with the IRA.

Ritual   An often-repeated pattern of behaviour. May involve symbols, but is primarily about behaviour and actions.

Saved   Another way to describe being born-again (see above).

SDLP   Social Democratic and Labour Party. Moderate nationalist party that has traditionally represented the bulk of Catholics in Northern Ireland but has recently conceded ground to Sinn Féin. Instrumental in paving the way for the current round of the peace process.

Secularization   The process by which religious beliefs, practices and institutions lose social significance. Secularization theorists argue that this process occurs inevitably in modern societies where religion becomes private and individualistic. Critics point to the continuing social salience and growth of Islam, evangelicalism, new religious movements as well as to the persistence of spirituality.

Sinn Féin   Currently the largest nationalist/republican political party in Northern Ireland. It is also an all-Ireland party with seats in the Dáil. The party sees itself as republican and left wing. It has historically had the closest relationship with the IRA and is now pursuing political methods to achieve Irish unity and equality.

Social structure   Refers to how relationships in a society are organized. May include religious, economic, political and other institutions as well as social norms and values. Social structure helps shape individuals ideas and behaviour.

Unionist   An individual who wishes to retain the union with Britain. May also express a British identity, but with regional Northern Irish/Ulster overtones.

UUP   Ulster Unionist Party. Until recently the largest unionist grouping. In favour of maintenance of the union with Britain, stressing a British identity, it is seen as more middle class than the DUP and is presently deeply divided over attitudes to the Good Friday Agreement.

Appendix
Notes on methods

The interview data

This book is concerned with how religion influences individuals' identification processes as people give meaning to social and political relationships in contemporary Northern Ireland. The research explores how the world is interpreted, understood, experienced and (re)produced – in other words, how reality is constructed by different actors. Understanding comes from inside a social situation, by trying to work out how individuals interpret their lives and experiences. Although we are working in the context of a complex, multi-layered social world with multiple subjective meanings, these meanings very often have coherence and can be understood. The aim of the interviews was to examine the subjective meanings given to self, other and people's sense of place in Northern Ireland.

The 35 interviews conducted for my doctoral research (Mitchell, 2001) were episodic (Flick, 1998). This is a mixture of narrative and semi-structured forms of interviewing where participants are invited to narrate/recount situations, episodes or experiences. These narratives are followed up with more pointed questions, trying to draw out subjective definitions and meanings. The narrative aspect is designed to give the interviewee the freedom to develop their story without intrusion by the researcher (Wengraf, 2001). The strength of this lies in the interviewee's selection of what she or he deems important, and the lack of input by the researcher whose questions may influence or lead responses. The assumption behind this form of interviewing is that participants' experiences of a certain domain are stored and remembered both in forms of narrative-episodic and semantic knowledge. Episodic knowledge is linked to experiences and concrete situations and circumstances, whereas semantic knowledge is based on assumptions and relations that are abstracted from these and generalized (Flick, 1998). The question-and-answer part of an episodic interview was designed to explore participants' subjective definitions of their faith, what role it plays in their life and their political ideas. In all cases, the priority was to allow interviewees freedom to talk about what they wanted to talk about, and large portions of the interviews were therefore unstructured.

There are of course some limitations to this method. As with all kinds of interviewing, the episodic model has limited access to peoples' activities and interaction, and simply provides interviewees' subjective viewpoints. In these interviews, interaction and experiences with others were narrated but not observed first hand. So if we follow Hajer (1995) in arguing that meaning is made through the interaction between agents and structures, it is important to consider that these interviews concentrate simply on people's *accounts* of their interactions. However, subjective meanings constitute the social world, at least partially, and they are socially real in so far as they define the terms of how we feel and act in given social situations.

A second limitation is my own role in the production of information. Although agnostic on the religious question, and having a 'foot in both camps' with dual Irish and British citizenship, I was perceived as a Protestant in these interviews. Communal background in Northern Ireland can usually be easily worked out (Burton, 1978; Cairns, 1980), and is an unavoidable dynamic of social interaction. If asked, I made my own views known: broadly that as a young person I supported the Agreement, but that I could understand why some people have problems with aspects of it. If pushed for a party identification, I said the Women's Coalition, which many interviewees seemed to think was not overly confrontational. If asked about my religion, I told the truth, which is that although I had been brought up a Protestant, I did not attend church and considered myself to be religiously agnostic. In all cases, I tried as far as possible to see things from the individual's point of view, and to create a relaxed and open atmosphere. It is certain that judgements were made of me, and that people may have measured their words at times to adapt to their perception of the social situation. However, I feel that the rewards of this openness far outweighed its possible limitations of refusing to reveal aspects of myself that would have been inferred anyway.

There were however, some significant differences in my interviews with Catholics and Protestants. All Protestant interviewees assumed I was also a Protestant. The advantage of this was that people seemed to feel we shared the same opinions and terms of reference without my having said anything to agree or disagree. Some interviews took on an unintentional, almost conspiratorial tone, for example, one Protestant man told me, 'They haven't got rid of Sam and they haven't got rid of Claire out of the country … You see they want to ride us out, clear us out altogether. Their idea was exterminate us and get us to go. Because they say that I'm a planter and you're a planter, you were brought in here, so you're not Irish – we're British and that's it.' In some cases, I think that the assumption that we were somehow on the same side allowed for greater freedom of expression of opinions.

When interviewing Catholics, the situation was sometimes different. With some individuals my background was not discussed and I do not know what assumptions may have been made. The fact that I had been living in Dublin for six years at the time may have reduced some of the constraints of my communal background. I was often questioned about my politics. People sometimes made comments like, 'I shouldn't be saying this to you' and stopped themselves from finishing sentences they had started. People often checked that I understood terms like confirmation and other aspects of Catholic doctrine and practice. Some were quite frank and said they felt uncomfortable talking to me about some issues, and at times I felt frustrated by these barriers. Having said this, I feel that good relationships were established with most people. It was sometimes remarked to me that I was OK – for a Protestant – or that they had never met a Protestant like me.

Overall, I felt that interviews with Catholics were more difficult. Despite their unfailing friendliness and generosity, I was aware of being perceived as an outsider.

This is in itself an interesting finding of this research. Despite my Irish passport, I was surprised to realize that the research process made me feel like a reluctant Protestant community member who does not identify with the kind of politics she is supposed to, but who is almost forced by others into a (loose) communal identification, because she cannot find acceptance elsewhere, as described in Chapter 4. The research process itself also drew out the contextual dimensions of identification. It was only when forced to confront the issue, and in certain social contexts, that I remembered I was being seen as a Northern Ireland Protestant, which in turn constrained my behaviour in certain ways. As a young, mobile, agnostic, multiply-identifying woman, I was struck by these contextual constraints on my interactions.

Another methodological limitation is that these narratives were produced in a specific political, as well as relational, context. Interviews were conducted over the years 2000 and 2001, which saw many regional, and localized, crises and conflicts. These have a bearing on the types of ideas that arose, feelings expressed and even the language used. As such, these are particular, context-bound and temporary accounts of the world. However, there are also advantages to this as increased sensitivity to context allows us to explore the dynamic and fluid aspects of the identification process.

A final limitation concerns representativeness. This type of interviewing is more suitable for deep rather than wide samples. Interviews are long and open-ended, requiring trust to be established, interviewees to be as comfortable as possible, and necessitating very detailed later analysis. With the resources at hand, it was not possible to work with a large representative sample of the Northern Ireland population. Thus, a sample of 30 to 40 people altogether was aimed for. Initial contacts were made with community figures across Northern Ireland and using these leads, a snowballing technique was used to elicit further participants. In the end, 35 people were interviewed, 17 Protestants and 18 Catholics. Certain broad categories were designed, and people asked to participate usually when I had a rough idea of which category they would fit into, and little or no idea of their religious and political attitudes. Interviewees were not pre-selected, rather invited to take part on an ongoing process of snowball sampling, according to the existing balance of, for example, churchgoers and nonchurchgoers. There was also an attempt to include some deviant cases to maximize variety (Patton, 1990).

Categories designed were churchgoing, age, and geographic region. Getting a range of political views and support for parties was also an aim, but was not a criterion for inclusion. A priority was to compare those actively involved in religious life and those who do not practise but maintain a religious affiliation. This was to explore and compare ideas of the churched and the unchurched. In sum, eight Protestants were churchgoers and nine were nonchurchgoers. Of the Catholics, nine attended mass and nine did not. Age was included to give some idea of generational variation. In total, 20 interviewees were under 45, 15 were over 45. The youngest was 18 and the oldest was 73. Twelve were women. Geographical residence was also considered in terms of getting participants from minority and majority communities. Two towns, one a predominantly Protestant town in Co. Down, the other a predominantly Catholic town in Co. Armagh were chosen, along with Belfast, as sites for the research. Both the Protestant and Catholic samples reflected a wide range of socio-economic backgrounds from the unemployed through to higher professional. Of course, quantitatively, this means that the sample is spread very thinly across cells. However, the aim was not to provide representative groups for each category, but rather to explore the dynamics of identification through a broad variety of individuals' life stories from which we could begin to understand the social meanings of religion (see Miller, 2000).

The formal interviews lasted between one and three hours. The interviews were tape-recorded and transcribed verbatim (Reissman, 1993). Notes were made on the banter before and after the interviews and on perceived nonverbal cues to aid interpretation of the data. In the text, all names have been replaced, and occupations changed to similar. Further details are not given to avoid the possibility of participants being recognized. As space is too limited below to allow room for more, small representative quotations have been used to demonstrate the frequency with which an idea is articulated. Speakers have been chosen in so far as they illustrate a common theme from the empirical data, rather than being selected to prove the point at hand.

The analysis focuses on how people talk about and present themselves, and how they present other people. These presentations can be used to examine how people construct meaning, what is important to them and how they feel they fit into society. Through this lens, we gain access to a wide range of cultural knowledge as to what it is like to be a Catholic or Protestant in Northern Ireland. We examine how stories mark out identities, how identities mark out differences, how differences define the 'other', and how the 'other' helps structure the moral life of culture, group and individual (Plummer, 1995). As well as opinion and argument, the texts contain multiple stories about life, work, love, friends, experiences and feelings. They often mark out epiphanies, experiences or events that have constituted a turning point in someone's life. They frequently highlight actors, agents who perform actions – in other words, self and other are often presented as active/passive, and very relevant in this research, as victors/victims. We also look at the language people use to talk about themselves, others and the political situation, and how this constructs morality and values. Through this lens, access is gained to a wide range of cultural knowledge as to what it is like to be a Catholic or Protestant in Northern Ireland. This data does not allow observation of how people interact and what they *do*. The interview data is used in the book to analyse how people construct reality – and the social roles of these constructions (Berger and Luckmann, 1967).

The approach taken here is not the only relevant one in relation to religion and politics in Northern Ireland. However, it is the type of analysis that the literature is most badly in need of, and one that was necessary to pull together and make sense of the research that preceded it. Up until now, work on religion has generally been based methodologically on quantitative analysis, for example, of correlations between church attendance or theological position and political attitudes. Theoretically, it has been based on assumptions that the role of religion can be measured in terms of ethnic overlap, the actions and ideas of powerful agencies or theologically derived politics. The approach taken here focuses on how meaning is constructed from the bottom up. It starts with individuals and deals with their subjective experiences of the world. The human voice is something which has been often given space in literature on Northern Ireland (O'Connor, 1993; McKay, 2000), but which is seldom treated with analytical or methodological rigour, particularly in recent times (important exceptions include Bell, 1990; Millar, 1999).

There are of course limitations in this approach, not least in the constraints in generalizing from such a small sample. However, what *is* generalizable, are the types of identification processes at work here. In a sense, what this research has shown is not that there is something intrinsic about religion in Northern Ireland that makes people behave in a certain ways, or feel certain things – but that religion is only politically meaningful in the context of interactions with others. This is a dynamic process that can only be understood by asking people, getting inside their shoes and working out how they make sense of the world. It is an approach that can usefully be harnessed to analyse religion and social and political relationships in many other areas of social conflict as well as Northern Ireland.

Additional data

A further body of interviews is drawn on here, although as these represent work in progress, no direct quotations or analysis are provided. The research in progress concerns why evangelical identifications change over time and is based on life history interviews. The first phase of this research was funded by Diageo Ireland as part of a Newman Fellowship in British-Irish Studies, held at the Institute for British-Irish Studies, University College Dublin 2001–2003. Thus far, over thirty interviews have been conducted in 2002, twenty of which are with conservative evangelicals, eight of whom were liberal evangelicals and two of whom were ex-evangelicals. Participants come from nine different denominations: Baptist, Elim, Independent Methodist, Church of Ireland, Methodist, Presbyterian, Free Presbyterian, Evangelical Presbyterian and Pentecostal. Like the previous research, sampling for the project is not random, but aims to select participants from a range of conservative to liberal evangelical traditions. Initial field contacts, based on a variety of personal recommendations and introductions, were made with a variety of individuals and organizations across Northern Ireland and using these leads, a snowballing technique is being used to elicit further participants.

Whilst the data is not used directly for this book, these interviews have thrown much light on the dynamics of religious ideology and theology, as well as providing insights into the role of the churches within evangelical culture. This has made an invaluable contribution to the present work and I am indebted to these participants for the time, personal stories and knowledge they have shared with me.

In addition to formal interviews, this research is also underpinned by extensive observation and participation in events in Northern Ireland from 1999 to the present. This includes observation of a variety of religious events, visits to community centres and attendance at other social gatherings such as public meetings, parades and demonstrations. On many of these occasions, field notes were made and have added to the analysis presented in the book.

The Northern Ireland Life and Times Survey

The quantitative data in the book comes primarily from the Northern Ireland Life and Times Survey, 1998–2003, as well as the Young Life and Times Survey, 2003. These surveys are run jointly by Queen's University Belfast and the University of Ulster and are a constituent part of ARK, the Northern Ireland Social and Political Archive. All data is publicly available at <http://www.ark.ac.uk/nilt> and <http://www.ark.ac.uk/ylt>. The survey uses a simple random sample of addresses selected from the Postcode Address File (PAF), stratified by the three broad geographic areas of Belfast/East/West. On first contact, interviewers select one adult for interview at each address using a Kish Grid method. Face-to-face interviews are carried out using computer-assisted personal interviewing (CAPI), and there is a further self-completion questionnaire which respondents are asked to fill in. The total achieved sample is 1,800 interviews for the face-to-face element and approximately 1,440 of respondents carry on to complete the self-completion form. Response rates have averaged 65 per cent across the previous six survey sweeps. The website gives more information on the technical details of the survey, including sampling errors and confidence intervals for key variables, a breakdown of response rates for previous surveys and a sample characteristics comparison with the Continuous Household Survey on key variables. (<www.ark.ac.uk/nilt/techinfo.html>).

Notes

Chapter 1

[1] These include Morrow, Birrell, Greer and O'Keefe (1991) *The Churches and Inter-Community Relationships*, Coleraine: Centre for the Study of Conflict; Boal, Keane and Livingstone (1997) *Them and Us? Attitudinal Variation amongst Church-goers in Belfast*, Belfast: Institute of Irish Studies; McKay (2000) *Northern Protestants: An Unsettled People*, Belfast: Blackstaff; O'Connor (1993) *In Search of a State: Catholics in Northern Ireland*, Belfast: Blackstaff; Bell (1990) *Acts of Union: Youth Culture in Northern Ireland*, Basingstoke: Macmillan Education; Nelson (1984) *Ulster's Uncertain Defenders*, Belfast: Appletree Press; Harris (1972) *Prejudice and Tolerance in Ulster: a study of neighbours and strangers in the border community*, Manchester: Manchester University Press.

[2] 'The conflict in Northern Ireland is ethnonational, a systemic quarrel between the political organisations of two communities who want their state to be ruled by their nation, or who want what they perceive as "their" state to protect their nation' (McGarry and O'Leary, 1995, p. 354).

Chapter 2

[1] The 'no religion' option was first introduced in the 1991 census, and 3.7 per cent of the population chose this option. In some survey analyses, the 'no religion' and 'religion not stated' categories are grouped together. It is likely that a number of the not stated do have a religious affiliation, as there has been traditional non-compliance with the religious question, especially on census forms. However, non-compliance was at its height in the 1981 census in the wake of the Hunger Strikes and is likely to be less pronounced subsequently. It is estimated that the 2001 census results are in line with recent surveys, with around 10 per cent claiming no religion.

[2] Northern Ireland has the third highest attendance rate in Europe – east and west. Ireland comes joint second with Poland, surpassed only by Malta (Fahey et al., 2004).

[3] Trew points out (1996, p. 147) that Catholics who select a Northern Irish identification differ very little in background characteristics or attitudes from all Catholics, although they are slightly more likely to be better educated, of non-manual status and to want retain the union. Protestants, on the other hand, who

choose a Northern Irish identification differ significantly from Protestants in general. They are more likely to be younger, female, better educated and less likely to be unionists.

4   Catholics claiming a nationalist identity numbered 40 per cent in 1989, 51 per cent in 1991, 40 per cent in 1993, 54 per cent in 1994, 71 per cent in 1999 and 65 per cent in 2002. (Trew, 1996; NILTS 1999, 2002).

5   Protestant-unionist identity was 71 per cent in 1989, 73 per cent in 1991, 75 per cent in 1993, 76 per cent in 1994, 75 per cent in 1999 and 73 per cent in 2002 (Northern Ireland Social Attitudes Survey, 1995–96, the Fifth Report, p. 37; NILTS 1999, 2002). The 69 per cent of Protestants identifying as unionists in the 2003 Northern Ireland Life and Times Survey does therefore represent a decrease, but it is too early to say whether this trend will be sustained or will fluctuate.

6   Trew found (1996, p. 148–50) that amongst those of no religion with a Protestant origin, just over a third identified as unionist, 1 per cent as nationalist and nearly two-thirds as neither. Over two thirds identify as British (5 per cent Irish, 16 per cent Northern Irish). Forty-seven per cent had allegiance to a unionist party, 20 per cent to Alliance, 4 per cent for the SDLP and one-fifth had no party allegiance. We see the clear trend at work – less communal party identification, but little crossing of the boundary.

7   The number of Catholics expressing a preference for a united Ireland has fluctuated, peaking in the early 1990s: 53 per cent in 1991, 49 per cent in 1993, 60 per cent in 1994, 58 per cent in 1999 and down to 46 per cent in 2002 (Breen, 1996, p. 35; NILTS, 1999, 2002).

8   The referendum in Northern Ireland was carried out on a single-constituency basis so it was not possible to give a breakdown of the 'yes' and 'no' figures for Protestants and Catholics. The best estimates indicated that the overwhelming majority of Catholics/nationalists voted yes – about 96–7 per cent. This is estimated at around 51–3 per cent for Protestants/unionists. Perhaps this disparity is an issue of social acceptance and over-statement of moderate views in survey data, and must be taken into consideration in the discussion of the analyses. (See Martin Melaugh and Fionnuala McKenna <http://cain.ulst.ac.uk/issues/politics/election/ref1998.htm> accessed 7 June 2004.)

9   For Catholics in the 18–24 age group, 62 per cent said they would be willing to marry a Northern Ireland Protestant (although more would marry an English or black partner). Amongst the university educated, 46 per cent said they would marry a Northern Ireland Protestant (Boal et al. 1997, pp. 50–51).

10   See McGarry and O'Leary 1995, pp. 195–8.

Chapter 3

1   The civil rights campaign, 1964 to 1972, aimed to highlight a range of inequalities experienced by Catholics under the unionist-controlled Stormont government. It held a number of marches, the last of which in 1972 culminated in 'Bloody Sunday', where the British Army shot dead 13 demonstrators (see Ó Dochartaigh, 1997).

2   Drumcree in Portadown, Co. Armagh, became the focal point for protests over Orange Order marches in the late 1990s and early 2000s after the Parades Commission forbade the Order to march down the predominantly Catholic Garvaghy Road (see Bryan, 2000).

3   Paddy Devlin, one-time leader of the SDLP, left the party because he felt that it was becoming too friendly with the Catholic Church, was concerned mainly with consolidating the Catholic vote, and as a result, was too conservative socially and economically (Murray, 1998, pp. 63–6). In policy terms, the SDLP shares some interests with the Church – such as opposition to abortion – however, on other issues such as integrated education, homosexuality and divorce, the SDLP is more liberal.

4   For example, Brenda McCartney, republican ex-prisoner states, 'Up until the troubles started, I just accepted that the priest was the one you revered and respected, and the hierarchy would look after you and all your interests: you were the flock, the sheep. But I've seen that the sheep can be savaged, the sheep can be stood upon, and the sheep can bleat – and they will turn a blind eye. That is my experience' ('The Church: The way forward – a public inquiry', 1995, Belfast: Linenhall Library pamphlet collection, p. 12).

5   In the 1980s, the Church was employed by the British government to play an administrative role in employment and training schemes – in fact, funding was withdrawn from non-Church schemes. Some of the community-based training and employment schemes were thought to have links with the IRA. As such, British government funding to the Church in republican areas was designed to marginalize Sinn Féin at community level. As a result, the Church was accused of compliance with the British government. Whilst the Church's involvement in daily life increased, it was harshly criticized and resented by some (Morrow et al., 1991, p. 159)

6   Subsequently, the Jesuits scaled back their activities in the Garvaghy Road because they wanted to avoid accusations of the Church meddling in politics, thereby antagonizing Protestants.

7   Revd Robert Coulter, UUP in North Antrim; Revd Ian Paisley, DUP in North Antrim; Revd William McCrea, DUP in Mid Ulster. The latter two are Free Presbyterian ministers whilst Revd Coulter is a Presbyterian.

8   Long claims (n.d.) that the Orange Order has had members of the Alliance party and the Northern Ireland Labour Party as initiates. In other words, the Order is theoretically open to anyone who is not a Catholic, nationalist or republican.

9   BBC News (2005) 'Orange Order severs its links with the UUP' BBC Northern Ireland (Saturday 12 March available at <http://news.bbc.co.uk/1/hi/northern_ireland/4342429.stm>, accessed 13 October 2005.

10   Only two UUP MLAs declare an interest or membership in the Orange Order, Black Preceptory or Apprentice Boys on the party website <http://www.uup.org>, accessed 6 April 2004. Fourteen (out of 33) DUP MLAs do. The Order itself estimates that 35 of the 60 Unionist members returned to the Northern Ireland Assembly in June 1998 were Orange Order members, most of whom were in the UUP <http://www.grandorange.org.uk/history/Orange_Institution_Ulster_Unionist_Council.html>, accessed 6 April 2004. Similarly, of the present

101-member executive of the UUP, an estimated 84 members are thought to have direct or indirect links to the Order, with a similar percentage on the present UUP Council (ibid).

[11] The Free Presbyterian Church is numerically small. It has 68 congregations scattered throughout Northern Ireland, and the total membership is 11,989. The 2001 census gave two different figures, for Free Presbyterian (11,902) and Free Presbyterian Church of Ulster (87). These figures should most likely be combined (Table S308, NISRA 2001, <http://www.nics.gov.uk/nisra/census/> accessed 6 April 2004).

[12] Interestingly, Fawcett (2000, p. 133) turned the question around and asked her interviewees how far they felt their ministers addressed such issues. A significant minority (25 per cent in one congregation) felt that they did not. She also found (2000, pp. 130–31) that a substantial minority of her interviewees were not aware that their (Presbyterian) church had been involved in talks with the IRA in 1992. We should not then assume that all Protestants are aware of the official positions the churches take.

[13] The Church of Ireland, whilst it has no formal links with the Orange Order, still has informal points of contact: many of the laity are members of both organizations, some Church services are attended by the Orange Order, and some Orange Order halls are used for Church activities (Sub Committee on Sectarianism Report, 1999). However, in the same report the Church of Ireland distances itself from the Orange Order theologically and practically, and argues that the Church of Ireland has changed. It calls on the Orange Order to consider reform and has argued that the exclusivity of the Order is opposed to the teachings of Christ. The report concludes that its church at Drumcree can still be used on the condition that there is obedience to the law, no action that would diminish the sanctity of worship, and no civil protest after the service. So ambiguity remains. Similarly, Canon Charles Kennedy has complained that although there is a group in the Church of Ireland opposed to Drumcree, their position is often ignored in the General Synod (RTE 1 *Today Programme*, 5 July 2001).

[14] Fawcett's (2000, pp. 109–11) research supports the idea that the linkages between the Presbyterian Church, the Church of Ireland and the Orange Order are loosening. She quotes the Church of Ireland primate, Archbishop Dr Robin Eames in 1997, cautioning Orangemen at Drumcree to behave with dignity and honour, and not in a way that would question the integrity of the Church. Similarly, the then Moderator of the Presbyterian Church, Dr Sam Hutchinson, issued a statement asking both Orangemen and the Garvaghy Road Residents' Association to consider waiving their right to march and protest. After the sectarian murders of the three Quinn children in 1998, in the height of Drumcree protests, Robin Eames, the new Presbyterian Moderator Dr John Dixon, and various other clergy publicly distanced themselves from events at Drumcree.

Chapter 5

1   The idea of community in pre-Vatican Two Catholic social thinking was very much linked to power and ideological antipathy to modernism. Todd argues (1990, p. 35) that the Church had a theological interest in unity and cohesion, as 'The very concept of community is central to Catholic social thinking, and is seen to counter the trends of secularism, individualism and normless pluralism.' This could be described as a principled form of social control, concerned with the perils of materialism, rationalism and their impact on morality, especially sexuality. Since Vatican Two, there has been more ideological openness from the centre of the Church, and more accommodation of 'modern values' in practice. However, concerns with unity and the relational context of faith are still overriding.

2   It could also be argued that 'inclusion' is a conservative notion, and has meant for many Catholics that all other Christian churches must unite with the Catholic Church, rather than meeting somewhere in between. Certainly, ideas of the 'one true church' and Cardinal Ratzinger's (now the Pope) statement in September 2000, *Dominus Ieusus*, arguing the Catholic Church was the mother of churches rather than a sister, supports this view. However, the Church has gone through both liberal and conservative phases, and both interpretations are viable.

Chapter 6

1   Indeed, the idea that the other is less truthful does not need to come from theology, and is a well-documented dimension of othering. See, for example, Pitt-Rivers' analysis of an Andalucian town, which reveals a similar attitudes to difference: always it was the outsiders who caused trouble, stole crops, whose wives were unfaithful, who lied, swore and drank too much (cited in Cohen, 1985, p. 110).

2   Other strands of Catholic theology, such as millenarianism and liberation theology, stress improving conditions in this world. Connolly, for example, points out (1985, pp. 23–4) that in nineteenth-century Ireland, millenarianism – belief in the imminent second coming of Christ – existed, arguing that 'Among the poor and the powerless such ideas, holding out the prospect of a divinely-ordained overthrow of the existing social and political order, has been one classic response to conditions of upheaval, anxiety or deprivation.'

3   In 1981, a number of republican prisoners went on hunger strike to achieve recognition of their political status from the British government. In the end, political status was not recognized and ten prisoners died. However, the hunger strikes catalysed much sympathy for the republican movement as well as electoral success for Sinn Féin (see Beresford, 1987).

Chapter 7

[1]   Although in the Scottish League, Celtic and Rangers are the football teams most associated with sectarianism in Northern Ireland: Celtic with Catholics, and Rangers with Protestants.

Bibliography

Akenson, D. (1992) *God's peoples: Covenant and land in South Africa, Israel, and Ulster*. Ithaca, NY: Cornell University Press.

Ammerman, N. T. (1997) 'Organized religion in a voluntaristic society', *Sociology of Religion*, 58 (3), 203–15.

Aughey, A. (1995) 'The idea of the union' in J. Wilson Foster (ed.). *The idea of the union: Statements and critiques in support of the union of Great Britain and Northern Ireland*. Belfast: Blackstaff Press, pp. 8–19.

Aughey, A. (1989) *Under siege: Ulster unionism and the Anglo-Irish Agreement*. Belfast: Blackstaff Press.

Barritt, D. P. and Carter, C. F. (1962) *The Northern Ireland problem: A study in group relations*. Oxford: Oxford University Press.

Barth, F., ed. (1969) *Ethnic groups and boundaries: the social organization of culture difference*. London: Allen & Unwin.

Baston, C. D., Schoenrade, P. and Ventis, W. L. (1993) *Religion and the individual: A social-psychological perspective*. Oxford: Oxford University Press.

Bell, D. (1990) *Acts of union: Youth culture and sectarianism in Northern Ireland*. Basingstoke: Macmillan Education.

Bellah, R. (1970) *Beyond Belief*. New York: Harper.

Bellah, R., Madsen, R., Sullivan, W. M., Swider, A. and Tipton, S. M. (1985) *Habits of the heart: individualism and commitment in American life*. London; Berkeley: University of California Press.

Beresford, D. (1987) *Ten men dead: the story of the 1981 hunger strike*. London: Grafton.

Berger, P. (1999) 'The desecularization of the world: A global overview', in P. Berger (ed.). *The desecularization of the world: Resurgent religion and world politics*. Washington, DC: Eerdmans, pp. 1–19.

Berger, P. (1967) *The sacred canopy: Elements of a sociological theory of religion*. London: Doubleday.

Berger, P. and Luckmann, T. (1991 [1967]) *The social construction of reality: A treatise in the sociology of knowledge*. Harmondsworth: Penguin.

Bew, P., Gibbon, P. and Patterson, H. (1973) *The state in Northern Ireland 1921–72: Political forces and social classes*. Manchester: Manchester University Press.

Beyond the fife and drum (1994) Report of a conference held on Belfast's Shankill Road, October. Island Pamphlets.

Bishop, P. and Mallie, E. (1988) *The Provisional IRA*. London: Corgi.

Boal, F. Campbell, J. and Livingstone, D. (1991) 'The Protestant mosaic: A majority of minorities', in P. J. Roche and B. Barton (eds). *The Northern Ireland question: Myths and reality*. Aldershot: Avebury Press.

Boal, F., Keane, M. and Livingstone, D. (1997) *Them and us? Attitudinal variation among churchgoers in Belfast*. Belfast: The Institute of Irish Studies, Queen's University Belfast.

Bourdieu, P. (1991) 'Genesis and structure of the religious field', *Comparative Social Research: A Research Annual*, 13, 1–43.

Bourdieu, P. (1990) *The logic of practice*. Cambridge: Polity Press.

Breen, R. (1996) 'Who wants a united Ireland?: Constitutional preferences amongst Catholics and Protestants' in R. Breen, P. Devine and L. Dowds (eds). *Social attitudes in Northern Ireland: The 5th report*. Belfast: Appletree Press, pp. 33–48.

Breen, R. and Hayes, B. C. (1997) 'Religious mobility and party support in Northern Ireland', *European Sociological Review*, 13 (3), 225–39.

Brewer, J. D. (2004) 'Continuity and change in Ulster Protestantism', *Sociological Review* 52 (2), 265–83.

Brewer, J. D. (2003) 'Northern Ireland', in M. Cejka and T. Bamat (eds). *Artisans of peace*. Maryknoll, NY: Orbis Books, pp. 67–95.

Brewer, J. D. (2002) 'Are there any Christians in Northern Ireland?' in A. M. Gray, K. Lloyd, P. Devine, G. Robinson and D. Heenan (eds). *Social attitudes in Northern Ireland: The 8th report*. London: Pluto Press, pp. 22–38.

Brewer, J. D. (1998) *Anti-Catholicism in Northern Ireland 1600–1998*. London: Macmillan.

Brewer, M. B. (2003) *Intergroup relations* (2nd edition). Buckingham: Open University Press.

Brown, R. (2000) *Group processes: Dynamics within and between groups*. Oxford: Blackwell.

Brown, T. (1981) 'The majority's minorities: Protestant denominations in the North', *The Crane Bag*, 5 (1), 22–5.

Brubaker, R. and Cooper, F. (2000) 'Beyond "identity"', *Theory and Society*, 29 (1), 1–47.

Bruce, S. (2003) *Politics and religion*. Cambridge: Polity.

Bruce, S. (2001) 'Fundamentalism and political violence: The case of Paisley and Ulster evangelicals', *Religion*, 31 (4), 387–405.

Bruce, S. (1997) 'Victim selection in ethnic conflict: Motives and attitudes in Irish republicanism', *Terrorism and Political Violence* 9 (1), 56–71.

Bruce, S. (1996) *Religion in the modern world: From cathedrals to cults*. Oxford: Oxford University Press.

Bruce, S. (1994) *The edge of the union: The Ulster loyalist political vision*. Oxford: Oxford University Press.

Bruce, S. (1986) *God save Ulster: The religion and politics of Paisleyism*. Oxford: Clarendon Press.

Bruce, S. and Alderdice, F. (1993) '*Religious belief and behaviour*' in P. Stringer and G. Robinson (eds). *Social attitudes in Northern Ireland: The 3rd report*. Belfast: Blackstaff Press, pp. 5–20.

Bryan, D. (2000) *Orange parades: The politics of ritual, tradition and control*. London: Pluto Press.

Bryan, D., Fraser, T. G. and Dunn, S. (1995) *Political rituals: Loyalist parades in Portadown*. Coleraine: Centre for the Study of Conflict.

Buckley, A. (1985) 'The chosen few. Biblical texts in the regalia of an Ulster secret society', *Folk Life*, 24, 5–24.

Buckley, A. and Kenny, C. (1995) *Negotiating identity: Rhetoric, metaphor and social drama in Northern Ireland*. Washington, DC: Smithsonian Institution Press.

Buckley, P. (1994) *A thorn in the side*. Dublin: O'Brien Press.

Burton, F. (1978) *The politics of legitimacy: Struggles in a Belfast community*. London: Routledge.

Cairns, E. (1980) 'The development of ethnic discrimination in young children in Northern Ireland' in J. Harbinson and J. Harbinson (eds). *Children and young people in Northern Ireland: A society under stress*. Somerset: Open Books, pp. 115–27.

Calhoun, C. (1994) *Social theory and the politics of identity*. Oxford: Blackwell.

Casanova, J. (1994) *Public religions in the modern world*. Chicago, IL: University of Chicago Press.

Castells, M. (1997) *The power of identity*. Oxford: Blackwell.

Chong, K. H. (1998) 'What it means to be Christian: The role of religion in the construction of ethnic identity and boundary among second-generation Korean Americans', *Sociology of Religion* 59 (3), 259–86.

Church of Ireland (1999) *Sub-Committee on Sectarianism Report*, General Synod Book of Reports.

Clayton, P. (1998) 'Religion, ethnicity and colonialism as explanations of the conflict in Northern Ireland' in D. Miller (ed.). *Rethinking Northern Ireland*. London: Longman, pp. 40–54.

Cochrane, F. (1997) *Unionist politics and the politics of unionism since the Anglo-Irish Agreement*. Cork: Cork University Press.

Cohen, A. P. (1985) *The symbolic construction of community*. London: Tavistock.

Connolly, S. (1985) *Religion and society in nineteenth century Ireland*. Dublin: Economic and Social History Society of Ireland.

Coulter, C. (1999) *Contemporary Northern Irish society: An introduction*. London: Pluto Press.

Coulter, C. (1994) 'The character of Ulster Unionism', *Irish Political Studies*, 9, 1–24.

Crilly, O. (1998) 'The Catholic Church in Ireland' in N. Richardson (ed.). *A tapestry of beliefs: Christian traditions in Northern Ireland*. Belfast: Blackstaff Press, pp. 23–44.

Cruise O'Brien, C. (1994) *Ancestral voices: Religion and nationalism in Ireland*. Dublin: Poolbeg.

Daly, C. (1991) *The price of peace*. Belfast: Blackstaff Press.

Darby, J. and Dunn, S. (1987) 'Segregated schools' in R. D. Osborne, R. J. Cormack and R. L. Miller (eds). *Education and policy in Northern Ireland*. Belfast: Queen's University and the University of Ulster, Policy Research Institute, pp. 85–98.

Davie, G. (2000) *Religion in modern Europe: A memory mutates*. Oxford: Oxford University Press.

Davie, G. (1994) *Religion in Britain since 1945: Believing without belonging*. Oxford: Blackwell.

Davie, G. (1992) 'You'll never walk alone: The Anfield pilgrimage' in I. Reader and T. Walter (eds). *Pilgrimage in popular culture*. London: Macmillan, pp. 201–19.

De Graaf, N. D. and Need, A. (2000) 'Losing faith: Is Britain alone?' in R. Jowell, J. Curtice and A. Park, et al. (eds). *British social attitudes: the 17th report – Focusing on diversity*. London: Sage Publications, pp. 119–36.

Demerath, N. J. III. (2001) *Crossing the Gods: World religions and worldly politics*. New Brunswick, NJ: Rutgers University Press.

Demerath, N. J. III. (2000) 'The rise of cultural religion in European Christianity: Learning from Poland, Northern Ireland, and Sweden', *Social Compass* 47 (1), 127–39.

Devine, P. and Schubotz, D. (2004) 'Us and them?', Northern Ireland Life and Times Survey, research update no. 28. Belfast: ARK.

Douglas, M. (1966) *Purity and danger: An analysis of concepts of pollution and taboo*. London: Routledge.

Durkheim, E. (1915) *The elementary forms of religious life*. London: Free Press.

Elliott, M. (1985) *Watchmen in Sion: The Protestant idea of liberty*. Derry: Field Day Pamphlet no. 8.

Evans, G. and Duffy, M. (1997) 'Beyond the sectarian divide: The social bases and political consequences of nationalist and unionist party competition in Northern Ireland', *British Journal of Political Science*, 27 (1), 47–81.

Fahey, T., Hayes, B. C. and Sinnott, R. (2004) *Two traditions, one culture? A study of attitudes and values in the Republic of Ireland and Northern Ireland*. Dublin: Institute of Public Administration.

Faul, D. (2000) 'Editorial', *Irish News* (29 November).

Fawcett, L. (2000) *Religion, ethnicity and social change*. London: Macmillan.

Fay, M., Morrisey M. and Smyth M. (1999) *Northern Ireland's Troubles: The human costs*. London: Pluto Press.

Fentress, J. and Wickham, J. (1992) *Social memory*. Oxford: Blackwell.

Finlayson, A. (2001) 'Culture, politics and culture politics in Northern Ireland', *New Formations*, 43, 87–102.

Finlayson, A. (1997) 'Discourse and contemporary loyalist identity' in P. Shirlow and M. McGovern (eds). *Who are 'the people?: Unionism, Protestantism and loyalism in Northern Ireland*. London: Pluto Press, pp. 72–94.

Flanagan, K. (2000) 'Sociology and religious difference: Limits of understanding anti-Catholicism in Northern Ireland', *Studies* 89 (355), 234–42.

Flanagan, K. (1996) *The enchantment of sociology*. New York: St. Martin's Press.

Flick, U. (1998) *An introduction to qualitative research*. London: Sage.

Fox, C. (1997) *The making of a minority: Political developments in Derry and the north 1912–25*. Londonderry: Guildhall Press.

Fraser, G. and Morgan, V. (1999) *In the frame: Integrated education in Northern Ireland – the implications of expansion*. Coleraine: Centre for the Study of Conflict.

Fulton, J. (2002) 'Religion and emnity in Northern Ireland: Institutions and relational beliefs', *Social Compass* 49 (2),189–202.

Fulton, J. (1991) *The tragedy of belief: Division, politics, and religion in Ireland.* Oxford: Clarendon Press.

Gallagher, A. M. (1989) 'Social identity and the Northern Ireland conflict', *Human Relations* 42 (10), 917–35.

Gallagher, E. and Worrall, S. (1982) *Christians in Ulster 1968–1980.* Oxford: Oxford University Press.

Ganiel, G. (2002) 'Conserving or changing? The theology and politics of Northern Irish fundamentalist and evangelical Protestants after the Good Friday Agreement', IBIS Working Paper no. 20, Dublin: Institute for British-Irish Studies.

Gans, H. J. (1994) 'Symbolic ethnicity and symbolic religiosity: Towards a comparison of ethnic and religious generation', *Ethnic and Racial Studies* 17 (4), 577–92.

Garland, R. (1997) *Gusty Spence.* Belfast: Blackstaff Press.

Glock, C. Y. and Stark, R. (1965) *Religion and society in tension.* Chicago, IL: Rand McNally.

Gramsci, A. (1994) *Letters from prison*, edited by F. Rosengarten, translated by R. Rosenthal. New York: Columbia University Press.

Hajer, M. (1995) *The politics of environmental discourse.* Oxford: Oxford University Press.

Harris, M. (1993) *The Catholic Church and the foundation of the Northern Irish state.* Cork: Cork University Press.

Harris, R. (1972) *Prejudice and intolerance in Ulster: A study of neighbours and strangers in a border community.* Manchester: Manchester University Press.

Hayes, B. C. and McAllister, I. (2004) 'The political impact of secularisation in Northern Ireland', IBIS Working Paper no. 36, Dublin: Institute for British-Irish Studies.

Hayes, B. C. and McAllister, I. (1999a) 'Ethnonationalism, public opinion and the Good Friday Agreement' in J. Ruane and J. Todd (eds). *After the Good Friday Agreement: Analysing political change in Northern Ireland.* Dublin: University College Dublin Press, pp. 30–48.

Hayes, B. C. and McAllister, I. (1999b) 'Generations, prejudice and politics in Northern Ireland' in A. F. Heath, R. Breen and C. T. Whelan (eds). *Ireland north and south: Perspectives from social science.* Oxford: Oxford University Press, pp. 457–91.

Hayes, B. C. and McAllister, I. (1995) 'Religious independents in Northern Ireland: Origins, attitudes and significance', *Review of Religious Research* 37 (1), 65–83.

Herbermann, C., Pace, E., Pallen, C., Shahan, T. and Wynne, J. (1911) *The Catholic encyclopaedia: Work of reference on the constitution, doctrine and discipline and history of the Catholic Church, Volume 12.* New York: Robert Appleton Company.

Hervieu-Léger, D. (2001) '*The twofold limit of the notion of secularisation*' in L. Woodhead, P. Heelas and D. Martin (eds). *Peter Berger and the study of religion.* London and New York: Routledge, pp. 112–25.

Hervieu-Léger, D. (2000) *Religion as a chain of memory.* Cambridge: Polity Press.

Hervieu-Léger, D. (1994) 'Religion, memory and Catholic identity: Young people in

France and the new evangelisation of Europe', in J. Fulton and P. Gee (eds). *Religion in contemporary Europe*. Lampeter: Edwin Mellen Press, pp. 125–38.

Hickey, J. (1984) *Religion and the Northern Ireland question*. Dublin: Gill and Macmillan.

Higgins, G. I. and Brewer, J. D. (2003) 'The roots of sectarianism in Northern Ireland', in O. Hargie and D. Dickson (eds), *Researching the Troubles: Social science perspectives on the Northern Ireland conflict*. Edinburgh: Mainstream, pp. 107–22.

Hogg, M. and Abrams, D. (eds) (2001), *Intergroup relations*. Philadelphia, PA: Psychology Press.

Hogg, M. and Abrams, D. (1988) *Social identifications: A social psychology of intergroup relations and group processes*. London: Routledge.

Holmes, F. (1981) *Henry Cooke*. Belfast: Christian Journals.

Hornsby-Smith, M. (1987) *Roman Catholics in England: Studies in social structure since the Second World War*. Cambridge: Cambridge University Press.

Howard, K. (2004) 'Constructing the Irish of Britain: Ethnic recognition and the 2001 UK census', Working Papers in British-Irish Studies, no. 37, Dublin: Institute for British-Irish Studies.

Hurley, M. (1994) 'Introduction' in M. Hurley (ed.). *Religion and reconciliation in society*. Belfast: Institute of Irish Studies, pp. 1–5.

Inglis, T. (1998) *Moral monopoly: The rise and fall of the Catholic Church in modern Ireland*. Dublin: University College Dublin Press.

Jarman, N. (1997) *Material conflicts: Parades and visual displays in Northern Ireland*. Oxford: Berg Publishers.

Jenkins, R. (2000) 'Categorization: Identity, social process and epistemology', *Current Sociology* 48 (3), 7–25.

Jenkins, R. (1996) *Social Identity*. London: Routledge.

Johnston, R. K. (2000) 'Evangelicalism' in A. Hastings, A. Mason and H. Pyper (eds). *The Oxford companion to Christian thought*. Oxford: Oxford University Press, pp. 217–20.

Jordan, G. (2001) *Not of this world? Evangelical Protestants in Northern Ireland*. Belfast: Blackstaff Press.

Juergensmeyer, M. (2000) *Terror in the mind of God: The global rise of religious violence*. Berkeley: University of California Press.

Kelley, J. and de Graaf, N. D. (1997) 'National Context, Parental Socialization, and Religious Belief: Results from 15 Nations', *American Sociological Review* 62 (4), 639–59.

Kennedy, L. (1996) *Colonialism, religion and nationalism in Ireland*. Belfast: Institute of Irish Studies.

Kertzer, D. (1988) *Ritual, politics, and power*. New Haven, CT: Yale University Press.

Kertzer, D. and Arel, D. (2002). *Census and identity: The politics of race, ethnicity and language in national censuses*. Cambridge: Cambridge University Press.

Lambkin, B. (1996) *Opposite religions still? Interpreting Northern Ireland after the conflict*. Aldershot: Avebury Press.

Larkin, E. (1976) *The historical dimensions of Irish Catholicism*. Dublin: Four Courts Press.

Long, S. E. (n.d.) *The Orange Institution*, pamphlet in Linenhall Library, Belfast, Political Collection.

MacDonald, M. (1986) *Children of wrath: Political violence in Northern Ireland*. Cambridge: Polity Press.

Martin, D. (1997a) *Does Christianity cause war?* Oxford: Clarendon Press.

Martin, D. (1997b) *Reflections on sociology and theology*. Oxford: Clarendon Press.

McBride, I. (1998) *Scripture politics: Ulster Presbyterians and Irish radicalism in the eighteenth century*. Oxford: Clarendon Press.

McCullough, C. (1994) 'Bible and reconciliation' in M. Hurley (ed.). *Religion and reconciliation in society*. Belfast: Institute of Irish Studies, pp. 28–42.

McElroy, G. (1991) *The Catholic Church and the Northern Ireland crisis 1968–86*. Dublin: Gill and Macmillan.

McEvoy, J. (1986) 'Theology and the Irish future: Viewpoint of a northern Catholic', in E. McDonagh (ed.). *Irish challenges to theology*. Dublin: Dominican, pp. 21–41.

McGarry, J. and O'Leary, B. (1995) *Explaining Northern Ireland*. Oxford: Blackwell.

McIntyre, A. (2000) 'The Good Friday Agreement and modern Irish Republicanism', paper presented to the Department of Politics, University College Dublin, 7 February.

McKay, S. (2000) *Northern Protestants: An unsettled people*. Belfast: Blackstaff Press.

McLellan, D. (1995) *The thought of Karl Marx*, 3rd edn. London: Papermac.

McVeigh, J. (1989) *Religion, politics and justice in Ireland*. Cork: Mercier Press.

Millar, A. (1999) 'The constitution of republican identity in Belfast: A Lacanian psychoanalysis', unpublished PhD thesis, University College Dublin.

Miller, D. W. (1978a) *The Queen's rebels: Ulster loyalism in historical perspective*. London: Gill and Macmillan.

Miller, D. W. (1978b) 'Presbyterianism and "modernization" in Ulster', *Past and Present* 80, 66–90.

Miller, R. (2000) *Researching life stories and family histories*. London: Sage Publications.

Mitchel, P. (2003) *Evangelicalism and national identity in Ulster 1921–1998*. Oxford: Clarendon Press.

Mitchell, C. (2004a) 'Is Northern Ireland abnormal? An extension of the sociological debate on religion in modern Britain', *Sociology* 38 (2), 237–54.

Mitchell, C. (2004b) 'Saving Ulster or saving souls?: Evangelical Protestants adaptation to political change in Northern Ireland', paper presented to the Sociological Association of Ireland's annual meeting, Athlone, April 2004.

Mitchell, C. (2003a) 'From victims to equals? Catholic identification in Northern Ireland after the Agreement', *Irish Political Studies* 18 (1), 51–71.

Mitchell, C. (2003b) 'Protestant identification and political change in Northern Ireland', *Ethnic and Racial Studies* 26 (4), 612–31.

Mitchell, C. (2001) 'Religion and politics in Northern Ireland after the Good Friday Agreement', unpublished PhD thesis, University College Dublin.

Mitchell, C. and Tilley, J. (2004) 'The moral minority: Evangelical Protestants in Northern Ireland and their voting behaviour', *Political Studies* 52 (4), 585–602.

Modood, T. (1997) 'Culture and identity' in T. Modood, R. Berthoud, J. Lakey, P. Smith, S. Virdee and S. Beishon (eds). *Ethnic minorities in Britain: Diversity and disadvantage*. London: Policy Studies Institute, pp. 290–338.

Morrow, D. (1997) 'Suffering for righteousness' sake? Fundamentalist Protestantism and Ulster politics' in P. Shirlow and M. McGovern (eds). *Who are 'the people'?: Unionism, Protestantism and loyalism in Northern Ireland*. London: Pluto Press, pp. 55–71.

Morrow, D. (1995) 'Church and religion in the Ulster crisis' in S. Dunne (ed.). *Facets of the conflict in Northern Ireland*. Basingstoke: Macmillan, pp. 151–67.

Morrow, D., Birrell, D., Greer, J. and O'Keefe, T. (1991) *The churches and inter-community relationships*. Coleraine: Centre for the Study of Conflict.

Moxon-Browne, E. (1991) 'National identity in Northern Ireland' in P. Stringer and G. Robinson (eds). *Social attitudes in Northern Ireland: The 1st Report*. Belfast: Blackstaff Press, pp. 23–30.

Moxon-Browne, E. (1983) *Nation, class and creed in Northern Ireland*. Hampshire: Gower Press.

Murray, D. (1985) *Worlds apart: Segregated schools in Northern Ireland*. Belfast: Appletree Press.

Murray, G. (1998) *John Hume and the SDLP: Impact and survival in Northern Ireland*. Dublin: Irish Academic Press.

Murtagh, B. (2002) 'Social activity and interaction in Northern Ireland', Northern Ireland Life and Times Survey, Research update no. 10. Belfast: ARK.

Nelson, S. (1984) *Ulster's uncertain defenders*. Belfast: Appletree Press.

O'Connor, F. (1993) *In search of a state: Catholics in Northern Ireland*. Belfast: Blackstaff Press.

Ó'Dochartaigh, N. (1997) *From civil rights to armalites: Derry and the birth of the Irish Troubles*. Cork: Cork University Press.

O'Duffy, B. (1995) 'Violence in Northern Ireland 1969–1994: Sectarian or ethnonational?', *Ethnic and Racial Studies* 18 (4), 740–72.

O'Leary, R. and Finnas, F. (2002) 'Education, social integration and minority-majority group intermarriage', *Sociology* 36 (2), 235–54.

O'Malley, P. (1990) *Biting at the grave: The Irish hunger strikes and the politics of despair*. Belfast: Blackstaff Press.

Opsahl, T., Pollak, A., O'Malley, P., Gallagher, E., Elliot, M., Faulkner, L., Lister, R. and Gallagher, E. (eds) (1993) *A citizen's enquiry: The Opsahl report on Northern Ireland*. Dublin: Lilliput Press for Initiative '92.

Orange Order (2000) 12th of July Resolutions, available at <http://www.grandorange.org.uk/press/12th:_resolutions/2004.html> accessed 6 May 2005.

Osborne, B. and I. Shuttleworth (eds) (2004) *Fair employment in Northern Ireland: A generation on*, Belfast: Blackstaff Press.

Patton, M. (1990) *Qualitative evaluation and research methods*. London: Sage Publications.

Pettersson, P. (1996) 'Implicit service relations turned explicit: A case study of the Church of Sweden as service provider in the context of the Estonia disaster', in B. Edvardsson and S. Modell (eds). *Service management: Interdisciplinary perspectives*. Stockholm: Nerenius and Santerus Publishing Co., pp. 225–47.

Phoenix, E. (1994) *Northern nationalism: Nationalist politics, partition and the Catholic minority in Northern Ireland*. Belfast: Ulster Historical Foundation.

Plummer, K. (1995) *Telling sexual stories: power, change and social worlds*. London: Routledge.

Poole, M. and Boal, F. (1973) 'Religious residential segregation in Belfast in mid-1969: A multi-level analysis' in B. D. Clark and M. D. Gleave (eds). *Social patterns in cities*, Special publication no. 5. Belfast: Institute of British Geographers, pp. 1–4.

Porter, D. (1996) 'Forward' in A. Thomson (ed.). *Faith in Ulster*. Belfast: Evangelical Contribution on Northern Ireland, pp. 6–7.

Putnam, R. (2000) *Bowling alone: The collapse and revival of American community*. New York: Simon & Schuster.

Rafferty, O. P. (1994) *Catholicism in Ulster 1603–1983: An interpretative history*. Dublin: Gill and Macmillan.

Rambo, L. R. (1993) *Understanding religious conversion*. New Haven, CT: Yale University Press.

Reissman, C. K. (1993) 'Narrative analysis' in P. K. Manning, J. Van Maanen and M. L. Miller (eds). *Qualitative research methods Vol. 30*. Newbury Park, CA: Sage Publications, pp. 1–25.

Richstatter, T. (1999) 'Mass and communion service: What's the difference?' *Catholic Update*, available at <http://www.americancatholic.org/newsletters/cu/ac0999.asp> accessed 6 May 2005.

Rose, R. (1971) *Governing without consensus*. London: Faber and Faber.

Ruane, J. and Todd, J. (forthcoming, 2005) *Dynamics of conflict and transition*. Cambridge: Cambridge University Press.

Ruane, J. and Todd, J. (1996) *The dynamics of conflict in Northern Ireland: Power, conflict and emancipation*. Cambridge: Cambridge University Press.

Samuel, R. and Thompson, P. (1990) *The myths we live by*. London: Routledge.

Shirlow, P. (2001) 'Fear and ethnic division', *Peace Review* 13 (1), 67–74.

Smith, C. (1998) *American evangelicalism: Embattled and thriving*. Chicago, IL: University of Chicago Press.

Smith, D. and Chambers, G. (1991) *Inequality in Northern Ireland*. Oxford: Oxford University Press.

Smith, D. and Chambers, G. (1987) *Equality and inequality in Northern Ireland. Part 2: The workplace*. London: Policy Studies Institute.

Smyth, C. (n.d.) 'Christian ethics and propaganda: A discussion of the Irish experience', pamphlet in Linenhall Library Belfast, Political Collection.

Somers, M. (1994) 'Narrative and the constitution of identity: A relational and network approach', *Theory and Society* 23 (5), 605–50.

Stevens, R. D. (2003) 'Irish religion: The empirical situation', speech to the Irish Assocation Armagh 11 November 2003, (available at <http://www.irish-association.org/archives/david_stephens10_03.html> accessed 30 January 2005).

Stewart, A. T. Q. (1986 [1977]) *The narrow ground: Aspects of Ulster 1609–1969*. London: Faber and Faber.

Storey, E. (2002) *Traditional roots: Towards an appropriate relationship between the Church of Ireland and the Orange Order*. Blackrock, Co. Dublin: Columba Press.

Tajfel, H. (1981) *Human groups and social categories*. Cambridge: Cambridge University Press.

Tara Proclamation (n.d.) Pamphlet, author's collection.

Taylor, P. (1999) *Loyalists*. London: Bloomsbury.

Thomson, A. (1998) 'Evangelicalism and fundamentalism' in N. Richardson (ed.). *A tapestry of beliefs: Christian traditions in Northern Ireland*. Belfast: Blackstaff Press, pp. 249–62.

Thomson, A. (1995) *The fractured family*. Belfast: Nelson and Knox.

Tillich, P. (1963) *Christianity and the encounter of the world religions*. New York: Columbia University Press.

Toborowsky, J. S. (2000) 'Dress at mass', *Homiletic and Pastoral Review*, June available at <http://www.catholic.net/rcc/Periodicals/Homiletic/2000-06/toborowsky.html> accessed 23 April 2004).

Todd, J. (1999) 'Nationalism, republicanism and the Good Friday Agreement' in J. Ruane and J. Todd (eds). *After the Good Friday Agreement: Analysing political change in Northern Ireland*. Dublin: University College Dublin Press, pp. 49–70.

Todd, J. (1998) 'Loyalism and secularisation' in P. Brennan (ed). *La sécularisation en Irlande*. Caen: Presses Universitaires de Caen, pp. 195–206.

Todd, J. (1995) 'Equality, plurality and democracy: Justifications of proposed constitutional settlements of the Northern Ireland conflict', *Ethnic and Racial Studies* 18 (4), 818–36.

Todd, J. (1990) 'Northern Irish nationalist political culture', *Irish Political Studies* 5 31–44.

Todd, J. (1987) 'Two traditions in unionist political culture', *Irish Political Studies* 2, 1–26.

Tonge, J. (2002) *Northern Ireland: Conflict and change* (2nd edn). London: Pearson Education.

Trew, K. (1996) 'National identity' in R. Breen, P. Devine and L. Dowds (eds). *Social attitudes in Northern Ireland: The 5th report*. Belfast: Appletree Press, pp. 140–52.

Tucker, R. (ed) (1978) *The Marx-Engels reader*. New York: Norton.

Turner, B. S. (1991) *Religion and social theory*, 2nd edn. London: Sage Publications.

Walter, T. (1991) 'The mourning after Hillsborough', *Sociological Review,* 39 (3), 599–625.

Warner, R. S. (1997) 'Religion, boundaries, and bridges', *Sociology of Religion* 58 (3), 217–38.

Weber, M. (1958 [1915]) *The Protestant ethic and the spirit of capitalism*. Boston, MA: Beacon.

Wengraf, T. (2001) *Qualitative research interviewing: Biographic narrative and semi-structured methods*. London: Sage Publications.

Whelan, K. (1998) 'Sectarianism and secularism in nineteenth-century Ireland', in P. Brennan (ed.), *La sécularisme en Irlande*. Caen: Press Universitaires de Caen, pp. 71–90.

White, R. W. (1997) 'The Irish Republican Army: An assessment of sectarianism', *Terrorism and Ethnic Violence* 9 (1), 20–55.

Whyte, J. H. (1990) *Interpreting Northern Ireland*. Oxford: Clarendon Press.

Whyte, J. H. (1983) 'How much discrimination was there under the Unionist regime, 1921–68?', in T. Gallagher and J. O'Connell (eds). *Contemporary Irish Studies*. Manchester: Manchester University Press, 1–35.

Whyte, J. H. (1980) *Church and state in modern Ireland*. Dublin: Gill and Macmillan.

Wigfall-Williams, W. and Robinson, G. (2001) 'A world apart: Mixed marriage in Northern Ireland', Northern Ireland Life and Times Survey, research update no. 8. Belfast: ARK.

Wilson, B. (1979) *Contemporary transformations of religion*. Oxford: Clarendon Press.

Wilson, D. (1985) *An end to silence*. Cork: Mercier Press.

Wright, F. (1973) 'Protestant Ideology and Politics in Ulster', *Archives Europeennes De Sociologie* 14 (2), 213–80.

Index